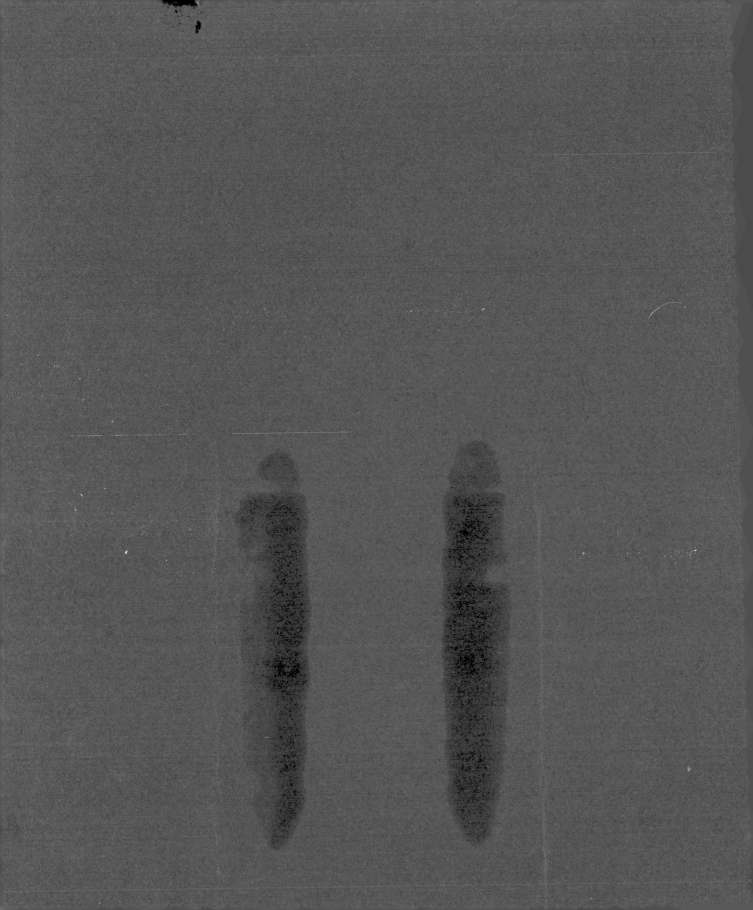

GREEN MAGIC

Previous page: Woodbine. From Walter Crane, *Flowers from Shakespeare's Garden*, 1906.

Opposite: Cockle. From Walter Crane, *Flowers from Shakespeare's Garden*, 1906.

A *Webb&Bower* BOOK
Edited, designed and produced by
Webb & Bower Limited, Exeter, England

Designed by Jacqueline Small

Picture Research by Anne-Marie Ehrlich

Copyright © Webb & Bower Limited 1977
All rights reserved

Published in 1977 by The Viking Press
625 Madison Avenue, New York, N.Y. 10022.
Published simultaneously in Canada by
Penguin Books Canada Limited.

LIBRARY OF CONGRESS CATALOGING IN
PUBLICATION DATA
Gordon, Lesley.
 Green magic.
 (A Studio book)
 Includes index.
 1. Plant lore. 2. Flowers (in religion, folk-
lore, etc.) I. Title.
GR780.G67   398'.368   77-6338
ISBN 0-670-35427-9

Text set in 10/11 Baskerville

Printed in Great Britain by
Jolly & Barber Limited
Rugby Warwickshire.

Bound by Webb, Son & Company,
London and Wales.

GREEN MAGIC

Flowers Plants & Herbs in Lore & Legend

LESLEY GORDON

A Studio Book
THE VIKING PRESS
NEW YORK

CONTENTS

FOREWORD

It may be the annual death and resurrection of plants and flowers, the continuous waxing and waning of petal and leaf, the mystery of the green pulse beneath the earth's brown, set into motion who knows when, that has caused man to seek for meaning in all growing things. Flowers have been used from earliest times as emblems of propitiation and thanksgiving in the most diverse forms of religious belief. In ancient manuscripts, wall decorations and sculptured reliefs, the lily, rose and crocus, and the leaves of acanthus, palm and oak were reproduced, not only for their beauty of form, but for the mystical meaning with which men had endowed them. These natural plant forms were the loveliest tribute men had to offer to their gods, and in so offering, honour was done to the flowers themselves.

The fragile beauty that yet held in every curve an unbelievable strength, that could adapt to climate and adversity, making the most of every nook and cranny, must have a message, people believed, for those that sought one. And so, the qualities of love and purity and innocence were attributed by man to the rose, the lily and the daisy.

By the nineteenth century flowers were playing a double rôle – the rose was not only offered in reverence to Mary, herself the Mystic Rose, but it could be handed shyly, as a token of love, to the girl next door. The age of the Language of Flowers had begun.

The magic of green life will always be with us, for it is both evanescent and permanent. We still decorate our churches for festivals of life, death and thanksgiving as we have done for centuries, and belief in herbal medicine is stronger than ever.

A symbol to some, and a mere visiting card to others, as when Francis Kilvert stuck a cowslip or an ivy leaf in the door-latch when he visited his parishioners and found they were not at home. A happy thought, meaning, 'Francis Kilvert has been here'. But to the Reverend Kilvert, the sight of a growing daffodil could also mean, 'God has been here'.

We speak of a pride of lions –
surely one may have a pride of grandchildren?

To Deborah, Richard, Jonathan, Piers and Lucy, with pride.

When men turned blindly to their gods to praise or blame some force bigger than themselves for the good and evils of life, it was natural that the beauty of trees and flowers should appeal to them as the best they had to offer by way of propitiation. From these acts of dedication arose the mythology that surrounds the flowers of the ancient world, and flower- and tree-names were linked with the names of gods and goddesses.

The goddess of love, the Greek Aphrodite or the Roman Venus, was offered the myrtle. In one legend, the myrtle was said to be the creation of Venus, who was crowned with its blossoms at the judgement of Paris. In some parts of Greece she was known as Myrtilla, or Myrtea. She was also associated with the apple, the quince, the violet and the rose, and the rose campion was supposed to spring from her bath.

Apollo, the sun god, was offered the cornel tree. There was a festival in his honour in Lacedemonia called Cornus, held as an appeasement, because the Greeks had incurred Apollo's displeasure by cutting down the cornel trees which grew in a consecrated thicket on Mount Ida. He was also offered the bay and the heliotrope, whose name derives from the Greek and means turn-to-the-sun, the flower that turns to Apollo.

Athena, or the Roman Minerva, was offered the olive. Athena caused the olive to spring from the ground at the foundation of her city, the City of Athens, and Pliny wrote that in his time the same tree was growing within the citadel of Athens. The olive being the symbol of peace, and Athena the goddess of war as well as of wisdom, it may also have been proffered as the ultimate aim and end of war.

A temple surrounded by oak trees was consecrated to Jupiter, the god of thunder, at Dodona, where thunderstorms rage more frequently than anywhere else in Europe. When the leaves rustled and the wind was still, Jupiter announced his supreme will to man.

To Mars, the god of war, the ash was dedicated; for Mars seized ashen poles to put into the hands of his warriors, and the spears of the Amazons and of the mighty Achilles were made of its wood.

I
Flowers and the Gods

The name of Bacchus or Dionysus was linked with the vine, as one would suppose, but also with fir cones and ivy; the latter because it was regarded as an antidote for drunkenness. Bacchus drank his wine from beechen bowls, cut from the purple beech, which still shows wine stains in its leaves. He was usually represented as carrying a wand of twined olive branches, bearing three leaves, which later was translated into two snakes, enlaced and kissing. This *thyrsus*, or *caduceus*, as it was called, was used to touch earth-dwellers, to teach them eloquence, as wine does, and to endow them with beneficent qualities, like the good fairy's wand. The enchanting *putti* (small boys), who accompanied Bacchus in his revels, as well as Mercury, also carried these wands.

The poppy was offered to Ceres, the earth-mother, but so was the narcissus, presumably for its narcotic perfume. The lily and the iris were Juno's flowers; Juno, the queen of heaven, and sister and wife of Jupiter. She was identified with the Greek Hera.

Dis, god of the underworld, was placated with cypress, the sad tree, and also with maidenhair (the hair of Proserpina?), narcissus and mint. Mint is called after Minthé, who was a favourite of Pluto. Proserpina, in a fit of jealousy, turned her into the herb we know. It is a fable of life and death, of sickness and health. Minthé, about to be taken by Pluto, was cured when she was turned into a medicinal herb.

To Hercules, the mighty, branches of a powerful beech tree were offered. The beech was also dedicated to Diana, and it was the tree in whose branches Athena and Apollo sat, in the form of vultures, watching the conflict between the Greeks and the Trojans. The fir was also offered to Diana, the huntress, and to Pan, as god of huntsmen. Huntsmen suspended a wolf's head from the branches of a pine or fir to secure their protection. Dittany was dedicated to the moon, and so to Diana. Diana was represented as the moon, for the light of the moon was propitious to huntsmen. Dittany had the quality of drawing out splinters of wood, of considerable service to a huntress, no doubt. Tasso says that when

Godfrey, the chief of the Crusaders, was wounded with an arrow, an 'odoriferous panacy' distilled from dittany was applied to the wound, whereupon the arrowhead fell out, and the wound immediately healed.

In time, some of these flowers and their symbols became confused, and merged in to one another. The poppy head became the pomegranate with its multitude of seeds, an image of life and fertility to painters and sculptors. The pomegranate is the Jewish and Christian symbol that we see pictured in the hand of the Infant Christ of Fra Angelico and of Botticelli, and came from the Byzantine poppy head, which in time merged with grapes and palm fruit. The palm became confused with the Greek iris, which in turn became the fleur-de-lys. A twelfth-century craftsman possibly took the thistle for the poppy-head, and the thistle leaf for the acanthus. The pineapple became confused with the pine-cone. Some of these pagan flower symbols, such as the lily and the rose, were adopted by the Christian faith.

In the mythology of Greece and Rome, every grieving god was turned into a blossoming plant or tree, and so was every frightened nymph. Flowers sprang from the blood of slain heroes; and they were to gods and men alike a refuge and a release. The legends of the gods have a sad similarity of love and death, with a haunting refrain in which the notes are flowers.

On the twin-headed mountain of Parnassus, one of whose summits was consecrated to Apollo and the Muses, the other to Bacchus, legendary flowers rose from which are descended the flowers in our own gardens. Thyme spread a scented carpet on Mount Hymettus, the honey mountain. Quinces, the golden apples which lost the race for Atalanta, grew in the Gardens of the Hesperides. Proserpina, happily gathering flowers in the meadows of Sicily,

Herself a fairer flower, by gloomy Dis
Was gathered,

and taken off to the Underworld to be his bride. In her terror she dropped her

flowers which were turned into daffodils for us. Proserpina is the Roman personification of the seasons; for the six months which she spends in Olympus give us the soft and gentle time of flowering and growing, and the six months that she is forced to spend in Hades, she grows stern and terrible, and the world becomes harsh and bitter.

Naiads peopled the lakes and streams, and dryads and hamadryads guarded the sacred groves of the classical world. Dryads, those beautiful flower-crowned female spirits, were free to wander at will, but hamadryads were doomed to live and die in the trees to which they were rooted. They carried hatchets to protect the trees on which their existence depended. Naiads, beautiful as they were, like mermaids, seemed to offer a threat to Greek and Roman youths:

Naiads, the dread of rustic wight,
Led the gay dance, and revell'd through
* the night.*

There is jealousy among the goddesses, and confusion between their Greek and Roman names. Venus was adorned with myrtle when Paris awarded her the prize for beauty, and so myrtle was hateful to Juno and Minerva, and was excluded from a Roman festival when all other flowers and shrubs might be used. The lotus and the lily – the names were interchangeable in mythology – were flowers of Juno, and odious to Venus. In fact, these goddesses behaved with all the unseemliness of the fourth form in a girls' boarding-school. But the passionate rivalries of the goddesses were healed, and their symbolic flowers forgotten, when these same flowers were laid at the feet of Our Lady at the coming of Christianity.

The legends of Venus are varied and conflicting. In Roman mythology she was the goddess firstly of vegetable gardens, later of sensual love, of little importance until she was later identified with the Greek Aphrodite, and she became the goddess of love and wedlock. In the ancient world, the Greeks considered the rose, of which they knew four varieties, the most beautiful flower,

Page 9: Narcissus; from G. P. Fauconnet, *Flower-name Fancies*, 1918. Insensible to love, Narcissus was caused by Nemesis to worship his own image reflected in the water – a shadow he could never embrace.

Opposite: Venus, Queen of Love; detail from *Primavera*, by Sandro Botticelli (1447–1510). Venus is the name given to the second planet from the sun, and the nearest heavenly body to the earth except the moon. Plants under her influence were used for the indispositions and sicknesses of love.

Below: Bacchus. Section of Attic red-figured plate. Corinth Museum. In Roman mythology the god of wine. In peace his robe is purple; in war he is covered with a panther's skin.

as Aphrodite was the most beautiful of women.

> *She wrapped her flesh in raiment which*
> *the Hours*
> *And Graces made and dipped in*
> *springtime flowers,*
> *All that the Hours bring forth. Crocus*
> *they bring,*
> *Bluebell and Violet brave – blossoming,*
> *Roses with lovely buds and nectarous*
> *scent,*
> *Ambrosial petals of the jonquil blent*
> *With lily cups. So Aphrodite wore*
> *Clothes that the scent of every season bore.*

The first roses were without thorns, until one day Aphrodite's young son, Cupid, was smelling a newly-opened rose, when a bee stung him on the lip. Cupid ran weeping to his mother, who, to pacify him, strung his bow with bees, first removing their stings, which she placed upon the stem of the rose.

Cupid, with his bow-string of bees, bears a close resemblance to Kama, the Hindu god of love, who sprang from Brahma's heart. Kama, too, is armed with bow and arrows, the bow being of sugar cane, the bow-string a line of bees; and each of the five arrows is tipped with a distinct flower, supposed to conquer one of the five senses. He rides on a parrot or sparrow, attended by nymphs, one of whom carries his banner displaying the Makara, or a fish on a red ground. His wife is Rati, Pleasure, or Priti, Affection; his daughter, Trisha, Desire, and his son, Aniruddha, the Unrestrained.

But to return to Venus. Roses were all white until Venus,

> *Her naked foot a rude thorn tore*
> *From sting of briar it bled,*
> *And where the blood ran evermore*
> *It dyed the roses red.*

Another legend tells how the mischievous Cupid, dancing among the gods, upset a cup of nectar that not only turned the roses crimson, but gave them their scent as well. Because of Botticelli's much-loved painting, 'The Birth of Venus', we know her as a vision of beauty rising weightlessly from the sea on a delicate scallop shell, but in some

Left: Apollo pursues Daphne as she begins to change into a laurel tree. Painting attributed to Antonio and Piero del Pollaiuolo *c.* 1430–90.

Opposite: *Ceres and harvesting cupids,* by Simon Vouet (1590–1649). Ceres was the Earth-mother and protectress of agriculture and all the fruits of the earth. She was identified with the Roman Demeter.

13

accounts she was born from an egg which two fishes conveyed to the seashore. This egg was hatched by two white pigeons.

Venus once loved Adonis, a beautiful youth who died from the wound of a boar's tusk, received while hunting. Zeus, the god of gods, decreed that Adonis should spend half the year in the upper, and half in the lower world, typifying the death of nature in winter and its revival in spring; again, the cult of Persephone (Proserpina). The Adonis cult came to Greece by way of Asia Minor, next to Egypt under the Ptolemies, and then, at the time of the Empire, to Rome.

There was an annual feast of Adonis, in springtime, for which the Greeks grew jars of fennel and lettuce. They were called Adonis Gardens, and the morning after the festival these jars were thrown away; and so short-lived and perishable things were called Adonis Gardens. From the blood of Adonis, mingled with the tears of Venus, grew the scarlet Adonis flower, *Flos adonis*.

Crocus was another beautiful youth who loved a shepherdess, Smilax. Crocus was killed by a quoit, flung from the hand of Mercury, the son of Jupiter. 'Dipped into celestial dew', the body of Crocus was changed into the flower that bears his name while Smilax was changed into a yew tree. The flower was used in love potions.

A discus also caused the death of Hyacinthus, the son of Amyclas, king of Sparta. This is the story of the love of man for man – how the sun-god Apollo fell in love with the beautiful Hyacinthus, and aroused the jealousy of Zephyr, the west wind and son of Aeolus and Aurora, who also loved the boy. Finding that he was adored by a god, Hyacinthus cast aside his earthly love, Thamyris. One day, when Apollo and Hyacinthus were playing at quoits on the banks of the Eurotas, Zephyr, in his blind rage, turned aside the discus that the sun-god had thrown, so that it struck Hyacinthus and killed him. From his blood, Apollo caused the hyacinth to grow, and marked its petals AI, the Greek word for woe.

Sorrow and beauty go hand in hand in

Flora in a garden, by Pieter van Avont, Master of the Antwerp Gild (1600–1652). The flowers and trees are by Jan Breughel (1568–1625). Flora, the Roman goddess of flowers and spring, sits outside the balustrade of a formal garden. Here the *putti* play in a glorious riot of flowers.

the myths of the old world. Probably the best-known of all flower legends is that of Narcissus, son of Cephisus and Liriope. Narcissus, denying the love of man or woman, worshipped his own beautiful image, reflected in a pool. Trying to reach his shadow he fell into the water and was drowned. Echo, a nymph who had loved Narcissus in vain, came weeping with her sister nymphs to remove the body, but it had disappeared. Only a white flower floated on the water, but we can still hear Echo calling in the emptiness of deserted places. A sad story, but as Emilia said to her servant in *The Two Noble Kinsmen*,

That was a fair boy certaine, but a foole
To love himselfe; were there not maids
enough?

The gods and goddesses of Greece and Rome were full of human faults and frailties, as we have seen. Jealousy and hatred hang like dark clouds over Olympus, and envy curdles the far from constant sunshine of the classical landscape.

Io, the beautiful daughter of Inachus, was unfortunate enough to catch the eye of Zeus, an eye ever alert for the attractions of the priestesses of his wife Hera's temple. The affair ended in Io being changed into a white heifer, some say by Hera in jealous spite, others that Zeus himself contrived the transformation when caught in a compromising situation with the unlucky girl. In order to ease a distasteful situation, Zeus caused white violets to grow for Io to feed on. Io was placed under the care of Argus of the hundred eyes, but when Argus was killed by Hermes at the command of Zeus, the unfortunate heifer was maddened by a gadfly sent by the spiteful Hera, and fled to Egypt. Io eventually recovered her original shape and bore a son to Zeus. The myth is explained as the horned heifer, Io, symbolizing the moon, and the hundred-eyed Argus, the starry sky.

And Io's white violets? Cupid so admired their purity and sweetness that Venus turned them blue, a petty meanness that seems to have misfired, since blue, or more accurately purple, violets

are among the best-loved flowers still. When reading of the gods, we are able to view human failings in a more charitable light.

The charitable light is still required when reading of Hebe, the daughter of Jupiter and Juno. Some say that this beautiful girl was the daughter of Juno only, for it was rumoured that Juno conceived the child after eating lettuces. Hebe, the ever-fair, the ever-young, was made the goddess of youth, and cupbearer to the gods. Poor Hebe! The honour was soon snatched away. The incident occurred when she was pouring out nectar at a grand festival. Reading between the lines it appears that the anxious girl, tasting the nectar before offering it to Jupiter, and unused as she probably was to the heady syrup of Olympus, happened, according to well-established authority (Lemprière's *Classical Dictionary*), to fall down 'in an indecent posture'. She was instantly dismissed. Keats took a kindlier view of the accident.

With a waist and with a side
White as Hebe's, when her zone
Slipt its golden clasp, and down
Fell her kirtle to her feet,
While she held the goblet sweet,
And Jove grew languid.

But Jove was far from languid. Olympian etiquette was not to be flouted, and the envied post as cup-bearer was offered to Ganymede. To reinstate the girl, Juno employed her to harness the peacocks to her chariot; a humbler task, but in the circumstances, one not to be refused.

The story ends happily. Hebe married Hercules and had two sons; in spite of which, she is usually represented as a young virgin, crowned with flowers and arrayed in a variegated garment, which, we hope, was sufficiently secured. Her plant, as might be expected, is a tender shrub, with both leaves and flowers firmly attached.

Many and vengeful are the stories of the gods, but two more only may be included. The first, the story of Daphne and Adonis. Cupid, the cause of so much trouble in the old world and the new,

and himself constantly in trouble with the gods, was rebuked by Apollo for some mischievous act, and in swift revenge shot the sun-god with his golden arrow. He then shot a second arrow of lead, and from here the story has two versions. The golden arrow caused the victim to love the first woman that he should meet; in this case, Daphne, the daughter of a river-god.

In one version, the leaden arrow struck the breast of Daphne, so that instead of returning Apollo's love, she fled from him in fear. The second version tells how the leaden arrow, following the flight of the golden shaft, struck Apollo a second time, causing him to arouse repugnance in the terrified girl. In either case the result was the same. Daphne fled, but with little chance of escape. With failing strength she prayed to the gods for help, and with Apollo's outstretched arms about to seize her, the gods took pity, and she was turned into a laurel tree. But Apollo's love, caused by the golden arrow, proved constant, and he chose the laurel for his sacred tree, and wore a wreath of its scented leaves in Daphne's memory.

The last legend, the story of the poppy, is included because of its link with the cult of Persephone. When Persephone was borne off to the Underworld by Dis and winter began, Ceres, her mother, inconsolable for the loss of her daughter, set out to seek her throughout Sicily. When darkness fell she climbed Mount Etna, and at its flame lit two torches to light her way through the night. The gods, unable to help her in her distress, caused poppies to spring up around her feet, whose flowers glowed redly in the flickering light. Ceres stooped, breathing in their bitter scent, and tasted their narcotic seeds. (In fact, the seeds have no narcotic properties, but this is the story.) Overcome by drowsiness, the sad earth-mother sank to the ground and slept among the poppies, and they have remained the symbol of forgetfulness in sleep.

That the Flanders poppy should be regarded as a symbol of remembrance, is just one of the strange turns of fate in plant lore. Its motto, 'Lest we forget', will stay with us for generations.

There is a tradition that the first churches were built of boughs as the pagan temples had been before them. Many sacred trees, or pillars formed of the living trunks of trees, were found in ancient Germany. They were called *Irmenseule*, and it is recorded that one of them was destroyed by Charlemagne in 772 at Heresburg, in Westphalia.

The instinct to use flowers and leaves as a means of decoration in architecture and painting, as well as directly, lies deep in human conception. Legends that arose from the contemplation of flowers, plants and trees in art and nature, stemmed from those same flowers that had flourished in the sunshine and rain of the ancient world. Roses, violets and lilies were adopted by the Christian church, unchanged in form, colour and perfume. Only the spirit of the stories changes from the dark and wavering passions of love and hate and jealousy, to reveal the glow of unquestioning faith – from thunder and lightning on Mount Olympus to the steady light of a star over a stable.

The Christian flower legends are very simple. They are stories from a lost world. Perhaps they are stories for a lost world, I do not know. But once upon a time – a lost phrase from a lost world – they were loved and believed in.

When Eve sat weeping outside Paradise, an angel was sent to comfort her. Since the Fall, no flower had bloomed, but the snow fell ceaselessly. As the angel talked with Eve, he caught a snowflake in his hand, breathed on it, and it fell to earth as the first snowdrop. No plot, no suspense, but a perfect symbol.

In Germany there is a different snowdrop legend. When at the Creation all things were coloured – the sky blue, the earth brown, the leaves green, the flowers of all colours – the snow complained to God that there was no colour left for him, and that he would be as little seen as the wind. God told him to go to the flowers and beg a little colour. One by one the flowers refused. At last the snowdrop said, 'If my white is any use to you, you are very welcome to it.' And so the snow became white, and in thanks it shelters the snowdrop and keeps it warm through the bitter winter.

II
Christian Flower Legends

Another German legend concerns the cowslip. Herb Peter was the name once given to the cowslip. One day, St. Peter heard a rumour that people were trying to enter heaven by the back door, instead of through the front gates of which he holds the key. He was so agitated at this lack of reverence, that he dropped his bunch of keys, which fell to earth, took root, and gave us the cowslips, which in Germany are known as *Himmelschlüsselchen*, the little keys of heaven. They were also called *Unsere Frauenschlüssel*, or Our Lady's key, *De heirathschlüssel*, the marriage key, and *Die schlüsselblume*, the key flower, which was believed to open rocks to reveal hidden treasure.

The touching story of the sainfoin is told in only a few words. When the Child was laid in the manger, all that could be found for bedding was some sun-dried hay. The flower of the lucern began to blossom, until a pink wreath encircled the small head. It was the flower of sainfoin, the Holy hay.

There are two attributes general to these short tales, love, and a simplicity that is not to be pitied. Walking through the Garden of Eden in the cool of the evening after the Creation, God noticed a small blue flower and asked its name. The flower, overcome by shyness, whispered, 'I am afraid I have forgotten, Lord.' God answered, 'Forget Me not. Yet I will not forget thee.'

Another German legend explains why the heartsease was known as Herb Trinity. Long ago the heartsease was valued for its perfume, even sweeter than the violet, as well as for its healing properties. It grew on cultivated land, and was so much sought after by the people that precious corn and vegetables were in consequence being trampled down and destroyed. This so grieved the flower that it prayed to the Holy Trinity to take away its perfume. The prayer was answered, and from that time the wild pansy, the heartsease, was known as *Dreifaltigkeits Blume*, or flower of the Trinity. It was also known in some parts of the Rhineland as *Je-länger-je-lieber*, 'the longer, the dearer'.

A story more familiar to us tells how the lavender was given its scent. Looking for

a place on which to hang the Child's washing, Mary chose a grey bush of lavender, and on this she spread the snow-white baby clothes. The sun and the wind dried the clothes, and when Mary came to take them in, the bushes were fragrant with the clean scent they still have. One of the most beautiful of our winter flowers is the Christmas rose, *Helleborus niger*. It was known in medieval times as the Flower of St. Agnes, and dedicated to her, but the Christian legend tells how, when the Magi came with their offerings of gold, frankincense and myrrh, a shepherd girl stood at a distance from the sleeping Child, quietly weeping. She was poor, and the weather cold, and she had nothing to offer the Baby, not the smallest flower. A passing angel saw her distress, stooped and throwing off a blanket of snow, disclosed roses blooming at her feet. They were the first Christmas roses.

There are some flowers that are traditionally connected with the Holy Family for which no story is told – the Madonna lilies, carried by the angel of the Annunciation, and which appear, together with the iris, in the foreground of so many of the Italian religious paintings; the cyclamen, with the blood-drop in its heart, because of the sorrow that pierced the heart of the Virgin; the Rose of Sharon, symbol of the Resurrection, and the poppy, bearing the Cross in its centre.

The Lily of the Valley, known as Ladders-to-Heaven; the Pimpernel that grew on Calvary; Aaron's Rod, Jacob's Ladder, Solomon's Seal and the Star of Bethlehem; each may have had a story that is now forgotten. Other biblical flower names, Grace-of-God for the hypericum; Gethsemane, an orchis; and Hallelujah for the oxalis, are not heard today. The tradition of the rustling of the leaves, when the thorn trees blossom on Christmas night to commemorate the Christ-child's birth, is almost forgotten, nor do we hear the German legend of the *nelka*, the carnation that bloomed on that same night. In Hampshire, when the leaves rustled at midnight, folk would go to the nearest cowstall to watch the animals rise and lie down on the other side, because on the

Page 17: The Moss Rose. From William Curtis, *Lectures on Botany*. The Moss Rose, a cosy Cabbage rose beloved of legend, valentines, scrap-books and the Language of Flowers. Believed to have originated in Italy and been brought to England in 1735. Its legend, therefore, is not ancient.

Left: *Virgin and Child with flowers*, by Carlo Dolci (1616–1686). The roses and lilies are Mary's own flowers, and there is a tradition that St Thomas refused to believe in her bodily assumption into Heaven, and asked that her tomb should be opened. This was done. The tomb was found to be full only of lilies and roses.

Below: The Tree of Jesse. Psalter, late 13th century. Ely. Jesse, the father of David, king of Israel. 'And there shall come forth a rod out of the stem of Jesse, and a Branch shall grow out of his roots.' Isaiah, 11:1.

night of the Nativity the oxen knelt. Walafrid Strabo, whose name means Walafrid the Squint-eyed, a monk who lived between 809 and 849, when he met his death by drowning in the river Loire, wrote in his *Hortulus* that the Rose symbolized Christ's death; 'dying, He gave its colour to the Rose,' and to the Lily he likened the purity of His life. In later medieval symbolism the Rose was given to Mary.

> *Mystic Rose! that precious name*
> *Mary from the Church doth claim;*
> *In the Lily's silver bells,*
> *The purity of Mary dwells.*
> *In the Myrtle's fadeless green,*
> *Mary's constancy is seen.*

In Christian art there was depicted a vine called the Root of Jesse, or a Rod out of the stem of Jesse. Here 'Rod' means literally a brilliant or shining bough. This vine traces the genealogy of Christ, 'a flower of the royal stem of Jesse.' Francis Quarles, in one of his Emblems, 1634, writes of 'Jesse's sov'reign flow'r,' by which he means Christ. The recumbent figure of Jesse is represented with the vine arising from his loins, and it can be seen in stained glass windows called Jesse windows, or it may be found embroidered on vestments, or as a branched candlestick.

The Passion Flower is perhaps not the least of the wonders that we owe to Columbus. To the newly-arrived Spanish settlers in South America, the superb climbing plants, whose intricate flowers of crimson, blue, flesh-coloured, yellow and greenish-white, known then as Murucuia or Maracoc, must have presented an arresting picture. Even today, it is impossible to pass one of the most common varieties without a second glance.

In their religious zeal, the Spaniards saw in this flower a God-given symbol of Christ's Passion, and hailed it as an assurance of the ultimate triumph of the Cross. Every part of the flower, leaf and stem seemed to be clearly designed for the purpose. It was pointed out to the natives that the leaf was a symbol of the spear, and the five anthers, the five wounds; and so the converted Mexicans called it *Flor de las Cinco Llagas*, the Flower of the Five Wounds. The tendrils were likened to the cords and whips, and the column of the ovary to the pillar of the Cross. The stamens symbolized the hammers, and the dark circle of threads – the dramatic centre of this extraordinary flower – the crown of thorns. The calyx represented the nimbus, and if the flowers were white it denoted purity, and if they were blue, heaven. The three days that were the life-span of the flower meant that so shall 'the Son of man be three days and nights in the heart of the earth.'

And so it was called *Flos-passionis*, changed by Linnaeus into *Passiflora*, the Passion Flower. It was thus held in veneration in South America, and nuns trained it round their dormitory windows. The flesh-coloured Passion Flower, *P. incarnata*, was the first species known in Europe, and it was introduced into England in 1629, the year of the publication of Parkinson's *Paradisus*. He was obviously disgusted at this superstitious nonsense, and he shows an engraving of 'The Jesuites Figure of Maracoc.' 'Some superstitious Jesuite would faine make me beleeve,' he says, 'that in the flower of this plant are to be seene all the markes of our Saviours Passion; and therefore call it Flos Passionis: and to that end have caused the figures to be drawn and printed, with all the parts proportioned out, as thornes, nailes, speare, whippe, pillar, etc; in it, and all as true as the Sea burnes.'

The common blue, *P. caerula*, which thrives in the open, arrived in 1690. Some varieties are edible, and these were once potted and trained round a wire framework, and served in full fruit on the table with the rest of the dessert, but this was before two world wars, and the peace that ushered in the frozen, pre-packaged, soon-prepared and as-soon-forgotten meal.

By the eighteenth century the flower legends lose their simplicity. They are moral but contrived. The parable of the Tulip and the Myrtle comes from the published letters between St Evremond and Edmund Waller, the poet. Together with the Sunflower and the Ivy, the Garden Rose and the Wild Rose,

and other similar fables, they were versified by Dr Langhorne in 1804. The worthy doctor sees to it that the Tulip, boastful creature that she is, is put firmly in her place by the Myrtle.

> *Deluded flower! the Myrtle cries,*
> *Shall we thy moment's bloom adore?*
> *The meanest shrub that you despise*
> *The meanest flower has merit more.*

The wanton beauty expands her petals to the sun, regardless of dark warnings from the Myrtle.

> *Those leaves, alas! no more would close;*
> *Relaxed, exhausted, sickening, pale;*
> *They left her to a parent's woes*
> *And fled before the rising gale.*

It is much as we expected.

The legend of the moss rose comes to us from Germany. One day, a tired angel was sleeping in the shade of a rose tree. When the angel awoke, he asked the rose what he could give her in return for her hospitality. The answer can be told in the words of Krummacher, which were translated and included in a few of our Victorian Language of Flowers books.

> *The spirit paused in silent thought –*
> *What grace was there that flower had*
> *not?*
> *'Twas but a moment – o'er the Rose*
> *A veil of moss the Angel throws,*
> *And, robed in nature's simplest weed,*
> *Could there a flower that Rose exceed?*

Although of an earlier date (the moss rose was first mentioned in a Dutch catalogue of 1720) both the moss rose and its legend are typical of the period when chair legs were modestly draped, and mantelpieces braided and fringed with green silk bobbles.

In the eighteenth century the flower legend suffered the vapours of the period; in the nineteenth it stifled and died in a feather-bed of morality.

Yet how flowers appeared has occupied the minds of men and women the world over, from the nebulous beginnings of thought, and still we neither know how, nor why.

FABLE VIII.

THE TULIP AND THE MYRTLE *.

'Twas on the border of a stream
A gayly-painted Tulip stood,
And, gilded by the morning beam,
Surveyed her beauties in the flood.

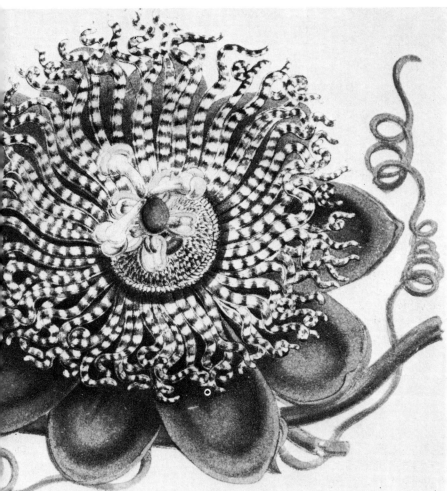

Top left: The Tulip and the Myrtle, from Dr Langhorne, *The Fables of Flora,* 1804. Dr John Langhorne was born at Winton, in Westmorland, 1735. He was a poet, and became rector of Blagdon, Somerset, where he died in 1779.

Top right: 'The Jesuites Figure of the Maracoc', from Parkinson's *Paradisi in Sole Paradisus Terrestris,* 1629. Figures of the flower were manufactured for devotional purposes, with iron nails for stigmas and real thorns for the thready rays.

Left: *Passiflora quadrangularis Decaisneana*, a crimson passion flower. From *The Floricultural Cabinet,* 1855. Associated with St Francis and his bride, the Lady Poverty, the passion flower climbed the Cross and covered its arms with flowers.

Overleaf: *Madonna and Child with pomegranate*; studio of Botticelli. National Gallery. The pagan symbol of the pomegranate was adopted by the Jewish and Christian religions, and its shape and internal structure used to symbolize the Oneness of the universe. It was also a symbol of fertility.

III
Plant Deities and Garden Saints

Pre-dating the saints, and anything but a saint himself, Priapus was worshipped by Greeks and Romans as the god of procreation, and so, of gardens and vineyards. Statues, later described as 'hideous, sensual and disgusting', were often placed in their gardens to serve a double purpose, that of protector against depredation, and that of scarecrow. One could imagine the race of leering dwarfs that today inhabit the gardens of suburbia to be the mini-progeny of this ancient horticultural figure.

Priapus, son of Dionysus and Aphrodite, or some say of a local nymph, was originally worshipped at Lampsacus, on the Hellespont, where asses were sacrificed in his honour. The story goes that an ass once brayed and awoke Lotis, a daughter of Neptune, who adroitly turned into a lotus-lily to escape the unwelcome attentions of Priapus. The potency of such a god was obviously in great demand, and he was taken over as the protector of shepherds, farmers and fishermen.

Flora was the Roman goddess of blossoming plants. A temple was built in her honour in 238 BC. Its dedication date was 28 April, and the Floralia was celebrated annually with dancing and games and the playing of indecent farces. Flora maintained a dubious respectability until May Day celebrations were abolished in England in 1644, and indeed, the scandalous behaviour objected to by the Puritans should not be laid at the door of Flora herself, but at that of her over-enthusiastic followers.

In 1661 a tract was published by Thomas Hall, entitled *Indictment of Flora*. In it Flora is brought to trial before a jury including the Holy Scriptures, Pliny, Charles II, the Ordinance of Parliament, and Ovid. The case commences:

> Flora, hold up thy hand, thou art here indicted by the name of Flora, of the city of Rome, in the county of Babylon, for that thou, contrary to the peace of our sovereign lord, his crown and dignity, hast brought in a pack of practical fanatics, viz. — ignorants, atheists, papists, drunkards, swearers, swashbucklers, maidmarians, morrice-dancers, maskers, mummers, May-pole stealers, health-drinkers, together with a rascallion rout of fiddlers, fools, fighters, gamesters, lewd-women, lightwomen, contemners of magistracy, affronters of ministry, rebellious to masters, disobedient to parents, misspenders of time, and abusers of the creature, &c.

After the various statements, the Judge sums up the case:

> Flora, thou hast been indicted for bringing in abundance of misrule

23

and disorder into church and state; thou hast been found guilty, and art condemned both by God and man, – by scriptures, fathers, councils, – by learned and pious divines, – and therefore I adjudge thee to

PERPETUAL BANISHMENT,

that thou no more disturb this church and state, lest justice do arrest thee.

After which, the followers of Flora settled down quietly to more innocent games on the village green, and may-poles were raised once more to celebrate the coming of spring.

The guileless Furry Dancers of Helston in Cornwall, decked in their bunches of lilies of the valley, happily dancing in the narrow streets, knocking at doors, bowing and curtseying to usher in the spring, might be a little startled to learn of their rakish antecedents. The Furry Dance takes place on 8 May, its name a corruption of Floralia; but Flora has learnt her lesson, and it is pleasant to know that she has lived down her disgrace, and that the good people of Helston may enjoy her festival with comparative decorum.

And in May, in countryside and garden, we may find her footprints.

Here! she was wont to goe! and here! and
here!
Just where those Daisies, Pincks, and
Violets grow;
The world may find the Spring by
following her.

Born to Priapus and the fruitful Flora was a son, Paralisos, who died of grief for his lost love. Paralisos, like most of those who died of love in those far-off days, was changed into a flower, a primrose, it is said. No flower could have been less well chosen to represent the son of such parents than the simple and delicate primrose, but there it is.

With the coming of Christianity, two saints were honoured as the patrons of gardens: St Phocas, the patron saint of gardeners and sailors, and St Fiacre, an Irish prince turned hermit, who looked after the cab-drivers of France, as well as

gardeners. This duplication of duties seems to have been the common fate of gods and saints alike.

St Phocas, whose brawny, bearded statue, dressed as a gardener and holding a spade, is still to be seen at St Mark's in Venice, cultivated his garden towards the end of the third century. All the flowers and vegetables he grew flourished, and he earned a living by the sale of his produce. When it came to the ears of the governors of Pontus, where he lived, that Phocas was a Christian, lictors (law enforcement officers) were sent to search for and kill him. The assassins failed to find him, but called at his house unknowingly and asked for shelter for the night.

Phocas gave them food and hospitality, as he did to all wayfarers, and during the course of the evening the strangers told him that they were in search of one Phocas, a Christian, and that it was their mission to kill him. Phocas said nothing. Late that night the travellers retired to bed, and Phocas went out into his beloved garden, and there, in the darkness, he dug his own grave among the flowers. He prepared his soul for death, and when morning came and his guests were ready to depart, Phocas told them that they need look no further, that the man for whom they searched stood before them. The lictors were horrified that they must kill their kindly host, but they obeyed their orders. And so Phocas was buried in the grave he had dug, a martyr to his faith, and men of the soil share with men of the sea his feast day on 3 July.

Three hundred years later, and in another part of the world, Fiacre, an Irish prince, left his own green land to join the new monastery of Saint Croix at Meaux, on the river Marne, near Paris. For a few years he lived there with the other brothers, until he was filled with a deep longing to live the life of a hermit, alone in the woods away from the monastery and his fellow men, in silent communion with God.

Fiacre, with the permission of his bishop, cleared a space in the woods, and built with his own hands an oratory to Our Lady, and a simple hut in which to spend his life. Around these primitive

buildings he began to dig a garden, with a spade of his own making. Self-denial has been called the luxury of saints, and here Fiacre lived in the luxury of happiness, growing what vegetables and fruit he needed to sustain life. Travellers would sometimes call on Fiacre, and their visits became more and more frequent, until he was forced to build another hut to shelter those who came from far away to consult him, or to be healed in times of sickness. Soon Fiacre found it necessary to go to the bishop to ask for more land. The bishop granted him as much land as he could enclose with his spade in one day.

Back went Fiacre to his forest clearing, and marked as much land as he could encircle in the time allotted him. An evil woman, going to the Bishop of Meaux, accused Fiacre of magic and of having dealings with the Devil, for a miracle had happened; the ground was cleared by a host of angels, and by sunset was ready for his building. From then onward all women were denied access to the oratory. Nearly a thousand years after his death, when Anne of Austria visited his shrine in the cathedral of Meaux, she did not enter the chapel but remained outside the grating.

In commemoration of the miracle, Fiacre became the patron saint of gardeners. He died in 670, and on the site of his cell a great Benedictine priory was built, where his body was kept, and people came to be healed, particularly of a disease that came to be called 'le fie de St Fiacre'. At the beginning of the seventeenth century his body was removed to the cathedral at Meaux.

In 1640, a man by the name of Sauvage started a business in Paris from which he let out small four-wheeled carriages for hire. He took a house in the Rue St Martin known as the Hotel de St Fiacre, and there was a figure of the saint over the doorway. Coaches hired from here began to be called fiacres, and drivers placed images of the saint on their carriages, and spoke of him as their saint. In England too, hackney coaches were known as fiacres. There are churches and altars to St Fiacre all over France, and the people of Brittany have a special Pardon of St Fiacre for penitents.

Page 23 above: St Phocas, Jacques Callot (1592–1635), *Les Images de tous les saintes*, 1636. St Phocas died willingly for God, and was buried in his garden. His flower is the common mallow.

Page 23 below: St Fiacre, from Jacques Callot, *Les Images de tous les saintes.* St Fiacre, son of an Irish king, was born in 600. He became the patron saint of gardeners and later, *c.* 1650, of cab drivers. His name was given to the hackney coach. His day is celebrated on 30 August.

Left: 'The Genius of Botany explaining to the Gardner the Characters of Plants, while Flora and Pomona offer him their choicest Products as Rewards of his labour'. John Hill, *A Compleat Body of Gardening*, 1757.

IV
The Doctrine of Signatures

Right: *Anemone (Hepatica) angulosa*, a rare alpine variety. From *The Floral World*, 1875.

Far right: 'The Mosse upon dead mens Sculls, *Muscus ex Craneo Humano'*, cured disorders of the brain and skull. From John Parkinson, *Theatrum Botanicum*, 1640. Cultivation of this whitish moss was attempted for medicinal purposes.

Many of the ancient herbalists believed that a number of plants had been stamped by God with the image of their properties, that those who gathered them might read. This likeness might be found in a knotted root, the shape of a leaf, or even the colour of the juices within the plant.

I have ofttimes declared, how by the outward shapes and qualities of things, we may know their inward virtues, which God hath put in them for the use of man. So in St. John's Wort we may take notice of the leaves, the porosity of the leaves, the veins – (1) The porosity or holes in the leaves signifies to us that this herb helps inward or outward holes or cuts in the skin. (2) The flowers of St. John's Wort, when they are purified, they are like blood; which teaches us that this herb is good for wounds, to close them and fill them up.

These perforations in the leaves are in fact glandular dots, which became the signature of wounds, serving to reinforce the signature of the red juice.) This theory, thus outlined by Paracelsus, who lived between 1493 and 1541, was taken up with enthusiasm by other physicians. Phillipus Aureolus Theophrastus Bombastus von Hohenheim, who conveniently Latinized the last part of his name to Paracelsus, was to some the father of modern chemistry, to others a mountebank and a quack. He was a German-Swiss physician and alchemist, and important in the history of medicine chiefly on account of the impetus he gave to the development of pharmaceutical chemistry. One of the many legends concerning him is that he kept a small demon or familiar in the hilt of his sword. Although the Doctrine of Signatures is usually associated with his name, the greatest exponent of the theory was Giambattista della Porta. It was laid down as a serious doctrine by Giambattista della Porta in 1588. One of the most gifted men of his time, he invented both the camera obscura and the telescope. He experimented in the art of distillation and cultivated rare plants in his garden at Naples, and in his

published work, *Phytognomica*, he stated his belief in the Doctrine of Signatures. In 1644 Robert Turner, an astrological botanist, added his support. He wrote, 'For what climate soever is subject to any particular disease, in the same place there grows a cure.' In a world so well organised, it would seem scarcely necessary for man to be afflicted with these ills in the first place. Nevertheless, it was a comforting idea that no doubt assisted the believer, and there were many, to a speedy recovery.

William Coles, in 1657, concluded that although a certain number of plants were endowed with signatures in order to assist man in his search for herbal remedies, others were purposely left blank, in order to encourage him to discover their properties for himself; a most accommodating notion. Searching for signatures as well as simples must have become an absorbing occupation. Simples, at that time, signified medicines made from a single herb. Those made from several were known as compounds. Coles was of the opinion 'that if those of these times would but be . . . as industrious to search into the secrets of the nature of Herbs, as some of the former times, and make a tryall of them as they did, [they] should no doubt find the force of Simples . . . no lesse

Effectuall, than that of Compounds, to which this present age is too much addicted. Thus have I broken the Nut of Herbarisme, do thou take out the Kernel and eate it and much good may it do thee'.

The theory, like the herb, was simplicity itself. Those with a yellow sap would cure jaundice; those whose surface was rough to the touch would heal all skin diseases. The stony seeds of gromwell, *Lithospermum officinale*, the 'stone seed' of Dioscorides, were good for gravel; the spotted leaves of pulmonaria or lungwort, or the inside of a foxglove flower, were a sovereign remedy for tubercular lungs, or a sore throat. The liver-shaped leaves of hepatica, or liverwort, were regarded as a certain cure for diseases of the liver. Even the habit of the saxifrage of growing in the fissures of rocks, as well as the formation of its root, caused it to be prescribed as a cure for stones in the bladder. The 'little knoppes like pearles' were sold to be boiled in wine, and taken to purify the kidneys. 'The little leaf-like tongue', known to William Coles as Horse-tongue, 'growing upon the greater is no light argument that this plant is effectual for sores in the mouth and throat . . . it is good also for those that have an imperfection in their speech.' Conjectures grew wilder. Flowers

Muſcus ex Cra= neo Hu= mano

shaped like butterflies would cure the bites of insects; roots with a jointed appearance, or the buds of a forget-me-not bent round in a spiral resembling a scorpion's tail, were sure remedies for the bites of serpents, and so forget-me-nots were called scorpion-grass at this time. The juice of celandine restored the sight of the swallow. 'It is called Celandine not because it first springeth at the coming in of Swallowes, or dieth when they go away . . . but because some hold the opinion, that with this herb the dames restore sight to their young ones when they cannot see.' Gerard, however, hastened to add, 'Which things are false'.

It was this persuasive doctrine that gave names to many of our herbs. Toothwort, *Lathraea squamaria*, with its white scales, was good for the teeth, self-heal, *Prunella vulgaris*, as a balm for all cuts and bruises, and feverfew, *Chrysanthemum parthenium*, as a soothing herb for all feverish diseases. Feverfew was later grown commercially as a medicinal plant. Tutsan, *Hypericum androsaemum*, used for all grazes and wounds, took its name from *toute-saine*, 'all wholesome'.

Viper's bugloss, *Echium chamaedrys*, with a stem speckled like a snake, was an antidote for snakebite and scorpion stings, a property believed to have been discovered by Alcibiades after a snake had bitten him in his sleep. Germander speedwell, *Veronica chamaedrys*, became known as Birds-eye, Cat's-eye or Angel's eye, from the belief that it was a cure for sore eyes. Clary or Clear-eyes, *Salvia horminoides*, was also prescribed for 'those who suffer from waterish humours, rednesse, inflammation, and divers other maladies, or all that happen under the eyes'; and so was Eyebright, *Euphrasia officinalis*, known to the poet Spenser.

Yet euphrasie may not be left unsung,
That gives dim eyes to wander leagues
around.

In 1855, Anne Pratt reported that 'on going into a small shop in Dover, she saw a quantity of eyebright suspended from the ceiling and was informed that it was gathered and dried as being good for weak eyes', and William Thistleton

28

Dyer, Director of Kew, confirmed that in country districts it was in use in 1888. It still keeps its place in modern herbals. Clover and trefoil became heart-clover and heart-trefoil, causing William Coles to announce that they were so-called 'not only because the leaf is triangular like the heart of a man, but also because each leafe doth contain the perfect icon (or image) of an heart, and that in its proper colour viz., a flesh colour. It defendeth the heart against the noisome vapour of the spleen'. So also the wood-sorrel, *Oxalis acetosella*, and the little wild pansy, the heartsease, *Viola tricolour*, were used as cordials.

Colours played an important part in the Doctrine of Signatures. Red roses were used for nose-bleeding. Mulberries and pomegranate seeds, the red root of the tormentil, *Potentilla erecta*, given 'in the water of a smith's forge, or rather the water wherein hot steele hath been often quenched of purpose', and the red leaves of herb-robert, *Geranium robertianum*, were all used to staunch blood. Jaundice was cured not only by the yellow juice of the celandine and the yellow bark of the barberry, *Berberis vulgaris*, otherwise known as jaundice-plant, but also by turmeric, a plant best known today as the source of a spice used in curry but formerly used for making dye. The freckled cowslip, *Primula veris*, was highly regarded by country girls when it was made into an ointment which 'taketh away spots and wrinkles of the skin', and which, it was claimed, 'adds beauty exceedingly'. A far-off echo of today's cosmetic advertisements.

Theorists went even further afield, and claims grew more extravagant. It was said that if moss were gathered from a skull, it was efficacious in treating disorders of the head and brain. Human skulls which before had accidentally gathered this particular kind of moss, were now placed where such moss was to be found, although how long the patient might expect to wait for his remedy to appear in sufficient quantity is not divulged. There is a description in the *Theatrum Botanicum* of 1640, with an accompanying illustration, of 'The Mosse upon dead mens Sculls, *Muscus ex craneo humano*', which reminds us of the ghost of

Hamlet's father and his 'fretful porpentine'; for each particular hair, or mossy particle, does indeed stand on end, thereby creating a similar reaction in ourselves, and providing yet another instance of the Doctrine of Signatures. 'Let me also adjoyne this kind of Mosse,' says the herbalist, 'not having any other place to insert it.

It is a whitish short kind of Mosse somewhat like unto the Mosse of trees, and groweth upon the bare scalpes of men and women that have lyen long, and are kept in Charnell houses in divers Countries, which hath not onely beene in former times much accounted of, because it is rare and hardly gotten, but in our times much more set by, to make the *Unguentum sympatheticum*, which cureth wounds without locall application of salves, the composition whereof is put as a principall ingredient, but as Crollius hath it, it should be taken from the sculls of those that have beene hanged or executed for offences.

Should the necessary lichen fail to materialize, brain troubles could also be treated with the encephaloid kernel of a walnut. 'Wall-nuts have the perfect Signature of the Head', said William Coles in 1675.

The outer husk or green Covering, represents the Pericranium, or outward skin of the skull, whereon the hair groweth, and therefore salt made of these husks or barks, are exceeding good for wounds in the head. The inner wooddy shell hath the Signature of the Skull, and the little yellow skin, or Peel, that covereth the Kernell, of the hard *Meninga* and *Piamater*, which are the thin scarfes that envelope the brain. The Kernel hath the very figure of the Brain, and therefore it is very profitable for the Brain, and resists poysons; For if the Kernel be bruised, and moystened with the quintessence of Wine, and laid upon the Crown of the Head, it comforts the brain and head mightily.

But perhaps the most indispensable item in the Doctrine of Signatures was the root of Solomon's seal, *Polygonatum multiflorum*, which, cut transversely, showed the characters of a seal. A seal for wounds, according to Gerard, who adds that 'the root of Solomon's Seale stamped, while it is fresh and greene, and applied, taketh away in one night, or two at the most, any bruise, black or blew spots, gotten by falls, or womens wilfulnesse in stumbling upon their hasty husbands' fists'. Without question, no family could afford to be without a root of Solomon's seal.

John Ray, in his treatise *The Wisdom of God in Creation* (1691), was among the first to express his doubts of the ingenious doctrine.

As for the signatures of plants, or the notes impressed upon them as notices of their virtues, some lay great stress upon them, accounting them strong arguments to prove that some understanding principle is the highest original of the work of Nature, as indeed they were could it be certainly made to appear that there were such marks designedly set upon them, because all that I can find mentioned by authors seem to be rather fancied by men than designed by Nature to signify, or point out, any such virtues, or qualities, as they would make us believe.

Having said which, he weakens his case by adding that

the noxious and malignant plants do, many of them, discover something of their nature by the sad and melancolick visage of their leaves, flowers or fruit. And that I may not leave that head wholly untouched, one observation I shall add relating to the virtues of the plants, in which I think there is something of truth – that is, that there are of the wise dispensation of Providence such species of plants produced in every country as are made proper and convenient for the meat and medicine of the men and animals that are bred and inhabit therein.

V
Plants and Planets

Side by side, or rather, strangely intermingled with the Doctrine of Signatures, was the theory of Astrological Botany, in which the ways of men and plants were influenced by the stars. 'There is not an herbe here below, but he hath a star in Heaven above, and the star strikes him with her beames, and says to him "Grow!"', wrote Thomas Vaughan. Paracelsus, having made his contribution to the Doctrine of Signatures, threw himself with his customary enthusiasm into Astrological Botany. He was full of botanical mysticism, and held that each plant was a terrestrial star, and each star a spiritualized plant. There were, of course, both critics and supporters of this theory. Francis Bacon was not uncritical, and stated his views with his usual clarity.

Some of the Ancients, and likewise divers of the Moderne Writers, that have laboured in *Naturall Magick*, have noticed a *Sympathy*, between the *Sunne*, *Moone*, and some Principall *Starres*; And certaine Herbs, and *Plants*. And so they have denominated some *Herbs Solar*, and some *Lunar*; and such like Toyes put into great Words. It is manifest, that there are some Flowers, that have *Respect* to the *Sunne*, in two *Kindes*; The one by *Opening* and *Shutting*; and the other by *Bowing* and *Inclining* the *Head*. For *Mary-Golds*, Tulippas, Pimpernell, and indeed most *Flowers*, doe open or spread their Leaves abroad, when the Sunne shineth serene and fair: And againe, (in some part) close them, or gather them inward, either towards Night, or when the Skie is overcast . . . . For the *Bowing* and *Inclining* of the Head; it is found in the great Flower of the Sunne; in Mary-golds; Wart-wort; Mallow Flowers; and others.

As Thomas Tusser had written in his *Five Hundred Points of Good Husbandrie* in 1562,

Sow peason and beanes in the wane of the moone,
  Who soweth them sooner, he soweth too soone,
That they with the planet may rest and arise,

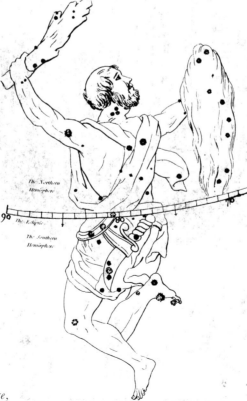

The Northern Hemisphere

The Ecliptic

The Southern Hemisphere

And flourish with bearing most plentiful wise.

It was not only plants, but men who were moon-governed. Charles Estienne wrote, seven years later, 'The farmer shall not be content to know what force and efficacy every quarter of the moon hath upon beasts, trees, plants, herbs, fruit, and other things: but shall also be carefull to observe what powers every day of the moon hath not only upon beast and plant, but also in the disposition and government of man'. Aubrey agreed that 'if a plant be not gathered according to the rules of astrology, it hath little or no virtue in it'. A useful tip came from John Woolridge:

The seeds from which you expect to have double Flowers, must be sown at the Full of the Moon, or in two or three days after. It hath been long observed that the Moon hath great influence over Plants . . . And if it hath any such influence, then surely it is in the doubling of Flowers.

William Turner had also supported the theory in his *New Herbal* (1551). But it was Master Nicholas Culpeper, who set up in Spitalfields as an astrologer and physician about 1640, who had the most to say on the subject. As peppery as the wild rocket he prescribes 'to increase sperm and venerous qualities', he hurls insults right and left at doctors and herbalists alike, calling as his witnesses Dr Reason and Dr Experience, with the assistance of Dr Diligence and Mr Honesty. The medical profession in general he describes as 'a company of proud, insulting, domineering doctors' – a clear case of pot calling kettle black – 'whose wits were born about 500 years before themselves'. Culpeper had studied the works of Hippocrates, Galen and Avicen, who regarded those who were ignorant of astrology as homicides. Paracelsus, indeed, had gone even further, and declared that a physician should be predestinated to the cure of his patient – the horoscope should be inspected and the plants gathered at the critical moment.

Lest the whole science should be regarded as too simple, and beneath the consideration of the learned, the Four Elements and the Four Humours were brought into the scheme of things. Every plant was allotted its share in the properties of Fire (hot and dry), Air (hot and moist), Earth (cold and dry), and Water (cold and moist) in various proportions. Cures were forthcoming according to whether the patient was considered to be Choleric or Melancholic, Sanguine or Phlegmatic, and according to the hot or cold nature of his disease. Sappy plants belonged to the moon. The bryonies, 'of a most loathsome taste ... are furious martial plants', while the innocent heartsease is 'saturnine, something cold, viscous and slimy', and under the celestial sign of Cancer. The signs of the Zodiac were as essential to Nicholas Culpeper's treatments as plant signatures were to the cures of William Coles. When he was not discussing his cases with Dr Reason or Dr Experience, or decrying the nitwitted treatments handed out by Dr Tradition, Culpeper was in communication with the planets, who acted as unpaid consultants over difficult cases. 'The other day Mars told me he met with Venus, and he asked her, What was the reason that she accused him for abusing women? He never gave them the pox. In the dispute they fell out, and in anger parted, and Mars told me that his brother Saturn told him, that an antivenerean medicine was the best against the pox.' And so the herb was given, and Culpeper turned to the next patient.

His theory that 'you may oppose diseases by Herbs of the planet', but that 'there is a way to cure diseases some-times by Sympathy, and so every planet cures his own disease', should have enabled him to die a wealthy man, when his planets finally tired in 1654. Nicholas, however, was as free of his purse as he was of his pen, and this was not the case.

To steer by the stars the botanical astrologer needed confidence, not to say effrontery, and more than a little luck. At any rate, that must have been the opinion of William Coles, who, although an advocate of the Doctrine of Signatures, refused to have anything to do with belief in the connection between stars and herbs.

It [the study of herbs] is a subject as antient as the Creation, yea more antient than the Sunne or the Moon, or Starres, they being created on the

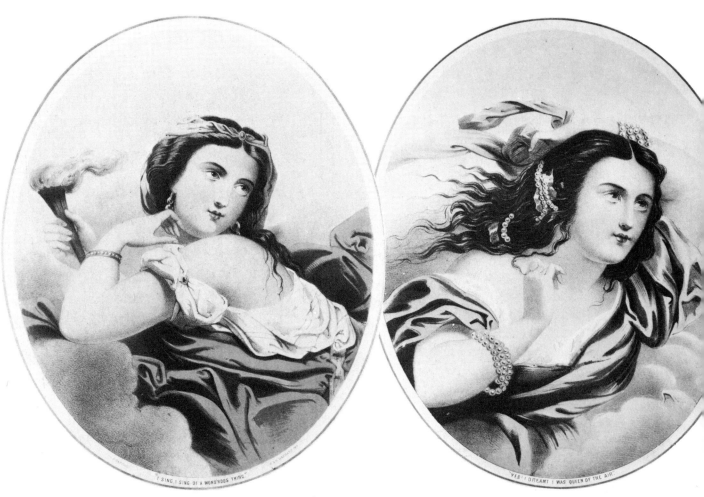

'I SING, I SING OF A WOND'ROUS THING'   'YES, I DREAMT I WAS QUEEN OF THE AIR'

fourth day whereas Plants were the third. Thus did God even at first confute the folly of those Astrologers who goe about to maintaine that all vegetables in their growth are enslaved to a necessary and unavoidable dependence on the influences of the starres; whereas Plantes were even when Planets were not.

Even as late as 1826, Dr Parkins, at the conclusion of his *English Physician*, gives tables and instructions for 'Gathering Herbs and Plants in the Planetary Hour', and 'How to find the Planetary Hours for each Day in the Week', 'to such as study astrology, who are the only men I know that are fit to study physic, physic without astrology being like a lamp without oil'.

Kennedy-Bell points out that although in Deuteronomy we read that precious

Below: The Four Elements, according to Aristotle, are Earth, Air, Fire and Water. Plants were governed by the Planets and influenced by the Elements, which were said to be 'hot and dry' (Fire), 'hot and moist' (Air), 'cold and dry' (Earth), and 'cold and moist' (Water). Here four Victorian beauties, symbolizing the Elements, embellish the ballads of their day. The Four Elements, by virtue of the theory of correspondences, may be associated with the Four Ages (waxing, fullness, waning and disappearing), and the four points of the compass.

Overleaf: *Ceres and the Four Elements*. The figures by Hendrik van Balen (1575–1632), the flowers, trees, birds and animals by Jan Breughel (1568–1625).

things are put forth by the moon, but precious fruits by the sun, it is a remarkable fact that, although through the ages the sun has been worshipped as the supreme luminary, from whose life-giving rays all vegetation draws its existence, at the same time, the growth and decay of plant life has been associated most intimately with the waxing and waning of the moon, and to this day the association persists.

The moon waxes and wanes, and stars shine with apparent indifference, while men theorize below them, but it is with Nicholas Culpeper, with his impatience, his hot temper, and his generosity, that we should leave the last word.

He that would know the reason of the operation of the Herbs, must look up as high as the Stars. ●

"THE BEAUTIFUL EARTH FOR ME"

"IN A ROAMER O'ER THE MOUNTAIN"

Presiding over the infernal regions, the Greek goddess Hecate taught magic, sorcery and witchcraft. To Hecate were dedicated the mandrake, the deadly nightshade, and aconite, azalea, cyclamen, mint, and osiers. She instructed her two daughters, Medea and Circe, in the properties and uses of herbs, and this had proved invaluable in the education of witches. Not only black witches, but the half-hearted grey ones, and white witches who only worked for good, were learned in plant lore, and so were the young and beautiful enchantresses, such as Morgan le Fay.

Controlling the birth, life and death of men and women were the three Fates: Clotho, who held the distaff, Lachesis, who spun the thread of life, and Atropos, who cut the thread when life was ended. It was after the cruel Atropos that deadly nightshade, *Atropa belladonna*, was named.

In the corner of the witch's garden there stood a cracked and skinny yew tree. The ground beneath was parched and

VI
Witchcraft and Wild Flowers

bare, for it is a well-known fact that nothing will grow beneath a yew. It wood was unsuitable for broomsticks although yew trees had been very highly thought of for making bows for archers The witch, therefore, had to depend on an ash, whose wood, used for a broom handle, would protect her from drowning. A bundle of birch twigs would be tied with osiers, Hecate's plant, and therefore a protection for witches, sorely needed in a precarious existence.

In her garden she grew hemlock, of course, and henbane, and there was a nice bed of deadly nightshade which would come in useful sooner or later Cinquefoil flourished, and so did vervain and endive, and the bryony might be needed when mandrakes were in short supply. She did not care for yellow or greenish flowers, with one or two exceptions, which included spurge and, of course, cinquefoil.

Fortunately the sun never shone on the witch's garden, for the least gleam would have ruined the medicinal prop rties of her herbs. A tall and straggly hawthorn hedge surrounded her modest property. 'Hedge' is derived from the same word as 'hag,' and hags, or witches, were believed to shelter in hedges, particularly hawthorn hedges; indeed, hags, hedges and hawthorn were always closely associated. So, for that matter, are hags and besoms, for difficult old ladies are often referred to as 'old besoms'.

Outside her hedge the witch would go hunting for other herbs: foxgloves or witch's bells, to decorate her skinny fingers; mullein or hag-taper for her candles; harebells for her thimbles; and ragwort, which had the useful property of turning into a horse, so that she could fly over the countryside when a broomstick was not at hand. Even a bundle of hay would serve, if she were hard put to it. No one ever saw the black witch picking her herbs, for they had to be harvested in secrecy, at certain phases of the moon and seasons of the year, and the signs of the Zodiac must be consulted.

Below: *Atropa belladonna*, the deadly nightshade, was named after Atropos, one of the Three Fates, whose duty was to cut the thread of life when it had ended. The name *belladonna* comes from its ancient use among Italian women ('beautiful lady') to make the eye lustrous by enlarging the pupils.

Opposite: Venomous snakes support the table on which Grandville's Hemlock-woman mixes her deadly brew. A mad March hare acts as a poison-taster, and a bloated toad has already succumbed. *Les Fleur's Animées*.

Her favourite herbs, such as the horned poppy, *Ficus infernalis*, caused hallucinations among the countryfolk she treated, an effect which gave her great satisfaction.

Ben Jonson in his portrayal of witches in his plays shows an intimate knowledge of herbs and their properties. In *The Sad Shepherd* he makes Alken, describing the witch of Popplewicke, Maudlin the Envious, say:

> *The venom'd Plants*
> *Wherewith shee Kills! where the sad*
> *Mandrake growes,*
> *Whose grones are deathfull! the dead-*
> *numming Nightshade!*
> *The stupifying Hemlock! Adders tongue!*
> *and Martagòn!*

Our flesh creeps and we shudder happily.

It is no great wonder that the witch was a little unbalanced in her behaviour, when one understands that so many herbs and plants, her very life blood,

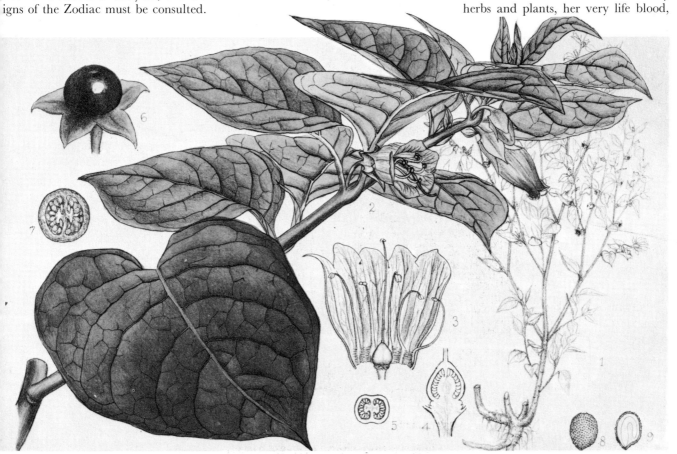

Left: *Departure for the Sabbat.*
Engraving by J. Aliamet, after
David Teniers (1582–1649). Traditionally, the witch's feet and
shoulders were anointed with the
fat of a murdered babe before she
mounted her broomstick to ride to
the Witches' Sabbat or Sabbath, a
feast of witches and demons,
which ended with a dance in which
they turned their backs to one
another. These orgies were held
four times a year, on Candlemas
(2 February), Walpurgis Night
(30 April), Lammas (1 August), and
Hallowe'en (31 October).

could equally well be turned against
her. Over the years the demands made
upon our herbs have been heavy. The
list of anti-witch plants is long, and beliefs in their efficacy were held in many
parts of the world. Elders, for instance,
could give the power to any baptized
man or woman, whose eyes had been
anointed with the juice, to see witches
be they never so far away, and so elders
were often planted near to cottages. In
Italy, branches of juniper were hung
over doorways to frighten them away.
The Germans, Norwegians and Danes
preferred rowan.

Rowan-tree and red thread,
Put the witches to their speed.

It is said that German witches hate marjoram, *Dost*, since it protects against
their spells, and drives away ghosts and
goblins.
Holy plants such as angelica were a
great protection. The holly, the holy
tree, with its prickly leaves signifying

Above: Discourse of Witchcraft, as
it was acted by the Family of Mr
Edward Fairfax of Fuystone, 1621.
From a MS in the British Museum.
The animals that surround the bent
figure muttering her spells are all
her 'familiars'.

thorns and its scarlet berries the blood of
Christ, were proof against the evil eye.
Consecrated flowers, or flowers and
leaves made into a cross, were also a sure
protection. Agrimony, maiden-hair and
ground-ivy were also of assistance
to witch-hunters, and so were wych- or
witch-hazel and the witch-elm. The
word 'witch' originally referred to the
pliant nature of the wood, and comes
from the Anglo-Saxon wic-en, to bend,
and wicce was an early name for
witches, hence confusion arose. However, folklorists seem to agree about the
magic and protective virtues of the tree.
The Reverend M. D. Conway, in *Mystic Trees and Flowers*, says that 'Groves
of Hazel or of Elm, which thence may
have been called Witch-Hazel (and
Witch-Elm) were frequently chosen by
the Saxons for their temples . . . the
Hazel being one of Thor's trees.' The
first Christian church in England was
built in Glastonbury of wattles of hazel;
and it was with a hazel bough that St
Patrick drove the snakes out of Ireland.

Hazel rods were not only used in water-divining, but in discovering buried treasure, and Brewer says that it is 'a shrub supposed to be efficacious in discovering witches. A forked twig of the hazel was made into a divining-rod for the purpose.'

In Sweden, oats fed to horses were touched with hazel boughs as a protection against the evil eye, and hazel nuts made their owners invisible. The nuts were also used for divination on Nutcrack Night on All Hallows' Eve.

In Germany, the witch-hazel is known as *Zauber-strauch*, the magic tree. In America the *Hamamelis* is also known as witch-hazel, because it too is made into divining-rods.

The greatest insult one could offer any witch was to lay a broom across the threshold. Curse she never so loud, there was no way in. With all these conflicting beliefs, the black witch lived on the very broom-edge of danger.

In Germany, France, Italy, Switzerland and in Scotland, witches, after enduring the most terrible tortures, were burned in the market place. In England they were hanged or strangled, and their bodies burnt thereafter. Poor old skinny hags were thrown into deep water to prove their innocence. They had their hands and feet tied together crosswise, the thumb of the right hand to the toe of the left foot, and vice versa. They were then wrapped up in a blanket and laid upon their backs in a pond or river. Let them prove that they aren't witches by swimming to the other side, people said. If they floated then of course they were witches, and would be suitably dealt with. If they drowned their characters would be cleared. It was cold, and damp, comfort for the witch, but at least it settled the point. A handful of ash or a sodden heap of old clothes at the bottom of a pond was all that was left, but it was enough; and when they were buried, what was left of them, in unhallowed ground, an aspen was laid on the grave to prevent them riding abroad.

Whatever evil was done by the witch was repaid in full, with the hounding to death of thousands of these miserable old bodies. Their witchcraft was of no avail; their magic herbs failed them.

Page 41: Title page from Gerard's *Herbal*; an early printed edition of 1597. Bodleian Library, Oxford. The *Herbal* contains 1,800 illustrations, much contemporary folklore, and an invaluable picture of the wild-flower life in London. Gerard was born at Nantwich in Cheshire in 1545. He died in 1611–12, and was buried in St Andrew's Church, Holborn. (Chapter 10, 'Some Herbals and Herbalists'.)

Page 42 Above: Victorian Children's Christmas Card. Victoria and Albert Museum. The favourite flowers of children such as these were 'three noble creatures, Hollyhocks, Canterbury Bells and Foxgloves. I cannot think of a garden without these three old favourites of history and folk-lore' Alice Morse, *Old Time Gardens*, Earle, 1902. (Chapter 15 'From Lady Mary's Purse.')

Page 42 Below: *The Language of Flowers.* Painting by G. D. Leslie, 1885. City of Manchester Art Gallery. An evocative period painting.

Unheeded flew the hours,
For softly falls the foot of Time
That only treads on flowers.

Anonymous
(Chapter 15, 'From Lady Mary's Purse'.)

Page 43: Astrological Chart from Andreas Cellarius, *Atlas Coelistis Hemisphaerium stellatum boreale antiquum, c.* 1660. In the astrologer's treatment of disease, the influence of the planet which governed the afflicted part of the body must be opposed by herbs under the influence of a contrary planet; or in some cases by sympathy, that is, each planet curing its own disease. (Chapter 5, 'Plants and Planets'.)

THE
HERBALL
OR GENERALL
Historie of
Plantes.

Gathered by John Gerarde
of London Master in
CHIRVRGERIE.

Imprinted at London by
John Norton.
1597

January

February

March

April

May

June

PHEBVS·

DAPHNE

FLEVVE·PE NEE

Amour premier au cueur de pheb⁹ nee
Ce fut Daphne fille au fleuue penee
Laquelle amour dauci cas diductur

Page 44-5 Below: Victorian fan-type New Year greeting card. Language of Flowers fans were sold also for birthdays and Christmas, some of them with real lace edging. 'Women are armed with fans as men with swords, and sometimes do more execution with them' – Addison in *The Spectator*, 1711. (Chapter 15, 'From Lady Mary's Purse.)

Page 45 Right: Delicate and lasting Pleasures arising from the Cup of Innocence. From Henry Phillips, *Floral Emblems*, 1825. Henry Phillips's flowery cup would have been of small appeal to Omar Kháyyám, for it is a symbol of Temperance. Here the sweet pea, *Lathyrus odoratus*, symbolizes Delicate and lasting Pleasure, and the daisies, Innocence. (Chapter 23, 'Floral Calendars'.)

Page 45 Top: Passion flower, *Passiflora caerulea*. From the Ware Collection of Blaschka glass models in Harvard University. A spray showing a bee entering the flower, which is in the second stage of development (anthers withered, pistils matured). (Chapter 22, 'Flowers and the Craftsman'.)

Pages 46-7: Emblems for the Calendar Months, 1825, by Henry Phillips (1780-1830). From Henry Phillips, *Floral Emblems*, 1825. Emblems existed before the days of the Pharaohs. An emblem unveils the inner meaning of things seen and unseen, and this is what Henry Phillips sets out to do. He symbolizes in flowers, time and the seasons of growing things, and the deep and trivial emotions of humanity. (Chapter 23, Floral Calendars)

Page 48: Apollo pursues Daphne. From a MS. in the Bodleian Library.

The Gods, that mortal beauty
    chase,
Still in a tree did end their race.
Apollo hunted Daphne so,
Only that she might laurel grow.

Andrew Marvell (1620-1678) 'The Garden,' (Chapter 1, 'Flowers and the Gods.')

The Devil, the lord and master of the witches, has left his name, as they did, along the hedgerows. On that never-to-be-forgotten day when he was cast out of heaven, he fell spinning and blaspheming through space, and landed in a blackberry bush. The Devil has a long memory, and he cannot forget or forgive such an indignity, and so every year, punctually on 11 October, the anniversary of his fall, he spits on the blackberries to make them unfit for us to eat. In another and entirely different version, his exit from Eden was slow and reluctant, leaving wormwood in his tracks. Mahomet says that garlic sprang from his left foot, and onion from his right when he was banished.

According to King James I, a vindictive witch-hunter and no friend to the Devil either, it was the Devil who invented tobacco, that noxious weed, and today there would be many who would agree. 'A Custom loathsome to the Eye, hateful to the Nose, harmful to the Brain, dangerous to the Lungs, and in the black stinking Fume thereof, nearest resembling the horrible Stygian Smoke of the Pit that is bottomless.' It must have been the Devil. So thought the Citizen's Wife in *The Knight of the Burning Pestle*, when she cried, 'Fie, this stinking tobacco kills me! would there were none in England! – Now, I pray, gentlemen, what good does this stinking tobacco do you? nothing, I warrant you: make chimneys of your faces!'

As well as the iniquity of having invented tobacco, he was known to lurk in the lettuce beds (although it may have been only the slugs), but it was with the parsley seed that he is usually associated. It is a well-known fact that parsley seed has to go seven times down to the Devil before it will send out roots. Many of the umbelliferous plants that still, but decreasingly, give our country lanes a delicate lace-edged border and make for every bank an altar cloth, have connections with Old Nick. Cow parsley, *Anthriscus sylvestris*, has a selection of names such as Bad Man's Oatmeal, Devil's Meal, Devil's Meat and Devil's Parsley, which must have come from the Old Man's Cook Book. Any wild plant resembling hedge parsley was liable to

VII
The Devil's Plant Lore

be so labelled, although upright hedge parsley, *Torilis japonica*, was known as Devil's Nightcap, surely too lacy and frivolous a decoration for an old gentleman; and fool's parsley, *Aethusa cynapium*, was Devil's Wand.

Pignut, *Conopodium majus*, found mostly in open woods and grassland, with its name of Bad Man's Bread, or Deil's Bread, and Deil's Oatmeal, also belongs to his pantry. How has it come about, then, that another of the *umbelliferae*, the abominable ground elder, *Aegopodium podagraria*, once a useful potherb but now the scourge of man, has escaped devilish nomenclature? We mildly call it Farmer's Plague or Garden Plague, instead of the Devil's Damnation that it is. Ruskin maintained that the Devil was mortally afraid of crocuses and wild roses.

Who sups with the Devil needs a long spoon, and these may be found in the broad-leaved pondweed, *Potamogeton natans*, or Devil's Spoons. Wood spurge, *Euphorbia amygdaloides*, provides his cup and saucer, out of which he may drink Devil's milk from the greater celandine, *Chelidonium majus*, or from the sun spurge, *Euphorbia helioscopia*. Unless, of course, he prefers it from the Devil's Milk Pail, known to us today as the dandelion, *Taraxacum officinale*. The common mallow, *Malva sylvestris*, gives him Old Man's Bread and Cheese. 'From its seeds a round knop like a little cake, compact or made up of a multitude of flat seeds like little cheeses', is Gerard's description.

His meat and parsley both come from the same source, cow parsley. Condiments are supplied by yarrow, *Achillea millefolia*, which gives him Old Man's Mustard and Old Man's Pepper. The latter may be found also in salad burnet, *Poterium sanguisorba*, or in sneezewort, *Achillea ptarmica*, Old Man's Pepper Box. His second course is rather limited, for deadly nightshade provides him with berries, cherries and rhubarb. If he dines by night he may have ground ivy, *Glechoma hederacea*, for his candlestick, and mandrake, *Mandragora officinarum*, for his candle, because its roots shine in the dark.

About the 17th, 18th and 19th of May,

there is a danger of the Devil blighting the apple trees with frost. This is the result of a bargain made with St Dunstan, who had set up as a brewer of ale at Glastonbury. The local cider was so popular that St Dunstan, anxious about the success of his ale, sold his soul to the Devil, who gave an undertaking that on three consecutive mornings there would be such frosts as would destroy the apple blossom for miles around. This unseemly pact is not mentioned in the Saints' Calendar.

Satan enlists the aid of a number of plants in the English countryside. Greater stitchwort, *Stellaria holostea*, an innocent-looking and starlike flower, has a surprising number of unflattering names: Devil's Corn, Devil's Eyes, Devil's Flower, Devil's Nightcap and Devil's Skirt Buttons. The ox-eye daisy, *Chrysanthemum leucanthemum*, was known as Devil's Daisy; and shepherd's needle, *Scandix pecten-veneris*, was the Devil's Darning Needle.

The poisonous plants seem more deserving of their names. Henbane, *Hyocymus niger*, is Devil's Eye; the evil fruit of the thorn-apple, *Datura stramonium*, is known as Devil's Apple, and that of the black bryony, *Tamus communis*, Devil's Berry; while hemlock, *Conium maculatum*, is Bad Man's Oatmeal, Devil's Blossom or Devil's Flower. The Devil's nutting bag is black, so it is inadvisable to carry a black bag for fear that you might be mistaken for him.

Gerard wrote of the Devil's-bit scabious, 'The great part of the root seemeth to be bitten away; old fantasticke charmers report, that the devil did bite it for envie, because it is an herbe that hath so many good vertues, and is so beneficial to mankinde.' As a healing plant its efficacy is somewhat impaired, but it is known as Devil's-bit scabious to this day. The American devilsbit, otherwise and probably more suitably known as Fairywand, is unrelated, and, as far as I know, unchewed.

Naughty Man, Old Man or even Old Uncle Harry, for mugwort, *Artemisia vulgaris*, are all Devil-names. One would scarcely expect the Old Man to be ignorant of natural aphrodisiacs, and here we have periwinkle, *Vinca*, Devil's Eye,

Right: Common houseleek, *Sempervivum tectorum*. 1812. Devil's Beard, or Welcome-home-husband-be-it-never-so-late. A clear case of the Devil looking after his own, for it is a plant that should never be uprooted.

Far right: Dandelion, *Taraxacum officinale*, known as the Devil's Milk Pail. To spite Old Nick the provident housewife may use its leaves for greens and salads, and its roots, roasted and ground, for coffee.

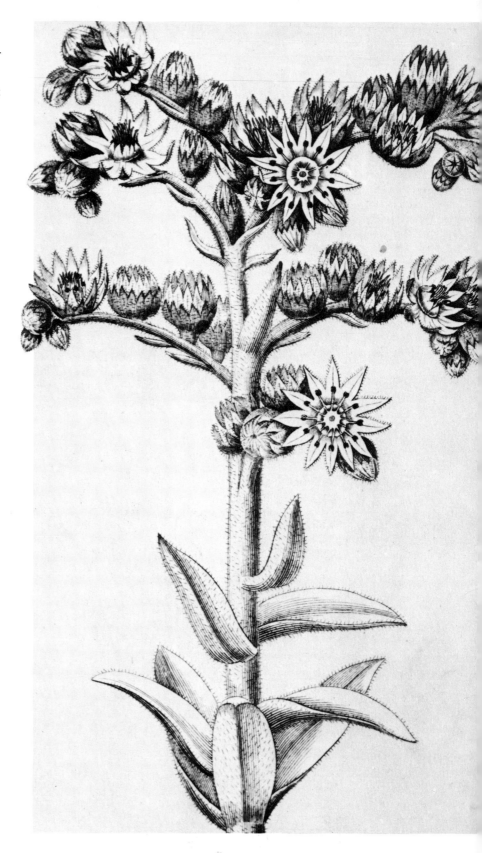

whose 'Leaves eaten by Man and Wife together, cause love between them', and Devil's Beard, houseleek, *Sempervivum tectorum*, another of whose names, 'Welcome-home-husband-be-it-never-so-late', has an encouraging sound. The sturdy spadix of the flower of the *Arum maculatum*, with its enveloping green spathe, has obvious sexual significance, and granted that one agrees that venery is of the Devil, then it depends upon one's social outlook as to whether it should be known as Lords and Ladies or the Devil's Men and Women.

The Devil, Old Nick, Naughty Old Man or what you will, seems to be on his home ground in Britain and has so far made only tentative attempts to settle in the New World. He has his Devilspaintbrush, in the orange hawk-weed, *Hieracium*, which he can hold in his Devilsclaw, but since this is one of the Sensitive plant family, *Mimoseacea*, whose leaves fold up at a touch, he is quite likely to drop his paintbrush. In this case, he can try again with another Devilsclaw, one of the Unicornplants, *Proboscidea*. His Devilshorn, *P. althae-folia*, is a smaller relative, and of course, he has a Devilstongue, a cactus. He has no choice of menu, being restricted to the Devilspotato, *Echites umbellata*, a prickly pear. One would hardly have thought it possible but the Devil is not yet fully established in America. He has also a foothold in Germany with the aconite, the *Teufelswurz*, or Devil's herb. The Devil's plants, as you will see, are many, but as with witches, there are anti-Devil plants for his undoing. Sometimes those same plants that he considered his allies could be turned against him to break his spells. Herb-bennet, the blessed plant, vervain, and dill are powerful Devil-deterrents, and he can find no footing in the gardens where they grow.

In *The Faithful Shepherdess*, Clorin, a shepherd, enters sorting herbs, and these are all herbs for the breaking of spells. There is much of the virtues of herbs and fountains, the ordinary course of the sun, moon and stars, and such like, in this charming play, and John Fletcher explains this in the foreword. 'Thus much I hope will serve to justify my poem, and make you understand it; to teach you more for nothing, I do not known that I am in conscience bound.'

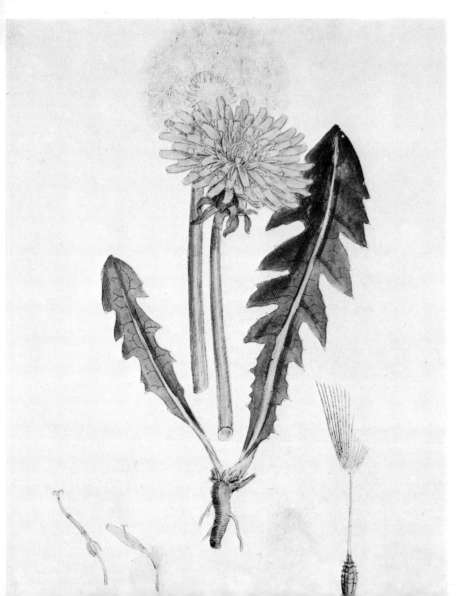

This is the clote [Burdock], bearing a
　　yellow flower;
And this, black horehound; both are very
　　good
For sheep or shepherd bitten by a wood
Dog's venomed tooth: these rhamnus'
　　[Buckthorn] branches are
Which, stuck in entries, or about the bar
That holds the door, kill all
　　enchantments, charms
(Where they Medea's verses), that do
　　harms
To men or cattle: these for frenzy be
A speedy and a sovereign remedy,
The bitter wormwood, sage and
　　marigold;
Such sympathy with man's good they do
　　hold:
This tormentil, whose virtue is to part
All deadly killing poison from the heart:
And, here, narcissus root, for swellings
　　best:
Yellow lysimachus [Loosestrife], to give
　　sweet rest
To the faint shepherd, killing, where it
　　comes
All busy gnats, and every fly that hums:
For leprosy, darnel and celandine,
With calamint, whose virtues do refine
The blood of man, making it free and
　　fair
As the first hour it breathed, or the best
　　air.

That our forebears had a taste for the 'fantasticke' in nature, which may at the same time have encouraged them in their credulity, is shown by this extract from a fifteenth-century manuscript: 'for to make that a pearl, or a prescious stone, or a farthing, or any other manner of thing to be found in an apple, take an apple or a pear after it has flowered, and somewhat waxen, and thrust in hard at the bud's end which one thou wilt of these things aforesaid, and let it grow, and mark well the apple that thou didst put in the thing, whatever it be'. Unfortunately, we learn no more of this promising experiment, although it hardly seems to have led to a marketable success. A basketful of diamond-centred apples would have won the heart of any but the most inflexible blonde, and today would surely have made headlines in the popular press, had this irresistible fruit still been available. From the same source, come helpful hints on the growing of cherries without stones, and peaches producing pomegranates, the latter, fortunately, a process doomed to failure.

Travellers in far-off countries returned with eye-witness accounts of plants bearing fruits that in turn produced embryo geese; others, no less strange, that were plant-animals, and bore little living sheep, suspended from a green stem; and other plants with roots that no man might dig up without fear of madness or death. These freaks of nature were pictured in old herbals, so that men could not possibly doubt of their existence, and worthy physicians and naturalists in learned societies would seriously discuss among themselves these wonderful works of God. Since there is always some basis of truth in these travellers' tales, decades, and even centuries might pass before fact was divorced from fantasy, and the mystery unravelled.

Feigned Plants

Gerard, who was completely convinced of the authenticity of the goose-bearing barnacle-tree, yet illustrates in his *Herbal* two 'Feigned Plants', one of which would be quite acceptable today as a species of *Hypoxis*, and the other instantly recognizable as the *Tigridia*,

VIII
Plant Fantasy

while at the same time disclaiming all belief in their reality:

I have thought it convenient to conclude the historie of the Hyacinth with these two bulbous Plants, received by tradition from others, though generally holden for feigned and adulterine. Their pictures I could willingly have omitted in this historie, if the curious eye could elsewhere have found them drawne and described in our English Tongue: but because I finde them in none, I will lay them downe here, to the end that it may serve for excuse to others, who shall come after, which list not to describe them, being as I said condemned for feined and adulterine nakedly drawne onely. The floures (saith the Author) are no lesse strange than wonderfull. The leaves and roots are like to those of Hyacinths. The floures resemble the Daffodils or Narcissus. The whole plant consisteth of a woolly or flockie matter: which description with the Picture was sent unto Dodonaeus by Johannes Aicholzius.

The second feigned picture hath beene taken of the Discoverer and others of late time, to be a kinde of Dragons not seene by any that have written thereof; which hath moved them to thinke it a feigned picture likewise; notwithstanding you shall receive the description thereof as it hath come to my hands. The root (saith my Author) is bulbous or Onion fashion, outwardly blacke; from which spring up long leaves, sharpe pointed, narrow, and of a fresh greene colour: in the middest of which leaves rise up, naked or bare stalkes, at the top whereof groweth a pleasant yellow floure, stained with many small red spots here and there confusedly cast abroad: and in the middest of the floure thrusteth forth a long red tongue or style, which in time groweth to be the cod or seedvessell, crooked or wreathed, wherein is the seed. The vertues and temperature are not to be spoken of, considering that we assuredly persuade our selves that there are no such

plants, but meere fictions and devices, as we terme them, to give his friend a gudgeon.

The two illustrations which Gerard would have omitted so willingly are 'The False bumbast Jacinth' and 'The floure of Tygris'.

The Goose Barnacle Tree

The myth of the Goose Barnacle Tree goes back to the twelfth century, when they were described as

like marsh geese but smaller. They are produced from fir-timber tossed about at sea and are at first like geese upon it. Afterwards they hang down by their beaks as if from a seaweed attached to the wood and are enclosed in shells that they may grow more freely. Having thus in course of time been clothed with a strong covering of feathers they either fall into the water or seek their liberty in the air by flight. The embryo geese derive their growth and nutriment from the moisture of the wood or of the sea, in a secret and most marvellous manner. I have seen with my own eyes more than a thousand minute bodies of these birds hanging from one piece of timber on the shore enclosed in shells and already formed . . . in no corner of the world have they been known to build a nest.

Giraldus Cambrensis, a zealous reformer of Church abuses and author of *Typographica Hiberniae* (1187), having thus described the creatures, finds cause for concern. 'Hence the bishops and clergy in some parts of Ireland are in the habit of partaking of these birds on fast days without scruple. But in doing so they are led into sin. For if anyone were to eat the leg of our first parent, although he (Adam) was not born of flesh, that person could not be adjudged innocent of eating flesh.' Indeed, a distressing thought.

Convinced of the reality of these barnacles, as well they might be, since their ever-increasing progeny surround our shores to this day, Jews in the Middle Ages were divided as to whether these barnacle geese were to be eaten as flesh or fish.

Travellers continued to report on this vegetable-fishfowl. Early in the fifteenth century Sir John Mandeville, his own identity as suspect as that of any barnacle goose, wrote in his *Voiage and Travaille*, 'In our Contree weren Trees, that beren a Fruyt, that becomen Briddes fleeynge; and tho that fallen in the Water lyven, and thei that fallen on the Erthe dyen anon; and thei ben right gode to mannes mete'. Holinshed in his *Cronycle* (1578) claims that with his own eyes he saw the feathers of these barnacles 'hang out of the shell, at least two inches'.

William Turner already having expressed his belief, in 1597 Gerard evidently felt safe in describing in detail, at the end of his *Herbal*, the Goose Barnacle Tree, or the Tree bearing Geese. He is also able to put a price on this delicacy.

. . . certain shells, in shape like those of the Muskle, but sharpe pointed, and of a whitish colour; wherein is contained a thing in forme like a lace of silke finely woven as it were together; of a whitish colour, one end whereof is fastned unto the inside of the shell, even as the fish of Oisters and Muskles are: the other end is made fast unto the belly of a rude masse or lumpe, which in time commeth to the shape and forme of a Bird: when it is perfectly formed the shell gapeth open, and the first thing that appeareth is the foresaid lace or string; next come the legs of the bird hanging out, and as it groweth greater it openeth the shell by degrees, til at length it is all come forth, and hangeth only by the bill: in short space after it commeth to full maturitie, and falleth into the sea, where it gathereth feathers, and groweth to a fowle bigger than a Mallard, and lesse than a Goose, having blacke legs and bill or beake, and feathers blacke and white, spotted in such a manner as is our Magpie, called in some places a Pie-Annet, which people of Lancashire call by no other name than a tree Goose; which place aforesaid, and all those parts adjoyning

do so much abound therewith, that one of the best is bought for three pence.

But at last, voices of doubt began to be heard. Parkinson, in *Theatrum Botanicum* (1640), under the heading Barnackles or Brant Geese, which he places for convenience with marine plants – in order, it seems, to prove that they do not exist – says, 'let me bring this admirable tale of untruth to your consideration, that whatsoever hath formerly beene related concerning the breeding of these Barnackles, to be from shels growing on trees, etc., is utterly erronious, their breeding and hatching, being found out by the Dutch and others, in their Navigations to the Northward'.

Considerably more than a century later, the Barnacle Goose was dealt an urbane but final blow by the Comte de Buffon. 'We need not remark on the absurdity of such a notion: Aeneas Silvius relates, that chancing to be in Scotland, he inquired particularly for the place of the wonderful metamorphosis of the Barnacle, but was referred to the remote Hebridies and the Orknies; and he adds pleasantly, that as he sought to advance, the miracle retired from him.'

The Scythian Lamb

During the rise and fall of the Barnacle Goose, another, more appealing, and infinitely more useful little creature was reported by those indefatigable travellers to stir the imagination of the stay-at-homes. As early as 445 BC Herodotus had written that 'Certain trees bear for their fruit fleeces surpassing those of sheep in beauty and excellence, and the natives clothe themselves in cloths made therefrom'. He also mentioned a corselet sent by the King of Egypt to Sparta as having been ornamented with gold and fleeces from the trees. This invaluable tree, already grown as a crop, was known as the wool-bearing tree. It was also mentioned by Pliny, Theophrastus and Strabo.

During the reign of Edward III Sir John Mandeville described and pictured 'a lytelle Best in Fleshe, in Bon and Blode, as though it were a lytylle Lomb with outen Wolle', which he called the

Vegetable Lamb Plant. 'And Men eten both the Frut and the Best, and that is a great Marveylle. Of that frut I have eaten.'

In the sixteenth and seventeenth centuries the Vegetable Lamb was made a subject of investigation and argument by some of the most celebrated writers of that period. Fortunio Liceti, Professor of Philosophy at Padua University, wrote in 1518 of a little beast like a lamb found within a fruit-pod when it bursts from over-ripeness. Sigismund, Baron von Herberstein, Ambassador to Emperors Maximilien I and Charles V, in his *Notes on Russia*, wrote of

a certain seed like that of a melon, but rather rounder and longer, from which, when it was set in the earth, grew a plant resembling a lamb, and attaining to a height of about two and a half feet . . . which was called in the language of the country, Borametz or Little Lamb . . . its hoofs were not horny, but like those of a lamb, but of hairs brought together in the form of the divided hoof of a living lamb. It was rooted by the navel in the middle of the belly, and devoured the surrounding herbage and grass, and lived as long as that lasted; but when there was no more within its reach the stem withered, and the lamb died. For myself, although I had previously regarded these Borametz as fabulous, the accounts of it were confirmed to me by so many persons worthy of credence that I have thought right to describe it.

In 1557, Girolamo Cardano of Pavia endeavoured to expose the absurdity of these beliefs. He argued that if it had blood, it must have a heart, and that the soil in which a plant grows is not fitted to supply a heart with movement and vital heat. Against which Claude Duret maintained that 'Of all the strange and marvellous trees, shrubs, plants and herbs which Nature, or, rather, God himself, has produced, or ever will produce in this Universe, there will never be seen anything so worthy of admiration and contemplation as these Bor-

Page 54: 'The Breede of Barnacles', from Gerard's *Herbal*, 1597. 'Upon this rotten tree I found growing many thousands of long crimson bladders, in shape like unto puddings newly filled, before they be sodden, which were very cleere and shining' (Gerard).

Page 55: *A Sense of Smell*, by Giuseppe Arcimboldo (*c.* 1527–1593). A pre-surreal and somewhat sinister anthropomorphic painting by the official portrait painter to Maximilian II, King of Bohemia, and to his successor, Rudolph II.

Below: 'Le Lin', a flower-fantasque by Albert Grandville, from *Les Fleurs Animées*. The fragile flax with its clear blue flower has ceased to be the flower of the spinster, as the spinster has ceased to be a woman who spins. No longer can it be said that 'Flax envelopes, conceals, and keeps from contact with the air the satin skins of our ladies' (Adam Karr, *A Tour Round My Garden*, 1859).

ametz of Scythia . . . If I did not entirely believe this I would denounce it as fabulous . . . but those who are in the habit of daily studying good and rare books, printed and in manuscript . . . know that there is no impossibility in Nature'. A French poem, written in 1578, and translated by Joshua Sylvester in 1584, described the astonishment of Adam as he wandered through the Garden of Eden, and came upon this striking spectacle.

> *True beasts, fast in the ground still*
>   *sticking,*
> *Feeding on grass, and th' airy moisture*
>   *licking,*
> *Such as these Borametz in Scythia bred*
> *Of slender seeds, and with green fodder*
>   *fed;*
> *Although their bodies, noses, mouths, and*
>   *eyes,*
> *Of new-yeaned lambs have full the form*
>   *and guise,*
> *And should be very lambs, save that for*
>   *foot*
> *Within the ground they fix a living root*
> *Which at their navel grows, and dies that*
>   *day*
> *That they have browzed the neighbouring*
>   *grass away.*

For yet another 150 years the learned professors argued. In 1641, the Professor of Mathematics at Avignon, Athanasius Kircher, declared, 'In order not to multiply miracles, we assert that it is a plant', but whether animal or vegetable, few by now doubted its existence. Parkinson's description follows that of Baron von Herberstein, and it is clear from the title-page of *Paradisi in Sole Paradisus Terrestris*, that a specimen flourished in the Garden of Eden, although Adam and Eve seem more interested in the giant cyclamen and strawberries nearby than in the Vegetable Lamb, modestly dangling from its stalk in the background.

Confusion was doubly confounded when this woolly wonder became entangled with the Astrakhan lamb-skins which were a valuable article of commerce. Jan de Struys, a Dutchman who travelled in Tartary between 1647 and 1672, found these skins a most satisfac-

58

A well-developed specimen of the Borametz or Tartarian Lamb, a tree bearing seed-pods which when they ripened and opened were believed to contain little lambs. From Henry Lee, *The Vegetable Lamb of Tartary*, 1887.

tory investment. 'I have myself paid five or six roubles for one of these skins, and doubled my money when I sold it again.' The fleeces of these unfortunate lambs were obtained before their birth to ensure a softer, whiter and curlier pelt and de Struys was of the opinion that some of these dried and shrunken skins may have found their way into museums, as examples of the Tartarian Lamb, and so come to be regarded as of vegetable origin.

In 1698, Sir Hans Sloane brought to the notice of the Royal Society yet another false claimant to the title of Tartarian Lamb. This proved to be the rhizome of one of the arborescent ferns of China shaped artificially into the rough likeness of a lamb, the root forming the body, and the foot-stalks, the legs. It was covered with a soft down, which was used in China for stopping blood, as cobwebs were used in the West. Dissatisfied with this scientific explanation of the mystery, travellers to Tartary still made the Vegetable Lamb their priority and John Bell, in about 1716, walked many miles in search of his quarry. He wrote of a certain shrub or plant called in the Russian language 'Tartasky Boraska, i.e. Tartarian Lamb, with the skins of which the caps of the Armenians, Persians, Tartars, etc are faced'. The creature's incredible habits were repeated to him, 'but all I could find out were some dry bushes, scattered here and there, which grow on a single stalk with a bushy top of a brownish colour; the stalk is about eighteen inches high, the top consisting of sharp prickly leaves. It is true that no grass or leaves grow within the circle of its shade – a property natural to many other plants here and elsewhere.' And what was more important, the Tartarians themselves were beginning to laugh at the fable.

The light was slow in dawning, however, for more than sixty years later two eminent botanical writers, Dr Erasmus Darwin and Dr De la Croix, gave vent to poetic expression on the subject of this creature, by now as much publicized as Mary's little lamb with fleece as white as snow. It is difficult now to believe that the following verses were written, and ead, in all seriousness, but so it was.

E'en round the Pole the flames of love
*   aspire,*
And icy bosoms feel the secret fire,
Cradled in snow, and fanned by Arctic
*   air,*
Shines, gentle Borametz, thy golden hair;
Rooted in earth, each cloven foot descends,
And round and round her flexile neck she
*   bends,*
Crops the grey coral moss, and hoary
*   thyme,*
Or laps with rosy tongue the melting
*   rime;*
Eyes with mute tenderness her distant
*   dam,*
And seems to bleat – a 'vegetable lamb'.

Dr Darwin bestows golden hair upon the unprotesting lamb, thus relating it to the fern-rhizomes of southern China, and so why he should have placed it to freeze in the Arctic air is no longer clear. Dr De la Croix composed his version of the fable in Latin, which was compared in all seriousness to Virgil's *Georgics*.

Upon a stalk is fixed a living brute,
A rooted plant bears quadruped for fruit,
It has a fleece, nor does it want for eyes,
And from its brows two woolly horns
*   arise . . .*

This was translated, all twenty-four lines of it, by Henry Lee, whose Sherlock Holmes-like exposition of the whole tangled woolly skein was published in 1887. He points out that the rhizome-lambs were not even intended to represent lambs by those that fashioned them, but made as little brownish toy dogs. 'The plant that set all Europe talking of the lambs that grew in fruits and on stalks of plants somewhere in Scythia was one of far higher importance and value to mankind than the childish knick-knacks made for amusement out of the creeping root-stocks of ferns.' Today we call it the cotton plant, *Gossypium herbaceum*. The Mystery of the Vegetable Lamb of Scythia, alias Borametz, alias the Tartarian Lamb, was solved at last by Henry Lee. As he might have said, 'Elementary, my dear Watson'.

The Upas-Tree, or Poison-Tree of Macassar

Part fact, part fantasy, the Upas-tree has so many horrific stories woven into its history, that its very existence came to be doubted. Tales brought back by travellers who had received them from yet other travellers, repeated possibly in good faith, told of a tree so deadly that its poisonous exhalations killed all vegetable and animal life for miles around it. Birds flying over the area where this baneful tree stood, fluttered to the ground and died instantly. Only the skeletons of men and animals were to be seen on the parched earth. A Dutch physician named Foersche, who was travelling in Java where it grew, claimed to have seen this leafy monster, and he published his account in 1783. 'Not a tree', he wrote, 'nor a blade of grass is to be found in the valley or surrounding mountains. Not a beast or bird, reptile or living thing, lives in the vicinity.' He added that 'on one occasion 1,600 refugees encamped within fourteen miles of it, and all but 300 died within two months'. The place became known as the Valley of Death.

The Russian poet Pushkin wrote of it, presumably at second hand. 'The poison, melted by the mid-day sun, percolates through the bark in drops, which in the evening are congealed into a thick and transparent gum. The birds avoid its very appearance, the tiger shuns it; a breath of wind rustles its foliage, and the passing wind is tainted.'

The story continues, that the Emperor of Java used the poison from the tree to despatch any persons who had the misfortune to offend him. Since there were obvious problems concerning the collecting of this deadly draught, only criminals condemned to death were employed. So reasonable were the Emperor's demands that the condemned criminals were given a choice – instant execution, or the chance of a visit to the Upas-tree, followed by a free pardon. Comparatively few availed themselves of the latter alternative. Those that did, made the journey in style, in their best clothes, with the blessing and instructions of the priest. They were each given a pair of leather gloves, and a leather cap that covered shoulders and chest. The caps were fitted with glass eye-holes, on the assumption that the trembling wearer wished to look out. They were also presented with long bamboo rods to catch the drops of poison, and a silver or tortoiseshell box in which to carry it.

The Upas-tree in fact grows in Celebes, Sumatra and Borneo, as well as in Java, and because of its reputation its name is applied to anything baneful or of evil influence. Its botanical name is *Antiaris toxicaria*, and it belongs to the order Urticaceae, which also includes the nettles, a little less deadly perhaps, but unpleasant enough. It grows to a height of 100 feet, and bears no branches up to 60 or 80 feet. The reddish-brown bark is smooth, and it has small flowers followed by a fruit like a plum.

Pushkin's description of its thick, transparent gum is accurate, for it exudes a gummy matter such as that found in gum-tragacanth, in which lies its poison. This hardens in the air, and if it touches the skin it occasions a slight eruption, but nothing more. The natives of Java, however, obtained from it an efficient poison for the tips of small darts, which they discharged through blow-pipes at their enemies. The inner bark of the tree contains a fibrous substance which has been converted into ropes, and also made into a kind of linen, which was found to cause an intolerable itching if insufficiently prepared.

The tree is not poisonous to the plants in its vicinity, nor is it dangerous to walk in its shade, and birds may feel free to roost in its branches. A Upas-tree flourishes amidst other hot-house plants in Kew Gardens, if anyone cares to visit it.

The Arabian Tree

'For as there is but one phoenix in the world, so there is but one tree in Arabia wherein she buyldeth.' A mythical tree to provide a suitable throne for a mythical bird. When the weakness of old age overtakes the phoenix, she spreads her weary wings and flies across the sea to the sole Arabian tree. There she builds her nest of aromatic twigs, cassia and frankincense, and burning in her own

Dunstan, Archbishop of Canterbury. From a MS. of the 12th century. This worthy painter, jeweller and blacksmith held the Devil by the nose with his red-hot pincers until he promised never to tempt him again.

ying ardour, she is consumed to ashes. From these ashes her beauty of gold, of purple, of azure-blue and rose-carnation arises into new life, and with the rebirth of the phoenix, is reborn the sole Arabian tree.

Bartolomaeus Anglicus wrote of it in 1495, quoting Pliny, but Shakespeare seems to doubt the existence of this fabulous bird in its mythical tree. In *The Tempest*, Sebastian, lost on a magical island, is half-willing to believe in beast and tree, and bird of imagery.

> *Now I will believe*
> *That there are unicorns; that in Arabia*
> *There is one tree, the phoenix' throne; one phoenix*
> *At this hour reigning there,*

but there is doubt in his protestations of belief. Shakespeare mentions the tree again, in the opening verse of *The Phoenix and the Turtle*.

> *Let the bird of loudest lay,*
> *On the sole Arabian tree,*
> *Herald sad and trumpet be,*
> *To whose sound chaste wings obey.*

Both bird and tree are emblems of immortality, and because there can be but one, the bird is used as an example of uniqueness. Hence, 'a phoenix among women'.

> *If she be furnished with a mind so rare*
> *She is alone the Arabian bird.*

The Dream-Tree of Dunstan

Dunstan was born at Glastonbury in about 924. The talented son of a West-Saxon noble, he was brought up at the Abbey of Glastonbury, and at the court of Aethelstan. He was an artist-craftsman and a musician, but he devoted his young manhood to the revival of a stricter monasticism throughout England, for the clergy had sunk into worldliness and ignorance. In this he was greatly helped by Oswald and Aethelwold, of the sees of York and Winchester. One night Dunstan dreamed of a wondrous tree of great height, with branches that stretched all over Britain, its boughs loaded with countless cowls, and the top of which was crowned with a cowl larger than all the others. The tree, as Dunstan interpreted his dream, was the England of the future, and the largest and highest cowl, that of Aethelwold.

Dunstan was appointed Archbishop of Canterbury in 959, and he died in 988. At his canonization he was given the monkshood as his flower, a symbol derived from his prophetic dream.

These vegetable lambs and fabulous trees we are told we need no longer believe in. What we must believe in, because it is listed and illustrated in one of our latest garden catalogues, is the Bat Plant, *Tacca chantrieri*, although in Malaya and Burma it is known as the Devil's Flower, from the way the 'eyes' seem to follow your every movement. Something between a bat and an aerial jelly-fish, the flowers have filaments or 'whiskers' up to twelve inches long, and it has a forked tail. This, we are assured, we may grow from seed, tame it and keep it in a pot in the house or in a greenhouse.

If Gerard in his *Herbal* had written about the Bat Plant or Devil's Flower, we should have smiled. ●

We are comfortably relaxed in the knowledge that many animals are vegetarians; it may be a little more difficult to accept the fact that, widely scattered over the world, there are numbers of plants that are carnivorous, or at least, insectivorous. We cannot help feeling that this is rather shocking behaviour on their part, and the fact that various pitcher-plants inhabiting a great part of the world from North America to Northern Australia have a highly-coloured and uncorseted appearance confirms us in a secret conviction that they are no better than they should be. If, however, we were to pick a sundew flower, which is like a small white saxifrage, or a butterwort, which resembles a violet, and we were to examine these flowers apart from their cunning and ingenious insect-trapping leaves, we should think that they were very 'nice' flowers indeed. Morally, it seems, then, that the families of *Drosera*, the sundew, and *Dionaea*, the Venus Flytrap, and *Pinguicula*, the butterwort, are even more to be deplored than the pitcher-plants, *Sarracenia*, *Darlingtonia* and *Nepenthes*, who are not quite so innocent-looking. It would be less than accurate to say that the Venus Flytrap makes no bones about its carnivorous predilections, because bones, or at least pathetic remnants of shards and broken wings and all the less enjoyable remains of its hapless victims, are exactly what it does make.

Perhaps, after all, morals have nothing to do with the matter, and Samuel Butler was right when he said, 'Whenever I hear a man say that a thing which manages its affairs with so keen an eye to the main chance as a nettle or a blackberry [or in this case, a sundew], has no intelligence, and does not understand its own business, on the ground that it shows no sign of understanding ours, I always feel that however little intelligence the plant may have the man has even less.'

In any case, it is not for us to criticize the life-pattern of such a charming family as the round-leaved sundew, *D. rotundifolia*, the long-leafed sundew, *D. longifolia*, and *D. anglica*, with still longer leaves. All three of these sundews

IX
Drosera or Dracula?

flourish in bogs, morasses, in sphagnum moss, and in other damp corners of the British Isles. There was a time, but it is long ago, when they could be found on Hampstead Heath.

Perhaps the round-leaved sundew is the prettiest of the three sisters, with its ruby leaves shaped like salt-spoons, covered on the inside with sticky hairs, and, as the herbalist Henry Lyte wrote, 'alwayes moyst and bedewed and the small leaves thereof alwayes full of little droppes of water, and the hoater the sunne shineth upon this herbe, so much the moyster it is'. Not only we, but the flies and midges of this boggy area are attracted by so much sweetness and bright colour, and, as we know from *The Beggar's Opera*,

> The fly that sips treacle is lost in the
>   Sweets,
> So he that tastes Woman, Woman,
>   Woman,
> He that tastes Woman, ruin meets,

and the fly that tastes the sundew also irrevocably comes to grief. Now the *femme fatale* shows herself for what she is. The red tentacles bend over, the leaf itself curls, and the sparkling dew is dew no longer, but a viscid liquid that envelops the helpless creature, and the process of digestion commences. The *Cyclopaedia of Botany* (c. 1820) states that the sundew is 'Good against convulsions, hysteric disorders and trembling of the limbs', but not the convulsions and hysteria of the captured fly; and his skinny little limbs tremble in vain, for he is doomed. When it is over, the leaf opens to its original position, the tentacles regain their erectness, their tips shine once more with their innocent-seeming dew, and – 'Won't you walk into my parlour says the sundew to the fly?'.

The old herbalists seemed unaware of this sinister aspect of the sundew, although they did accuse it of causing liver-rot to sheep, for which it was called Red-Rot in some places. Another name was Lustwort, 'because if Sheepe feede thereon they will go to the Ramme'. Sundew was used to cure warts and corns; diluted with milk it made an ex

Far left: Large-flowered butterwort, *Pinguicula grandiflora*. Also known as Bog Violets or Marsh Violets. The charming dairy-maids of the Scottish islands. They look as if they wouldn't hurt a fly, but no insect should trust them. However, they protect cows from elf-arrows, and their owners from witches. From *English Botany*, 1880, ed. John T. Boswell.

Left: Venus Flytrap, *Dionaea muscipula*. Innocent white flowers blandly ignoring a doomed victim below. From *Lectures on Botany* by William Curtis (1746–1799), who founded *The Botanical Magazine* in 1787.

X
Some Herbals and Herbalists

The history of the printed herbals stems largely from the manuscripts of two men, Dioscorides, a Greek physician, and Pliny the Elder, a Roman naturalist. Interest was already growing regarding the medicinal properties of plants; tentative experiments were being made, and who knows how many lives lost in the search for cures. By the first century AD there was already something to show for these patient experiments; some knowledge to pass on to future generations, and so the names of Pliny and Dioscorides will be found in most of the printed herbals of later centuries.

Pliny the Elder was a prolific author, although the only work that remains is his *Natural History*, a vast compilation in Latin of the writings of Greek authors, which contains a large section devoted to plants of every kind. Pliny died in his efforts to observe more closely the erup-

tion of Vesuvius in AD 79, and in his attempts to aid those who were in danger. An account of his uncle's death is preserved in a letter of Pliny the Younger. Gerard quotes him in his *Herbal* when writing of the birch tree. 'This tree, saith Pliny, in times past, the magistrats rods were made thereof; and in our time also Schoolmasters and Parents do terrifie their children with rods made of Birch.' Since that particular reign of terror lasted until Dickensian times and after, hatred of this graceful tree must have seared deeply into many childish hearts.

Dioscorides in *De Materia Medica* wrote of some 500 healing herbs, and his theories were frequently drawn on by succeeding herbalists. Gerard, for instance, in describing the Calves Snout, or Snapdragon, adds, 'They report (saith Dioscorides) that the herbe being hanged about one preserveth a man from being

66

bewitched, and that it maketh a man gracious in the sight of the people', and of black briony, 'The yong and tender sproutings are kept in pickle, and reserved to be eaten with meat, as Dioscorides teacheth'. Theophrastus, a Greek physician who lived between 372 and 288 BC, is another name that becomes familiar in the pages of the early English herbals. He was the author of *Researches about Plants* in nine books, and *Principles of Vegetable Life* in six, but in spite of this mountainous work, his plant descriptions were not always easy to identify by later herbalists.

These, then, were the principal roots from which our herbals grew.

Herb lore and folk medicine were inextricably mixed, as they have remained through the centuries, and each work as it was written and published reflected, not its own period, but the ages before, when basic knowledge and small discoveries were communicated by word of mouth. Rumours were exaggerated, mistakes repeated, and the early wood-cuts of the plants used over and over again, or copied, so that they became coarsened and debased. Many of the early works remain in manuscript only, in the libraries of universities and museums.

The earliest printed works on plants were translations from the Latin or the Saxon. It was Bartolomaeus Anglicus who wrote the first original work on herbs and their uses in 1495, in the seventeenth book of *De proprietatibus rerum*, and it is believed to contain the first botanical illustration to be published in an English book.

Banckes's *Herbal* (1525), the earliest English printed herbal, contains a reference to the tradition which has been repeated ever since, that rosemary 'passeth not commonly in highte the highte of Criste whill he was man on Erthe', and that when the plant attains the age of thirty-three it will increase in breadth but not in height. This book went into many editions.

This was followed by Peter Treveris's *Grete Herball* (c. 1526), a translation from the French. It was an important book, alphabetically arranged, and included the helpful information that

'Fungi ben musherons. There be two maners of them, one maner is deadly and sleeth them that eateth of them, and the other dooth not.' The occupational hazards of herbalism in ages now happily past must have been considerable. The herbal of William Turner marks the beginning of the science of botany in England. He studied at Cambridge and was a friend of Latimer and Ridley. Turner was a Reformer, and twice his books were prohibited and condemned to destruction. He travelled in Italy, where he received the degree of Doctor of Medicine, and he also studied in Germany and Holland.

He became Dean of Wells, but was exiled in Mary's reign, although he was reinstated on the accession of Elizabeth. The Father of English Botany, as he was called, dedicated his *Libellus de Re Herbaria* to Henry VIII in 1538. In 1548 he published *The names of herbes in Greke, Latin, English, Duche, and Frenche, with the common names that Herbaries and Apotecaries use*. He dedicated the first part of his great *Herbal* (1551) to the Duke of Somerset, Edward VI's uncle and at that time Lord Protector; the second part, to his old patron, Lord Wentworth; and the complete work to Queen Elizabeth. In the Preface he reminds the Queen of a conversation he had had with her, eighteen years before, at the Duke's house, when he was his physician.

A small book which contains a great deal of curious herb lore, among other 'marvaylous thinges of the world', is *The boke of secretes of Albartus Magnus of the vertues of Herbes, Stones, and certain beastes*. The author, who has never been identified with certainty, writes of a herb that he calls 'roybra' that 'yf it be put with the juyce of houselyke and the bearers hands anoynted with it and the residue be put in water if he entre in ye water where fyshes be they wil gather together to his hands', a useful hint that does not seem to have been put into practice by Izaak Walton. Perhaps more hopeful is his report on verbena. 'Infants bearing it shal be very apte to learne and loving learninge and they shal be glad and joyous.' Verbena is a pleasant plant for any garden, and one can but try.

Most of the herbals at this time were all-embracing volumes, with lengthy titles offering the promise of 'Joyfull newes out of the new-found worlde Wherein are declared the rare and singular vertues of divers Herbs, Trees, Plantes, Oyles and Stones', or 'A greene Forest, or a Naturall Historie, Wherein may bee seene first the most sufferaigne Vertues in all the whole kinde of Stones and Metals: Foules, Fishes, creeping Wormes and Serpents', and so on.

Thomas Newton, in 1587, published the first *Herbal For the Bible*, 'taken from Herbs, Plants, Trees, Fruits and Simples, by observation of their Vertues . . . and by the Holie Prophets, Sacred Writers, Christ himselfe and his blessed Apostles . . .'. This seems to have been the only herbal of the period where responsibility for the information given was placed firmly with a higher authority.

Herbals were by this time numerous, and their history involved, so often were they copied from one another, and the same illustrations used.

Not perhaps the greatest, but the best known and loved herbalist, is John Gerard. His *Herbal*, first published in

1597, is too full of other men's flowers to be called the greatest book on the subject. It is founded largely on the earlier work of Dodoens, from a translation made by Doctor Priest, Gerard himself not being sufficiently expert in Latin. Dr Priest died when the work was still unfinished, and Gerard published it as his own, stating that the doctor 'meant to publish the same, but being prevented by death, his translation likewise perished'. The herbal was corrected and enlarged by Thomas Johnson in 1633, and in the Preface Johnson wrote, 'I cannot commend my author for endeavouring to hide this thing from us'.

That a lovable character speaks to us from the open pages cannot be denied, but is it the personality of Gerard or of Dodoens that we warm to? Gerard writes of many old friends, and their gifts of rare plants and seeds from all over the world. When we read of Gerard's friend Stephen Bridwell, 'a learned and diligent searcher of simples in the West of England'; of Lord Zouche, who sent him rare seeds from Crete, Spain and Italy; and of Nicholas Lete, a London merchant, who is 'greatly in love with rare and faire flowers, for which he doth carefully send into Syria', we know that there is enthusiasm for the beauty of flowers, as well as for their medicinal value, in every line. With 'the purple pasque floures, which do grow very plentifully in the pasture or close belonging to the parsonage house of a small village six miles from Cambridge, called Hildersham: the Parson's name . . . was Mr. Fuller, a very kind and loving man, and willing to show unto any man the said close, who desired the same', we are finally convinced that John Gerard also was a kind and loving man, and we forgive him his literary trespasses.

For all his little weaknesses, he writes as a modest man. In comparing different varieties of dock and monk's rhubarb, he says, 'other distinctions and differences I leave to the learned Physitions of our London colledge, who are very well able to search this matter, as a thing far above my reach, being no Graduat, but a Country Scholler, as the whole frame of this historie doth well declare:

But I hope my good meaning will be well taken, considering I do my best: and I doubt not but some of greater learning wil perfect that which I have begun according to my small skill, especially the ice being broken to him, and the wood rough-hewn to his hands'. Rembert Dodoens, in spite of the fact that he may have written the bulk of this very bulky book, remains a pale shadow in the background, and it is the Country Scholler, with his passionate love of growing things, that we remember.

Gerard's own garden was situated in what is now Fetter Lane. It must have been a wonderful garden indeed, containing over a thousand herbs, many of them rarities at that time. In 1596 he published a 24-page catalogue of his plants – the first complete catalogue of plants in any garden. From the surrounding lanes he could gather mallow, shepherd's purse, sweet woodruff, bugle and paul's betony, and in the meadows nearby there grew red-flowered clary, white saxifrage, rocket, yarrow, lesser hawkweed and the strawberry-headed trefoil. Walls and rooftops were pleasant with wallflowers and stonecrop. Two hundred years later, Henry Phillips described the change that had come to Holborn since Gerard had cultivated his garden there.

> What would be the astonishment of this excellent old herbalist, could he be recalled, to see each avenue of his garden formed into streets; houses erected on his parsley beds, and chimneys sprung up as thick as his asparagus; churches occupying the site of his arbours, and his tool-house, perhaps, converted into the British Museum, where is safely housed the lasting memorial of his labours. In vain would he now seek wild plants in Mary-le-bone, where each blade of grass is transformed into granite, and every hawthorn hedge changed for piles of bricks: carriages rattling where snails were formerly crawling. His ear would be assailed by the shrill cry of 'Milk below', and the deep tone of 'Old clothes', where he had formerly retired to listen to the melody of the early lark, or the plaintive tones of the nightingale.

Left: A page from Culpeper's *Complete Herbal*, 1826, with 'their medicinal and occult properties, and upwards of fifty choice receipts selected from the author's last legacies'. The water flag, bottom right, was one of the ingredients of mithridate (see Chapter 13).

Page 73: Pliny handing his work to the Emperor Titus (AD 40 or 41–81), who was called, on what authority it can only be surmised, 'the delight of mankind'. The work offered by Pliny to the Emperor was an inexhaustible storehouse of information, which influenced thinking for centuries to come. Pliny, *Historia Naturalis*. 12th century.

The commonest of our garden herbs are the most valuable, if we put them to their various uses. Herbs and aromatic shrubs have been known in cosmetics, cookery and cures since the ancient Egyptians. Women of the old world dyed their hair and eyebrows with walnut juice, myrtle, cypress or St John's Wort. They made face masks of rye flour mixed with perfumed oil. Men also scented their bodies with mint, thyme and marjoram. Unguents were kept in alabaster boxes and flasks, so that the perfume exhaled through the alabaster. The first known perfume formula occurs in the Book of Exodus (XXX. 34–35). 'And the Lord said unto Moses, Take unto thee sweet spices, stacte, and onycha (a rock rose) and galbanum;

XI
Bouquet Garni

these sweet spices with pure frankincense: of each shall there be a like weight. And thou shalt make it a perfume, a confection after the art of the apothecary. . . .'

In cookery, a delicate blend of herbs was used in food and wines, and today many of the same herbs appeal even more to the sophisticated palate than to the country cook. That those herbs could be used and still are used in homoeopathic medicine as well as other medical treatment, is an extra gift that growing things add to the pleasures of sight and taste and smell. Hippocrates, one of the earliest physicians, has left a valuable description of the herbs in use in about 400 BC. Many of them, including balm, basil, horehound, ivy, rue and sage, are

still in use today. And so we commence with our four indispensables: mint, thyme, parsley and sage.

Mint *(Mentha)*

Medicinally the peppermints are derived from *M. piperita*, peppermint oil being utilized in pharmaceutical preparations and medicines requiring a masking flavour. Medicine apart, our bathrooms would not be the same without its fresh tingle in our toothpaste; and more recently, the cool, green, mint-scented soaps that are so popular today, a revival of the old practice of scenting a bath with a sprig of mint.

For commercial uses, peppermint is grown near lavender, so that the same stills can be used. Mint tea is a refreshing aid to the digestion, and can be taken for calming the nerves; for migraine, and for soothing sleep.

Culpeper tells us that mint 'is a herb of Venus . . . It stirs up venery, or bodily lust'. It isn't just something you eat with lamb. It also 'helps the biting of a mad dog . . . and as Simeon Sethi saith, it helps a cold liver', even if it doesn't cure a lisp. After giving us two columns of cures, one would think that there is nothing that mint cannot do, but we are told that it is 'extremely bad for wounded people; and they say that a wounded Man who eats meat will never be cured, and that is a long day'.

Pliny said that 'the smell of Mint doth stir up the minde, and the taste to a greedy desire of meat', so evidently he enjoyed his mint sauce as much as we do. It may also be used in sweets and soups. Try chopped mint and sugar on pineapple or grapefruit for a starter; and finely-cut mint leaves pounded with cream cheese make a delicious garnish for potatoes roasted in their jackets.

Dried mint is pleasant in small sachets in cupboards and drawers, where it will repel clothes moths. Outside the house it helps to keep away ants and the cabbage white butterfly caterpillar.

Thyme *(Thymus)*

Like mint and sage, thyme was introduced into Britain by the Romans. We can walk on it, eat it, and it is traditionally used to accompany us to the next world; and it enables us to see fairies, although results are not guaranteed. It is good to walk on a thyme lawn or path, because the delicious scent that we release gives us strength and courage. Thyme became the symbol of bravery, and medieval ladies embroidered it on scarves for their knights before a tourney, to give them courage.

In England thyme was associated with murdered men, whose souls inhabit the flowers; which, we hope, is some consolation to those unhappy spirits. In Wales, it was planted on graves, and it is a grave-plant also to the Oddfellows, who, at funerals, carry sprigs which are dropped onto the coffin of their dead colleague.

For the living, it is nature's remedy for coughs, a general tonic, and a preventative of bad dreams. It gives us the antiseptic oil known as Thymol. Thyme used in the bath is said to improve the skin, and tone up the nervous system. It is a bee plant, and was always planted near hives, and the leaves rubbed on the hives. It can be used sparingly in most savoury dishes, and it complements the flavour of all roast meats. The green leaves should be taken from the plants when in flower, but only from non-flowering shoots. Courgettes, thinly sliced, and gently cooked in butter, with pepper, salt and a teaspoonful of thyme, make a delicious entrée.

Fans of Gertrude Lawrence will remember her singing a catchy little duet entitled 'Wild Thyme'.

> SHE: *I'm very fond of wild thyme.*
> HE: *I've had a wild time, too!*
> SHE: *Grow it in your garden, won't you make a note?*
> HE: *Yes, I'll grow it in a line with where I sowed a wild oat.*

Does anyone remember it?

Parsley *(Petroselinum crispum)* and Parsley piert *(Aphanes arvensis)*

The wild parsley, also called Parsley Breakstones, was an almost unfailing remedy for stone in the kidney, because it can break its way through stony ground, and therefore it was constantly employed in the Doctrine of Signatures.

Left: Grandville's unconventional application of a herb that may be used as a demulcent, emollient and laxative. Marsh mallow is not, however, to be found in the pink and white gelatinous sweets sold by confectioners under that name. From *Les Fleurs Animées*.

Under the dominion of Mercury, it was good for coughs. The distilled water of parsley, like dill water, was a familiar medicine for nurses to give to their charges when they were troubled with 'the frets', which was their name for wind. It was evidently a poor man's herb, for Culpeper says, 'It were good the gentry would pickle it up as they pickle up Samphire [and still do, in the coastal areas of Britain] for their use all the Winter. I cannot teach them how to do it, yet this I can tell them, it is a very wholesome herb.'

Wild parsley has a remarkable record of success with all problems relating to anaemia, rheumatism, sciatica and jaundice, and for treating tumours and boils. It is rich in vitamins and good for the complexion. If eaten after onion or garlic, it removes all traces on the breath.

Sow your seeds on Good Friday for luck.

Sage *(Salvia officinalis)*

It grows best for the wise, but it withers when the master of the house is ailing; but, as the proverb says, 'Why should a man die who has sage in his garden?' So neither man nor sage it seems, need die, if proper care is taken. John Evelyn said that 'it is a plant indeed with so many and wonderful properties that the assiduous use of it is said to render men immortal'. It seems that the sage in John Evelyn's garden must have withered. And when, in spite of all that sage can

do, that sad time comes, it is strewn on the grave, as rosemary is, as a sign of remembrance.

Purple-leaved sage is mainly used in pharmaceutical products; wood sage, for gargles; and the garden sage for cookery. The plant is under Jupiter, and helps the memory, warming and quickening the senses. Added to rosemary, honeysuckle and plantain, and boiled in water with a little honey, it is good for gargles. The plant is most beneficial in the spring, and this is the best time for drying. A country hair tonic is made from tea and dried sage, in equal parts, covered with boiling water, and simmered for two hours. It was also used in herbal tobacco, and was commonly drunk as we drink tea. In Germany and Spain there is a considerable industry in sage oil.

In cooking, garden sage is used to flavour sausages, pâtés and terrines, and for stuffing veal, duck and goose. The flavour goes well with cheese; it improves Welsh Rabbit, and is delicious beaten with cream cheese and a few drops of lemon, as a sandwich spread. Sage cheese is a regional speciality of Derbyshire, and in some parts of the country it is used to flavour bread. The chopped leaves in batter make excellent pancakes. The leaves are best gathered before the plant has flowered.

Marjoram *(Origanum)*

This is a herb of Mercury, and under

Aries, and therefore an excellent cordial for the brain. It is a cheerful herb, as we learn from its name, *Origanum*, from the Greek *Oros*, mountain, and *ganos*, joy, from the gay appearance of the flowers on their native hillsides. It was probably this that caused Gerard to say, 'The leaves boiled in water, and the decoction drunke, easeth such as are given to overmuch sighing.'

If you are not given to sighing overmuch, it still might be interesting to learn that bears sought it for the same purpose, though presumably they did not find it necessary to boil the herb first. The prologue to *The Knight of the Burning Pestle* makes plain the dependence of the bear on marjoram as an anti-depressive drug. 'Where the bee can suck no honey, she leaves her sting behind; and where the bear cannot find origanum to heal his grief, he blasteth all other leaves with his breath.' It is the wild marjoram, *O. vulgare*, that is used in medicine. Its oil relieves painful swellings of rheumatic joints, and a bag of marjoram, plunged into boiling water and applied locally as hot as can be borne, will do the same. Oil of marjoram is used in ointments and salves, and in the making of perfumes. It is also a nature cure for indigestion and insomnia. It is cultivated in New England, where it is drunk as a herb tea. A tonic of marjoram and balm is given to cows after calving, to strengthen and content them.

As a savoury herb, sprinkle marjoram

over pork, veal and liver before cooking, and it is pleasant as a change from rosemary on roast lamb. It is used in stuffing, soups, stews, omelettes, cheese dishes and fish sauces. A little mixed in wine vinegar is excellent on salads. It improves shepherd's pie, and, like sage, can be used with cream cheese as a sandwich spread. Added to melted butter, it is an unusual garnish on vegetables.

Marjoram was an old strewing herb, and much use was made of it in potpourri, 'swete bags', 'swete powders', and 'swete washing water'.

Fennel *(Foeniculum officinale)*

A herb of Mercury, under Virgo, and antipathetic to Pisces. It reached England from the Mediterranean, and it is now naturalized in some parts of the country. It is a handsome, feathery, green or bronze plant, strongly aromatic of anise, and it is used increasingly today in weight-watching diets. It stops hiccoughs, and if you are feeling choosy, 'takes away the loathings which oftentimes happen to the stomachs of sick and feverish persons'. It is an ancient remedy, often mentioned in Anglo-Saxon herbals.

In cookery it is principally used with fish, but those who enjoy its strongly aromatic flavour use it also in meat, cheese and egg dishes. Sweet fennel, *F. dulce*, has swollen stems, which are cooked as a vegetable. Thinly sliced, they may be served in a French dressing with cold chicken. A green sauce of fennel, with two or more of the following herbs, chives, parsley, sorrel or watercress, gives a fresh interest to cold meat or fish.

Rue *(Rue graveolens)*, the Herb of Grace

An old disinfectant herb, used in medicine, but only seldom in cooking. It was understood to be medicinally safe if gathered in the morning, but poisonous if picked later. As in most herbs, the shoots are best taken before the plant flowers. A useful medicine for coughs and croup, colic and flatulence, but it should never be taken in large quantities, nor if the patient is pregnant. It is now known to be the source of a valuable drug for treating high blood pressure.

Its well-known disinfectant properties were mentioned by Culpeper: 'the places of the body most troubled with vermin and lice washed therewith while it [the rue-water] is warm, destroys them utterly'. The juice is used to cure warts.

One of its uses, unchanged since the Middle Ages, is in the bouquet handed to the judge on his entry to the court, as a once-necessary protection against jail-fever that might be spread by the prisoners in the dock. At one time Holy water was sprinkled from brushes made of rue at the ceremony preceding the Sunday celebration of High Mass, for which reason it was known as the Herb of Repentance, as well as the Herb of Grace. Rue, the benign herb of Repentance and Sorrow, was once eaten to avoid talking in one's sleep; a useful herb for husbands, and for wives too, for that matter, and we hope of symbolic significance as well.

Sweet basil *(Ocymum basilium)*

Sweet basil came originally from India, and is sacred to Krishna and Vishnu; it is a cherished plant in Hindu homes, and it is the custom to lay a leaf of basil on the breast of the dead before burial. Provided that you firmly put out of your mind Keats' poem *Isabella*, based on Boccaccio's repellent story of the young woman, who kept her murdered lover's head in a pot of basil which she watered with her tears, this is a herb to enjoy. Basil tea is drunk as a tonic, and prescribed for colds and coughs. Added to stock and with a little wine, it is delicious with lamb's liver, and it improves tomato dishes and sausage meat.

Culpeper did not trust it, however. 'Something is the matter,' he said, 'this herb and rue will not grow together, no, nor near one another, and we know rue is as great an enemy to poison as any that grows.' This is interesting, as an early reference to incompatibility in plants, a subject which has only been taken seriously during the last twenty years or so.

It is now known that there is a scientific basis for the fact that a number of plants do not get on with each other, either in the flower bed or vase. Certain members of the daisy family treat their weaker relatives with extreme venom. If lily of the valley and narcissus, two prima donnas of perfume, are put together in one bunch, they will soon wither. Mignonette also shortens the lives of other flowers in the same vase, although it seems to like roses.

Whoever wrote 'To flower and plant and tree, the garden is a cloistered refuge from the battle of life', was not entirely accurate. Cloistered from the battle outside, perhaps, but what about each other? The lion may be persuaded to lie down with the lamb more easily than clover with buttercups. Mint and parsley dislike each other's company, and Henry Phillips in 1824 quoted Mr James Justice as saying that 'Carnations must never be planted in earth where Hyacinths have grown, they, from certain experience, being a sure poison to the Carnation, and vice versa'. It has been discovered since that some strongly aromatic plants, such as wormwood, because of their toxic root excretions may inhibit the growth of other plants as strongly aromatic, fennel, sage and caraway, for instance.

Fortunately there is a reverse situation, in which plants may encourage each other's growth; deep-rooted plants may prefer the company of shallow-rooted ones; tall plants may prefer low-growing neighbours. The expression 'rare buddies' applies to dill, coriander, mallow and chervil, for they bud most contentedly when sown together.

Apart from the useful lessons we may learn in studying the Biodynamic Method of Farming and Gardening, as it is called, the emergent fact that Some Plants are more cussed than Some People may cause a wry smile.

Tansy *(Tanecetum vulgare)*, Bachelor's Buttons

'Dame Venus was minded to pleasure Women with child by this herb, for there grows not an herb, fitter for their use than this is . . . Let those Women that desire Children, love this Herb, 'tis their best companion, their Husband excepted. . . . This,' said Cul-

Isabella and the Pot of Basil, by William Holman Hunt (1827–1910). Boccaccio's gruesome story of a woman who kept her murdered lover's head in a pot of basil and watered it with her tears was retold by Keats:

No heart was there in Florence but did mourn
In pity of her love, so overcast.

peper, 'is for the Garden Tansy.' As regards the wild tansy he is equally encouraging. 'Dame Venus hath fitted Women with two herbs of one name, the one to help conception, and the other to maintain beauty, and what more can be expected of her?' What, indeed?

Whatever it may have done for those women who consulted Culpeper for treatment and advice, it was the herb that made Ganymede, that most beautiful boy, the cup-bearer to the gods, immortal; and perhaps for that reason, it was used by the ancients to preserve dead bodies.

As a herbal cure today, tansy has settled down prosaically as a mildly narcotic tonic to be taken after exhaustion, diseases and fevers. Used externally, it is good for skin diseases and will relieve sprains and swellings, and a hot fomentation is used for rheumatic pains. It is not now a popular herb in cookery, except at Easter, for which there is an historic background. Tansy was eaten in the past in various forms, because it was considered very wholesome after the diet of salt fish which was consumed during Lent. Tansy tea and tansy puddings were allowed in Lent, and tansy cakes were eaten at Trinity College, Cambridge, on Easter Monday and Tuesday. Tansy was also served with fried eggs. Tansy cakes were competed for as prizes in the Easter Games, when even archbishops and bishops stooped to play handball with the men of their congregations.

Borage *(Borago officinalis)*

This, the most attractive of all herbs, well earns its country name of Herb of Gladness. The flowers, piercing blue and dramatically black-anthered, make a striking garnish for salads and drinks, and the leaves add a cool flavour of cucumber. They should only be used very young. 'The leaves and floures of Borrage put into wine make man and women glad and merry, driving away all sadnesse, dulnesse, and melancholy'; but at a pinch, one can do without the borage.

It is a herb of Jupiter, and under Leo, and it is employed to promote the activity of the kidneys, and for feverish

pulmonary and catarrhal complaints. It can also be applied externally, as poultices for inflamed swellings. The leaves are used as an ingredient in a cosmetic bath, not only to cleanse and beautify, but to strengthen the body.

Like rose petals, violets and primroses, borage flowers can be crystallized. Boil 1 lb of caster sugar in a cup of water. When it is bubbling hard, but in no danger of turning into toffee, drop two tablespoonfuls of the dried flowers into the saucepan and boil for one minute. Lift them out carefully with a perforated spoon, and separate them out on to foil. Cool off in a slightly warm oven. In *A Proper Newe Booke of Cokery*, there is a sixteenth-century recipe for 'a tarte of borage flowers'.

This herb is never dried, but always used green and young, owing to the rough texture of the leaves, which would grow rougher still in its dried state. Indeed, the dried leaves and stalks of the dead plants, encountered among the grass in the wild, are very unfriendly to bare legs and feet.

Lemon balm *(Melissa officinalis)*

A plant of Jupiter. Nothing but good can be said of this rather insignificant-looking and unassuming herb. It is a valuable bee-plant, and, according to Pliny, acted as a sort of sign-post, in case any bee was in danger of getting lost. 'Bees are delighted with this herbe above all others . . . when they are straied away, they do finde their way home againe by it.' The leaves of balm are still rubbed inside the hives after the hiving of a new swarm, to encourage the newcomers to stay.

Lemon balm is one of the most sweetly-smelling herbs in the garden, and it is naturalized in the south of England. Oil of balm is used in the making of perfumes, as well as in medicine. It is both a tonic and a sedative, and is excellent in the drying-up of sores and wounds. It makes a cooling tea for feverish patients, and has carminative properties. A carminative was once a charm medicine, when magic and charms were at one time the chief healers. The name is now given to a remedy for flatulence.

In cookery it may be used when any

lemon-mint flavour is desirable. Fruit, jellies and winecups are all improved by a few leaves, and it is pleasant in chicken stuffing. Try a leaf or two in the teapot with your usual tea, especially in summer-time. Mixed with French dressing and poured over orange segments, it is delicious served with roast duck.

Hyssop *(Hyssopus officinalis)*

A herb of Mars and a strongly-flavoured plant which is used rather more for cosmetics and medicine than for cooking, although it is useful for many purposes. It yields an essential oil, extremely valuable to perfumers. It is also employed in the manufacture of liqueurs, and is one of the 130 herbs that are blended in the making of Chartreuse. Hyssop honey is particularly appreciated. Hyssop tea is an old-fashioned remedy for rheumatism, and the green tops used in soups are given for asthma.

It was a strewing herb, and used in prophylactic nosegays. Hyssop is mentioned a number of times in the Bible but it is thought that the references are to another aromatic plant, the thorny caper, *Capparis Spinosa*.

Dill *(Anethum graveolens)*

Dill was grown in Greek and Roman gardens. The name is derived from a Saxon word meaning 'to lull', and it has been used for lulling babies to sleep for centuries. The old lullaby,

Lavender's blue, dilly dilly,
Lavender's green.
When you are king, dilly dilly,
I shall be queen

may be a reference to the dill-water that has just been administered to a restless child. Dill-water is a proprietary medicine, carminative for adults as well as for babies. It also has the reputation of protecting infants from witches.

Galen says 'Dill procureth sleep, wherefore garlands of Dill are worn at feasts'. An odd remark, since most of us prefer to keep awake at feasts. It is a herb of Mercury, and a native of the Mediterranean region and southern Russia, and is found growing wild in the cornfields of

with his memories of Christ's Hospital and 'boiled beef on Thursdays . . . with detestable marigolds floating in the pail to poison the broth', who has put us off. Maybe, if he hadn't called the vessel a 'pail', the contents might have sounded less repulsive. The marigold, if it is no longer 'sowen as well for the potte as for the decking of Garlands, bewtifying of Nosegayes, and to be worne in the bosome' (where it would very soon close itself into a tight roll, like a furled umbrella) still makes a brave show in our gardens, even if it does not appear in our broth.

Dandelion (*Taraxacum officinale*)

The ingratitude shown to the dandelion is almost unbelievable. We should be inviting it in to our gardens with low bows, rather than uprooting it with imprecations. Few gardeners take note of that word *officinale*, which points to the fact that the dandelion should be treated with respect as a herb used in medicine. Perhaps if we mentioned in passing to our neighbours that our *Taraxacums* were doing well this year, we might do a little to reinstate what is, after all, quite a handsome flower. But no, its old-fashioned names of Piss-a-bed in the United States and England, and Pissenlit in France, would rise, a guilty secret from the past, to smirch its already tarnished good name. There are other ways, too, in which the dandelion reveals its plebeian nature. Although it blooms heroically when and where almost every other plant will give up, when it is arranged in vases and out of its true element, it sulks and closes.

In medicine, the dandelion's principal use is in kidney and liver disorders. It is employed in many patent medicines in combination with other agents, for dyspepsia and skin diseases. It has been proved efficacious in the treatment of dropsy.

In cooking, the young leaves are used in salads, or cooked and served with butter and a scatter of other herbs. The young roots can be scraped and boiled, or fried. Dandelion wine is famous for its potency, but dandelion coffee is, well, dandelion coffee.

Perhaps one day a nurseryman by the

name of Henry Higgins will take this golden-haired slut of a dandelion – or rather, dandelioness, for she is undoubtedly female – restore her name of *Taraxacum*, or its female form of *Taraxaca*, and educate her to take her true place among the lilies and the roses.

Today's nostalgia for country ways and country receipts is not only reviving our interest in herbs and herbal remedies. It is introducing a freshness and zest in bathroom, bedroom and kitchen perfumes. Soaps, lotions and skin foods are more subtly and delicately coloured; we arise from our turquoise and emerald bubble baths spangled like so many Aphrodites; and our shampoos are sharply and deliciously redolent of wild apple. Our hair is set and sprayed and generally reconditioned with the oil of sunflowers, and our skin is cleansed with elderflower lotion. If we merely want to wash our hands, we may choose from among the perfumes of peaches and black cherries, cucumber, avocado and apricots, if we feel sophisticated, or marjoram, rosemary, thyme and honeysuckle to give us the aroma of the countryside that we hope to see at the weekend. And in these delights husband and children join us.

All this is not new. The desire for scented oils and cosmetics is as old as civilization itself, and the use of aromatic herbs and spices may well have originated with the embalming of corpses, and the burning of incense at funerals. But the Egyptian and Greek herbalists, and the Roman and Arabian chemists, improved the art of extracting essences from flowers, fruit, roots and barks, and new perfumes were

created for the living. The Greek historian, Herodotus, wrote that the Babylonians perfumed their bodies with expensive odours. The Romans invented indoor fountains that sprayed perfumed water, and thus the first scent spray was achieved.

Centuries were to pass before perfumed soaps and skin foods became an everyday need to the less wealthy; until all small houses had their still-rooms, a simpler version of the distilling-rooms which had been the centre of household activities in the manor houses of England. It is from the still-rooms of our ancestors that the secrets of the still-room receipt books have been handed down from mother to daughter, or left to moulder until brought to light once more.

In the seventeenth century, Parkinson recommended that the mountain primrose, the *Auricula*, could serve as rouge. If crushed and laid on the cheek 'of any tender skind woman, it will raise an orient red colour'; which is just what my grandmother did for my pale young mother when she was going to a party, and suffering from pre-party nerves – only on these occasions an artificial flower had to serve. A rose petal pulled off mama's bonnet, a little spit, a brisk rub, and the pale child was transformed. It was fortunate that parties were few, or mama's bonnet might have suffered.

Grandmama herself, with most of the rest of her contemporaries, did not approve of the more conventional cosmetics, contenting herself with a mere dusting of Sanitary Rose Powder, white, pink or cream, for sunburn or tender feet. She did, however, approve of 'elbow-grease', as applied to the polishing of silver, brass, copper and woodwork, provided, of course, that this unguent was supplied by the housemaid, and not herself.

Now, the furniture, the kitchen-ware, and even our floors and windows are fresh with the odours of lavender, lemon and lime, produced in the finest of sprays. Need I go on? It is all to be seen in the shimmering, misty, windswept world of commercial television. It looks effortless, and perhaps it is – almost – but it is not new.

peper, 'is for the Garden Tansy.' As regards the wild tansy he is equally encouraging. 'Dame Venus hath fitted Women with two herbs of one name, the one to help conception, and the other to maintain beauty, and what more can be expected of her?' What, indeed?

Whatever it may have done for those women who consulted Culpeper for treatment and advice, it was the herb that made Ganymede, that most beautiful boy, the cup-bearer to the gods, immortal; and perhaps for that reason, it was used by the ancients to preserve dead bodies.

As a herbal cure today, tansy has settled down prosaically as a mildly narcotic tonic to be taken after exhaustion, diseases and fevers. Used externally, it is good for skin diseases and will relieve sprains and swellings, and a hot fomentation is used for rheumatic pains. It is not now a popular herb in cookery, except at Easter, for which there is an historic background. Tansy was eaten in the past in various forms, because it was considered very wholesome after the diet of salt fish which was consumed during Lent. Tansy tea and tansy puddings were allowed in Lent, and tansy cakes were eaten at Trinity College, Cambridge, on Easter Monday and Tuesday. Tansy was also served with fried eggs. Tansy cakes were competed for as prizes in the Easter Games, when even archbishops and bishops stooped to play handball with the men of their congregations.

Borage (*Borago officinalis*)

This, the most attractive of all herbs, well earns its country name of Herb of Gladness. The flowers, piercing blue and dramatically black-anthered, make a striking garnish for salads and drinks, and the leaves add a cool flavour of cucumber. They should only be used very young. 'The leaves and floures of Borrage put into wine make man and women glad and merry, driving away all sadnesse, dulnesse, and melancholy'; but at a pinch, one can do without the borage.

It is a herb of Jupiter, and under Leo, and it is employed to promote the activity of the kidneys, and for feverish pulmonary and catarrhal complaints. It can also be applied externally, as poultices for inflamed swellings. The leaves are used as an ingredient in a cosmetic bath, not only to cleanse and beautify, but to strengthen the body.

Like rose petals, violets and primroses, borage flowers can be crystallized. Boil 1 lb of caster sugar in a cup of water. When it is bubbling hard, but in no danger of turning into toffee, drop two tablespoonfuls of the dried flowers into the saucepan and boil for one minute. Lift them out carefully with a perforated spoon, and separate them out on to foil. Cool off in a slightly warm oven. In *A Proper Newe Booke of Cokery*, there is a sixteenth-century recipe for 'a tarte of borage flowers'.

This herb is never dried, but always used green and young, owing to the rough texture of the leaves, which would grow rougher still in its dried state. Indeed, the dried leaves and stalks of the dead plants, encountered among the grass in the wild, are very unfriendly to bare legs and feet.

Lemon balm (*Melissa officinalis*)

A plant of Jupiter. Nothing but good can be said of this rather insignificant-looking and unassuming herb. It is a valuable bee-plant, and, according to Pliny, acted as a sort of sign-post, in case any bee was in danger of getting lost. 'Bees are delighted with this herbe above all others . . . when they are straied away, they do finde their way home againe by it.' The leaves of balm are still rubbed inside the hives after the hiving of a new swarm, to encourage the newcomers to stay.

Lemon balm is one of the most sweetly-smelling herbs in the garden, and it is naturalized in the south of England. Oil of balm is used in the making of perfumes, as well as in medicine. It is both a tonic and a sedative, and is excellent in the drying-up of sores and wounds. It makes a cooling tea for feverish patients, and has carminative properties. A carminative was once a charm medicine, when magic and charms were at one time the chief healers. The name is now given to a remedy for flatulence.

In cookery it may be used when any lemon-mint flavour is desirable. Fruit, jellies and winecups are all improved by a few leaves, and it is pleasant in chicken stuffing. Try a leaf or two in the teapot with your usual tea, especially in summer-time. Mixed with French dressing and poured over orange segments, it is delicious served with roast duck.

Hyssop (*Hyssopus officinalis*)

A herb of Mars and a strongly-flavoured plant which is used rather more for cosmetics and medicine than for cooking, although it is useful for many purposes. It yields an essential oil, extremely valuable to perfumers. It is also employed in the manufacture of liqueurs, and is one of the 130 herbs that are blended in the making of Chartreuse. Hyssop honey is particularly appreciated. Hyssop tea is an old-fashioned remedy for rheumatism, and the green tops used in soups are given for asthma.

It was a strewing herb, and used in prophylactic nosegays. Hyssop is mentioned a number of times in the Bible but it is thought that the references are to another aromatic plant, the thorny caper, *Capparis Spinosa*.

Dill (*Anethum graveolens*)

Dill was grown in Greek and Roman gardens. The name is derived from a Saxon word meaning 'to lull', and it has been used for lulling babies to sleep for centuries. The old lullaby,

> *Lavender's blue, dilly dilly,*
> *Lavender's green.*
> *When you are king, dilly dilly,*
> *I shall be queen*

may be a reference to the dill-water that has just been administered to a restless child. Dill-water is a proprietary medicine, carminative for adults as well as for babies. It also has the reputation of protecting infants from witches.

Galen says 'Dill procureth sleep, wherefore garlands of Dill are worn at feasts'. An odd remark, since most of us prefer to keep awake at feasts. It is a herb of Mercury, and a native of the Mediterranean region and southern Russia, and is found growing wild in the cornfields of

Spain and Portugal. In England it is
now cultivated in East Anglia for the
pharmaceutical market, and oil of dill is
used in the perfuming of soaps. In India
dill is used for flavouring pickles, and for
medicinal purposes.

Although much in use in Scandinavian
and Russian cookery, it is not in great
demand in Great Britain, except in the
making of pickles. 'I am always pleased
with that time of the year which is proper for the pickling of dill and cucum-
bers', remarked Addison in *The Spectator*. A recipe for dill pickle was found in
the Receipt Book of Joseph Cooper,
Cook to Charles I; and John Evelyn, in
Acetaria, A Discourse of Sallets, gives a
recipe for Dill and Colly Flower Pickle.
Its sharp, aromatic flavour lends an interest to egg and cheese dishes, cottage
and cream cheeses, and yoghurt and
soured cream. It may be used in salads,
or as a garnish to vegetables. In cooked
dishes, it should be added just before
completion, to keep its freshness of flavour.

Elecampane *(Inula helenium)*

The handsome plant with the legendary
name – Elecampane – it is poetry to
read or to write; no wonder Kipling
couldn't resist it; 'Eyebright, Orris and
Elecampane', it positively sings.

'Of the lamentable and pitifull teares of
Helena, Wife to Menelaus, when she
was violently taken away by Paris into
Phrigia, having this herbe in her hande.
Or as other doe say, this noble Helena
made a goodly medicine of this herbe,
against the deadly Venome, or poyson
of Serpents.' Sprung from the tears of
Helena, or fallen from her hands when
she was carried off by Paris, it makes no
matter. It is Helen's plant, and as
Helen's plant it was recommended for a
quaintly assorted trio of ills – convulsions, contusions, and the hip-gout.
Gerard recommends it for 'shortnesse of
breath, and an old cough, and for such
as cannot breathe unlesse they hold
their neckes upright', also, it is good for
them that are 'bursten'. It also fixes
loose teeth.

Helen's plant, under the dominion of
Mercury, is now a native of southern
England, and it has travelled to New

1 *Calendula multiflora maxima.*
The greatest double Marigold.

3 *Calendula minor polyanthos.*
The smaller double Marigold.

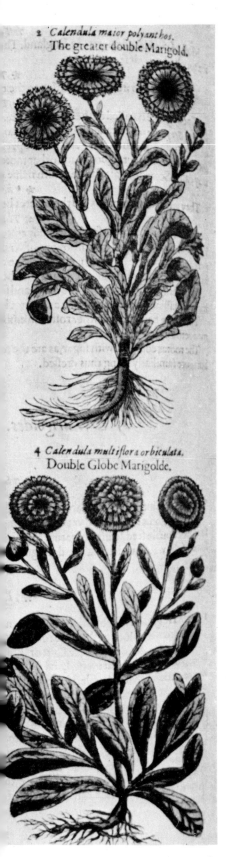

2 *Calendula maior polyanthos.*
The greater double Marigold.

4 *Calendula multiflora orbiculata.*
Double Globe Marigolde.

England with the settlers, until now it grows along the roadsides as though dropped by Helen herself. It is today considered beneficial for hay-fever, inflammation of the lungs, and urinary problems.

The Elizabethans made from it a candied sweetmeat, but it is of little use in cookery now. For us, if we care to plant it in the back of the border, it is a tall and handsome presence, the presence of the legendary Helen.

Marigold *(Calendula officinalis)*

When every garden was a herb garden, and herbs, vegetables and flowers grew side by side, the pot marigold might have been made the symbol of man's food, man's medicine, and man's delight. It was in fact known in some country districts as Summer's Bride, or Husbandman's Dial, because it followed the sun. It is a herb of the Sun and under Leo, and the traditional time for prescribing it is midday, when the sun is highest.

'The yellow leaves of the flowers', said Gerard, 'are dried and kept throughout Dutchland against Winter to put into broths, Physicall potions and for divers other purposes, in such quantity that in some Grocer's or Spice-seller's houses are to be found barrels filled with them, and retailed by the penny more or lesse, insomuch that no broths are well made without dried Marigolds.' It must have taken a great number of marigolds to fill a barrel, but the invigorating aromatic scent that arose when the petals were measured out for each customer must have more than balanced the smells of cheese and tallow and all the other musty comestibles in the grocer's shop.

Marigold flowers are useful for childish ailments such as measles. An infusion may be given internally or externally for chronic ulcers, varicose veins, etc., and it is also prescribed for fevers. The flower, rubbed on a wasp- or bee-sting is said to bring relief. A tincture made from the whole plant when in flower may be given, in small, well-diluted doses, in cases of anaemia.

Although marigolds still shine in every garden, they are little used in cookery today. Perhaps it was Charles Lamb,

Left: Greatest Double Marigold, Greater Double Marigold, Smaller Double Marigold, Double Globe Marigold. From Gerard's *Herbal*, 1597. Bodleian Library, Oxford. 'The Greatest Double Marigold', says Gerard, is 'called of the vulgar sort of women, Jacke-an-apes on horse backe . . . for this plant does bring forth at the top of the stalk one floure . . .'

Overleaf: An Alembic Oven, from Mattioli's *Commentaires*, Lyons, 1579. Used for distilling, the original alembic was an apparatus consisting of a *cucurbit* or gourd-shaped vessel, and the *cap* or alembic proper, the beak of which conveyed the products to a *receiver*. The alchemists attempted to turn base metals into gold and at the same time to achieve spiritual progress towards perfection.

with his memories of Christ's Hospital and 'boiled beef on Thursdays . . . with detestable marigolds floating in the pail to poison the broth', who has put us off. Maybe, if he hadn't called the vessel a 'pail', the contents might have sounded less repulsive. The marigold, if it is no longer 'sowen as well for the potte as for the decking of Garlands, bewtifying of Nosegayes, and to be worne in the bosome' (where it would very soon close itself into a tight roll, like a furled umbrella) still makes a brave show in our gardens, even if it does not appear in our broth.

Dandelion (*Taraxacum officinale*)

The ingratitude shown to the dandelion is almost unbelievable. We should be inviting it in to our gardens with low bows, rather than uprooting it with imprecations. Few gardeners take note of that word *officinale*, which points to the fact that the dandelion should be treated with respect as a herb used in medicine. Perhaps if we mentioned in passing to our neighbours that our *Taraxacums* were doing well this year, we might do a little to reinstate what is, after all, quite a handsome flower. But no, its old-fashioned names of Piss-a-bed in the United States and England, and Pissenlit in France, would rise, a guilty secret from the past, to smirch its already tarnished good name. There are other ways, too, in which the dandelion reveals its plebeian nature. Although it blooms heroically when and where almost every other plant will give up, when it is arranged in vases and out of its true element, it sulks and closes.

In medicine, the dandelion's principal use is in kidney and liver disorders. It is employed in many patent medicines in combination with other agents, for dyspepsia and skin diseases. It has been proved efficacious in the treatment of dropsy.

In cooking, the young leaves are used in salads, or cooked and served with butter and a scatter of other herbs. The young roots can be scraped and boiled, or fried. Dandelion wine is famous for its potency, but dandelion coffee is, well, dandelion coffee.

Perhaps one day a nurseryman by the

name of Henry Higgins will take this golden-haired slut of a dandelion – or rather, dandelioness, for she is undoubtedly female – restore her name of *Taraxacum*, or its female form of *Taraxaca*, and educate her to take her true place among the lilies and the roses.

Today's nostalgia for country ways and country receipts is not only reviving our interest in herbs and herbal remedies. It is introducing a freshness and zest in bathroom, bedroom and kitchen perfumes. Soaps, lotions and skin foods are more subtly and delicately coloured; we arise from our turquoise and emerald bubble baths spangled like so many Aphrodites; and our shampoos are sharply and deliciously redolent of wild apple. Our hair is set and sprayed and generally reconditioned with the oil of sunflowers, and our skin is cleansed with elderflower lotion. If we merely want to wash our hands, we may choose from among the perfumes of peaches and black cherries, cucumber, avocado and apricots, if we feel sophisticated, or marjoram, rosemary, thyme and honeysuckle to give us the aroma of the countryside that we hope to see at the weekend. And in these delights husband and children join us.

All this is not new. The desire for scented oils and cosmetics is as old as civilization itself, and the use of aromatic herbs and spices may well have originated with the embalming of corpses, and the burning of incense at funerals. But the Egyptian and Greek herbalists, and the Roman and Arabian chemists, improved the art of extracting essences from flowers, fruit, roots and barks, and new perfumes were

created for the living. The Greek historian, Herodotus, wrote that the Babylonians perfumed their bodies with expensive odours. The Romans invented indoor fountains that sprayed perfumed water, and thus the first scent spray was achieved.

Centuries were to pass before perfumed soaps and skin foods became an everyday need to the less wealthy; until all small houses had their still-rooms, a simpler version of the distilling-rooms which had been the centre of household activities in the manor houses of England. It is from the still-rooms of our ancestors that the secrets of the still-room receipt books have been handed down from mother to daughter, or left to moulder until brought to light once more.

In the seventeenth century, Parkinson recommended that the mountain primrose, the *Auricula*, could serve as rouge. If crushed and laid on the cheek 'of any tender skind woman, it will raise an orient red colour'; which is just what my grandmother did for my pale young mother when she was going to a party, and suffering from pre-party nerves – only on these occasions an artificial flower had to serve. A rose petal pulled off mama's bonnet, a little spit, a brisk rub, and the pale child was transformed. It was fortunate that parties were few, or mama's bonnet might have suffered.

Grandmama herself, with most of the rest of her contemporaries, did not approve of the more conventional cosmetics, contenting herself with a mere dusting of Sanitary Rose Powder, white, pink or cream, for sunburn or tender feet. She did, however, approve of 'elbow-grease', as applied to the polishing of silver, brass, copper and woodwork, provided, of course, that this unguent was supplied by the housemaid, and not herself.

Now, the furniture, the kitchen-ware, and even our floors and windows are fresh with the odours of lavender, lemon and lime, produced in the finest of sprays. Need I go on? It is all to be seen in the shimmering, misty, windswept world of commercial television. It looks effortless, and perhaps it is – almost – but it is not new.

Unlike most words, whose meanings are inclined nowadays to suffer from middle-aged spread, the word 'physic' has narrowed in its meaning. In the seventeenth century, 'physic' stood for natural science, and a physic garden was a scientific garden, not necessarily connected with drugs. The apothecary, once defined as 'the physician's cooke', after many vicissitudes succeeded in establishing his right to practise medicine, as well as to prepare it. Although this had been the situation for a long time, legal recognition did not come until 1721, when the College of Physicians prosecuted an apothecary named Rose for prescribing as well as compounding medicines. The College lost its case. In due course, the chemists and druggists rose in turn against the apothecaries, and a hundred years later the sale of drugs and medicines was safely in the hands of the druggists and the chemists. Today, the term apothecary is principally kept alive by the Society of Apothecaries.

In the old monastery and nunnery gardens, men and women had cultivated their vegetables for the pot, flowers for saints' days, and simples for the cure of disease. After the dissolution of the monasteries, a more scientific study of plants began in the gardens of the herbalists, and of the wealthy patrons of horticulture. Lord Zouche, who himself introduced several plants from abroad, was one of the greatest patrons, and he employed L'Obel, Botanist to King James I, as the supervisor of his physic garden in Hackney. Lord Zouche also did us the dubious service of introducing the thornapple to this country.

Medical gardens had already been established in Salerno in 1309 and Venice in 1333. At Padua, the first botanic garden was established two hundred years later. The Medicis founded a medicine garden in Pisa in 1544, and the famous botanic garden of Leyden followed in 1577. In this same year, there was translated into English by Barnaby Googe, a minor but lovable poet, the Four Bookes of Husbandry of Conrad Heresbach, who was Counsellor to 'the high and mighty Prince, the Duke of Cleve.' Published in one volume we find a lively

XII
The Physic Garden

description of the activities in a country house and garden, delivered by various characters each with a burning desire to instruct or be instructed; a method of imparting information which was to be continued with enthusiasm until the end of the nineteenth century. In this, a character named Marius shows clearly the growing interest in the art of cultivating medicinal herbs within easy reach of the household. In 1597 a garden was established in Paris to supply the court bouquets, and no doubt it was for antiseptic reasons and not merely for decoration that these bouquets were carried. Aromatic nosegays were regarded as necessary in all the great cities, and the nursery rhyme,

> *Ring-a-ring of roses,*
> *A pocketful of posies,*
> *A-tishoo, a-tishoo,*
> *We all fall down,*

is believed to refer to the Great Plague, and those poor wretches who fell dead in the streets. Probably the posies themselves were relics of an even earlier age when plants were thought to possess qualities to protect those who carried them from evil. In 1635, the medical garden in Paris became Le Jardin des Plantes.

The oldest physic garden in Great Britain was founded in Oxford in 1621. It was planted with 'divers simples for the advancement of the faculty of medicine', but at first, because of the Civil War, work there made little progress. The original curator of the garden was Jacob Bobart the Elder, who was noted, apart from his excellent work as gardener and botanist, for his cultivation of a splendid beard, which on 'rejoicing days' he wore tagged with silver, as if he, too, had burst into bloom. It is related that he walked attended by a goat, and if this is true, one would have thought that his herbs would have been at greater risk than had he been content with a mere dog, but doubtless he knew what he was doing. Another of his characteristic achievements were two large yews, clipped to resemble giants; one holding a bill and the other with a club over his shoulder.

An Accurate Survey of the Botanic Gardens at CHELSEA, with the Elevation and Ichnography of the Green House and Stoves and an Explanation of the Several Parts of the GARDEN shewing where the most considerable Trees and Plants are disposed The Whole carefully SURVEY'D AND DELINEATED BY John Haynes

Page 83: Linnaeus (1701–1775), in the dress he wore for his journey through Lapland, at the age of twenty-five. He carries the plant *Linnaea borealis*, named in his honour, and a Laplander's drum. After a painting by M. Hoffman, *c.* 1737

Left: *Chelsea Physic Garden*. An engraving by John Haynes, 1751, when Phillip Miller was Curator.

> The most hopefull and ever-flourishing
>   Sprouts of Valour,
> The indefatigable Centrys of the Physic
>   Garden.

Bobart died in 1679 at the age of 81, 'a Germane Prince of plants'. In 1726 Dr William Sherard, a plant collector and a patron of botanical science, made over to the Physic Garden an herbarium which, in the opinion of Linnaeus, made Oxford pre-eminent in this respect among the universities of Europe, and the Botanic Garden remains the mecca of plant-lovers from all parts of the world.

While Bobart was planting his 'divers simples' in Oxford, the Apothecaries, or 'potticaries', as they were often called, were by no means idle. The Apothecaries' Society was the creation of James I, whose interest in the culture of plants did not stop with his enthusiastic introduction of the mulberry tree. His dream of a flourishing silk-culture in England came to nothing – only a few noble trees remaining to remind us of a royal disappointment. With the Apothecaries he was more successful. In 1617, with the full backing of the king, the Apothecaries broke away from the Company of Grocers, to which they had belonged, and formed themselves into a City Company. The charter runs thus:

> James, by the grace of God, King, and Defender of the Faith . . . to all whom these present shall come greeting. Whereas . . . very many unskilfull and ignorant Men . . . do abide in our City of London . . . which are not well instructed in the Art or Mystery of Apothecaries, but . . . do make and compound many unwholesome, hurtful, corrupt, and dangerous medicines and the same do sell . . . to the great peril and daily hazard of the lives of our subjects . . . We therefore . . . thought necessary to disunite and dissociate the Apothecaries of our City of London from the Freemen of the Mystery of Grocers . . .

As might have been expected, nothing went smoothly. The Grocers resisted – the Apothecaries were doubtful – but King James stood firm. In 1624 the Lord Mayor was persuaded to petition the King to revoke the charter, but King James told the Mayor and Corporation that 'from his own judgement for the health of the people, knowing that grocers are not competent judges of the practice of medicine', the charter must stand. Cobham House, on the banks of the Thames, was purchased from Lady Howard of Effingham, and in December 1632 the Apothecaries' Company was installed.

One of the members, Thomas Johnson, presented the Company with his newly amended edition of Gerard's *Herbal*, a copy that was to be destroyed in the Great Fire of London. Johnson, who had published the first local list of wild flowers in England, fought and died in the Civil War, at the age of forty, leaving his country the poorer for his loss and the Johnsonias, a group of lilies, for his memorial. He had been the first to study native flora as a botanist instead of as a searcher after simples, and might have been the best herbalist in England had he lived.

Never were Apothecaries so greatly needed, for the Civil War, followed by the Great Plague and the cleansing Fire of London, were soon to come. The Apothecaries' Hall vanished, with their entire library, but the Company survived – survived to begin cultivation of the rare seeds and plants that were now coming from foreign lands. A garden was found in the pleasant village of Chelsea, and in 1673 they obtained a lease of it from Charles Cheyne, afterwards Lord Cheyne, for an annual rent of £5.

It was an excellent site for a garden, separated as it was from the smoke of London by the cultivated fields, meadows and ditches, and irrigated along its south side by the river Thames. But its $3\frac{1}{2}$ acres of garden were miles away from Blackfriars, where the master and wardens still had residence; workmen cheated; plants were stolen; there was no money, and it was proposed that it should be abandoned. The majority of the Company, however, decided to keep it, and a wall was built to shelter its

Flora, with usefully employed *putti*, welcomes the god of Horticulture. From Phillip Miller, *The Gardeners Kalendar*, 1745. Phillip Miller (1692–1771) was dismissed from the Physic Garden at the ripe age of seventy-nine, for 'obstinacy and impertinence'. He died the following year.

plants from the cold winds and thieving hands. The four famous Cedars of Lebanon, among the first in England, were planted about 1683. The last of these was cut down in 1903.

Then came the greatest event in the history of the Society. Sir Hans Sloane had purchased the manor of Chelsea some years before, and in 1722, for a yearly payment of £5, he made over the Physic Garden, with its greenhouse and stoves, to the Apothecaries' Society in perpetuity, 'for the manifestation of the power, wisdom and Glory of God in the works of the Creation', and to demonstrate how 'useful plants' may be distinguished 'from those that are hurtful'. In exchange, every year for forty years, fifty specimens of plants, all grown in the Garden, and no two alike, carefully dried, mounted and named, were to be sent to the Royal Society; they are now preserved in the Natural History Museum.

Phillip Miller was the first to be given the title of Curator of the Garden. After two years there he published his *Gardener's Dictionary*, which for a long time was the standard work on gardening. He was the first botanist to realize the part played by insects in the fertilization of flowers. Miller remained at the Physic Garden for almost fifty years, and on one eventful day he sent a small packet of seeds to the newly-founded American colony of Georgia, named after George II. The packet contained the seeds of the plant from which the greater part of the world's cotton is descended. Miller dedicated his *Gardeners Kalendar* (1745) to the 'Master and Wardens and the Rest of the Court of Assistants Of the Worshipful Company of Apothecaries of London'. Miller was followed by William Forsyth, whose name is remembered each spring in the golden showers of forsythia, one of our most beautiful hardy shrubs.

Famous trees and famous people all found their way to the Chelsea Physic Garden. John Evelyn wrote in his diary of a visit on 7 August 1685, when he saw for the first time 'the tree bearing the Jesuit's bark (the *Cinchona*, from which

quinine is obtained), which has done such wonders in Quartan Agues'. The botanical name of *Cinchona* is derived from the wife of the Spanish Viceroy, the Countess of Chinchón, who in 1639 had brought the Peruvian bark to Spain, to relieve the ague-stricken labourers on her husband's estate. Evelyn also remarked upon the stove under the conservatory, that made it possible to keep doors and windows open in the hardest frost, a considerable improvement on the charcoal-filled fire-baskets that were drawn up and down the greenhouses of Oxford's Botanic Gardens.

It was about the same time that the Botanic Garden of Edinburgh was established, with a catalogue of some 3,000 plants.

By 1730, John Bartram, Quaker, farmer, amateur doctor and devoted botanist, had started the first botanical garden in America, in the 5 acres of land surrounding his house by the Schuylkill river which flows through Pennsylvania and joins the Delaware at Philadelphia. But before that important event, we are given a picture of young John Bartram sitting under a tree, idly pulling a daisy to pieces, and then slowly being led to consider the small miracle he was destroying. After brooding on the subject for four days, he saddled a horse and rode into Philadelphia, went into a book-shop there, and asked for a book of instruction on the nature of plants. He came out with a botanical treatise in Latin, and a Latin grammar, under his arm. Later he was given Parkinson's *Theatrum Botanicum*, and began to botanize on the farm and in the surrounding country. He exchanged plants with foreign collectors and, his first wife having died, he married again, and bought the farm on the Schuylkill where he was to make his first botanical garden.

And so, in the eighteenth century, two small daisies died, but not in vain. One, as we have seen, gave America her first botanical garden in 1730. The other, an ocean apart, was unwittingly destroyed by a young Scottish farmer, the son of a nurseryman whose ancestors had farmed

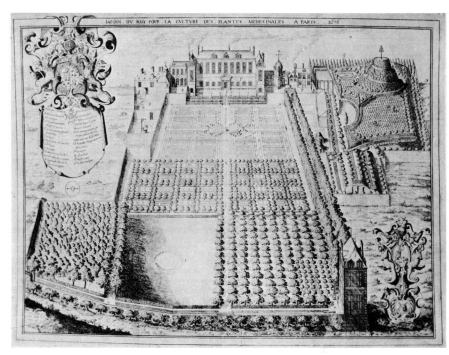

Right: Jardin des Plantes, Paris, 1636, a year after it was taken over from the original herb garden. In 1869 William Robinson described its 'vast zoological, botanical and mineralogical collections'.

Far right: America's first botanic garden by the Schuylkill river, with John Bartram's house, 1798. It is said that in the days of the Revolutionary War the shock of fear at the approach of the British army, and his concern for the safety of his plants, caused his death in 1777.

the highlands for generations. Robert Burns was the repentant murderer, and he wrote a memorial to his victim.

'To a Mountain Daisy'
On Turning One Down With a Plough, in April, 1786

Wee, modest crimson tipped flower,
Thou's met me in an evil hour;
For I maun crush amang the stoure [dust]
Thy slender stem;
To spare thee now is past my power,
Thou bonnie gem.

England's greatest botanical garden, and one of the most important scientific institutions in the world, the Royal Botanic Gardens of Kew, is beyond our present scope, and there is but one small part of it, the Physic Garden, which is needed to complete the story. Kew's Physic Garden was commenced in 1760, with the beginning of the Botanic Gardens in which it is set. It was devoted to herbaceous plants arranged in accordance with the newly-devised Linnean system. Two years later, Cambridge followed, when Richard Walker, the Vice-Master of Trinity College, presented some 5 acres of land in the city to the

university for a garden. It was laid out by the Professor of Botany, Thomas Martyn, with the help of Phillip Miller, whose son, Charles, was its first Curator. Physic gardens had by now merged with botanical gardens, and others were being established in many parts of the British Isles. Only the Chelsea Physic Garden kept and still keeps the boundaries of its original purpose. For this reason we will mention here a few more of the famous men who walked its paths in centuries past. The great Linnaeus, who, as has been mentioned earlier, brought order out of chaos in the naming of plants, was allowed the freedom of the garden on his first visit to England in 1736. That the name of Linnaeus, one of the most respected and respectable in botany and horticulture, should later sound in the narrow confines of the Passage de l'Opera in Paris, comes as a surprise to us, as it might have done to him. Heine, emigrating to Paris in 1831, and full of the excitement of adventure, writes of a charming encounter.

My French had grown rusty since the battle of Waterloo, but after half an hour's conversation with a pretty flower-girl in the Passage de l'Opera it soon flowed fluently again. I mana-

A Draught of John Bartram's House and Garden as it appears from the River 1758   Sent to P Collinson

Schuilkiln River 200 Yards wide

ged to stammer forth gallant phrases in broken French, and explained to the little charmer the Linnaean system, in which flowers are classified according to their stamens. The little one practised a different system, and divided flowers into those which smelled pleasantly and those which smelled unpleasantly. I believe that she applied a similar classification to men. She was surprised that, notwithstanding my youth, I was so learned, and spread the fame of my erudition through the whole Passage de l'Opera. I inhaled with rapturous delight the delicious aroma of flattery, and amused myself charmingly. I walked on flowers . . .

But the flowers of the Passage de l'Opera were to wither and die for this poor genius, and the Linnaean system become a mere echo of erudition to an unknown flower-girl.

In 1748, Peter Kalm, the Swedish botanist after whom the attractive shrub kalmia is named, was a visitor. On Sir Joseph Banks's return from Iceland in 1772, the first rockery for alpine plants was made in the Physic Garden. John Lindley, the author of many valuable books on botany; Sir Joseph Hooker, later to become Director of Kew; Robert Fortune, who founded the tea industry in India; Nathaniel Ward, the inventor of the Wardian case, by which means plants were enabled to survive the most difficult journeys; all these, and countless other great names are associated with Chelsea.

In 1899 the Chelsea Physic Garden was taken over from the Apothecaries' Society by the London Parochial Charities, supported by various smaller bodies, but still, after more than 250 years the planting and the research goes on. The gardens are not open to the public, but students and teachers work there as they have always worked. Botanical specimens are supplied to schools and hospitals, and the collection of plants is based purely on its suitability for teaching botany as a pure science – the Chelsea Physic Gardens are still there for 'the manifestation of the power, wisdom and glory in the works of the creation'.

XIII
Poison Gardens

Since King Attalus reigned over Pergamum in 138 BC, few people have deliberately set out to plant a poison garden.

For those that are so inclined, the approach is likely to be scientific or even romantic, rather than criminal. It is true that many gardeners are unrelenting in their campaigns against aphis, slugs and snails, and will stop at nothing in their murderous designs, but they usually have little desire to poison their fellows.

The veritable murderer, apart from the unlikelihood of a true murderer being a true gardener, would scarcely need to grow a gardenful of poisonous plants, when one good aconite would serve his purpose. As for that, a deadly nightshade or a hemlock, or better still, a thornapple, would do as well, and these can be obtained for free in waste land probably not too far away. In short, no would-be poisoner need go to the extreme lengths of planning a toxicological garden, unless he really enjoys gardening.

The name of King Attalus lives for 'his poysonous plantations of Aconite, Henbane, Hellabore, and plants hardly admitted within the walls of Paradise'. But was King Attalus sinner or saint, killer or curer? for a poison garden, treated with knowledge and caution, may also be a medicine garden.

Aconite, for instance, is one of our most useful drugs, often employed in homocopathy, but it is also a deadly poison; henbane has been used as a cure for toothache, neuralgia and rheumatism, but it can cause convulsions, and even insanity, and it is a narcotic poison. Hellebore has been proved of value in nervous disorders and hysteria, but it is violently narcotic. It is to be hoped that King Attalus was a cautious and kindly man. He was certainly an odd man, for he left his kingdom of Pergamum to Rome in his will, and it was duly handed over when he died in 133 BC.

Whatever the reasons for King Attalus' interest in poisonous plants, only a few years later, Mithridates, King of Pontus, pursued the same path with the purest of motives. Whether he, too, cultivated a poison garden, or whether

He gathered all that springs to birth
From the many-venomed earth,

in the surrounding countryside, we do not know, but he evolved the theory of the use of poisonous plants in the slow building up of a resistance against poison. This resulted in a composition containing seventy-two ingredients, which was to be administered in the form of an electuary, that is, a powder mixed with honey or syrup. This mixture became known as a Mithridate or Mithridatum in old pharmacy. Its fame, and presumably its use, continued for centuries, and it was mentioned in 1635 in *The Knight of the Burning Pestle*: 'What brave spirit could be content to sit in his shop . . . selling Mithridatum and dragon's water to infected houses?' Culpeper was his first avowed champion. 'The whole world, is at this present time beholden to him for his studies in physic', wrote Culpeper. 'And that he uses the quantity but of an hazel-nut of that receipt every morning, to which his name is adjoined shall to admiration preserve his body in health.'

After a life spent in winning and losing a number of bloody battles, Mithridates was captured and, ironically, attempted to commit suicide by poison. The reader must judge whether this is a chronicle of brilliant success or dismal failure. Mithridatum, the antidote, prevailed against the poison; Mithridates, the apothecary-king, and a failed suicide, was at his own request put to death by a Celtic soldier in 63 BC.

Writing of gardens and gardeners in *The Garden of Cyrus*, Sir Thomas Browne mentions 'Some commendably affected Plantations of venomous Vegetables', and that word 'commendably' seems to indicate good intentions. It may well be a case of 'a little more than a little is by much too much', as King Henry IV put it. A surprising number of the plants that are grown in the suburban gardens of today are capable of causing illness and even death if taken by mouth – and as every parent discovers, there is often a stage in childhood when the attraction of cramming illicit food down the infant gullet seems to be hard to resist. To avoid accidents it is very necessary to

keep an eye on children when they are too young to remember warnings, and to put an absolute ban on eating any part of a plant whatever as soon as they are old enough to understand. The alternative – to eradicate altogether from the garden plants which are potentially harmful – is unthinkable.

Consider what would be lost in so doing. To keep poisonous plants altogether from our gardens, would leave sad gaps in the shrubbery and herbaceous border. If in our efforts to save our children from death or disaster from eating the poisonous seeds of laburnum or daphne we ban from our garden the delicately perfumed golden chains of blossom in May, or the enchanting little cretonne sprigs that break along the leafless twigs of mezereum in early spring, how great a loss to our garden and to ourselves! And to what avail, since there are many potential hazards besides plants. If adult visitors insist on chewing our oleander flowers or our clematis stems it is their own affair; for although we may be forced to live without oleanders, we surely cannot be expected to exist without a clematis?

The poppy would have to go – not the field poppy, for that is only slightly narcotic; but we are not likely to cultivate field poppies on our own home patch. The white poppy, *Papaver somniferum*, which varies from white to reddish purple, is the source of opium, and has great powers for good or ill. As early as the 13th century it was known as 'a slepi herbe', and today it is used in morphine and codeine. It was known to be the gall which, mixed with vinegar, was offered to Christ by compassionate Roman soldiers at Golgotha. We know, too, that Christ refused the opiate, choosing to suffer the full measure of agony in order to redeem mankind.

We should also lose the foxglove, so handsome in the back of the border, and a valuable source of digitalis. It has been used from earliest times in diseases of the heart, but if given over a prolonged period can lead to hypertrophy; and readers of Mary Webb will remember how, in *Precious Bane*, Gideon Sarn poisoned his old mother with foxglove tea. Those given to brewing of mint, lemon

balm and other herbal teas, should remember to avoid foxgloves, and yet, so
strange are the properties of plants,
foxglove tea, added to the water in
vases, helps to preserve the life of cut
flowers.

The larkspur has exceedingly poisonous
seeds, which were used to destroy lice
and nits in the hair, but which we may
happily grow for decorative reasons
only. The kernels of the nuts on our
lovely almond trees contain prussic
acid. A tincture of the flowers of morning glory is used for headaches, rheumatism and inflamed eyes, but all the
parts of the plant except the roots contain a potentially dangerous halluci-
natory drug, and even the seeds worn as
bracelets or necklaces may cause a
rash. Monkshood, the name we have
given to the aconite since the Middle
Ages, is known in Germany as the *Eisen-
hut*, the Iron hat, or the *Sturmhut*, or
Storm hat. It is another handsome plant
which we should be loth to lose, but do
not plant it in the kitchen garden, for it
contains a deadly poison.

We may not, perhaps, cherish buttercups in our garden in spite of their
wonderfully varnished golden flowers,
but this is rather because of their repre-
hensible manner of spreading than the
fact that they possess the unamiable
property of blistering and inflaming the
skin. Some members of the Primulaceae
have this same effect on delicate skins.
The fresh bulbs of bluebells are poisonous, but when they are tucked safely
underground in our wild garden, we,
and they, are safe from harm. If you
must dig them up, however, they can be
used for book-binder's glue, or as a substitute for starch, should you need such
commodities. The bryonies, both black
and white, are strictly not garden
plants, although they are handsome
enough for any shrubbery, but we should

Page 90: *The Absinthe Drinker*, by
Degas (1834–1917). The brooding
young figure alone at a café table
is already familiar with the
bitterness of wormwood.
Absinthium, wormwood, has given
its name to absinthism, a disease as
demoralizing as alcoholism.

Above: Henbane, *Hyocyamus niger*.
From *Medicinal Plants*, 1880.
Anodyne necklaces, made of pieces
of root rounded and strung
together, were sometimes worn
round the necks of teething babies.

not introduce them, for the translucent gem-like red berries of the black briony, and the black berries of the white briony, could be attractive to children, and they contain a dangerous irritant poison.

Many of the handsome spurges, the *Euphorbias*, that are so popular today are extremely toxic, but like most of these Jekyll-and-Hyde plants they have good in them as well as bad. Even our gentle dove-plant, the columbine, whose leaves were made into lotions for sore mouths and throats, has been known to poison a child, if too large doses were taken. Herbals tell us that there have been several cases of poisoning from the eating of daffodil bulbs in mistake for onions. Tulip bulbs, however, became a common article of diet in Holland during the German occupation. The Dutch ate them boiled, baked and chipped, with the appetite of the desperate rather than the gourmet.

Although thrushes and blackbirds may eat our holly berries with impunity and impudence, to humans the berries are violently emetic. You should point out to your children that they are neither thrushes nor blackbirds. Houseleek juice is emetic and purgative – so keep it on the roof, where it will guard your house against fire and lightning. Unlike the true saffron, *Crocus sativus*, the corm and seeds of the meadow saffron, *Colchicum autumnale*, are very poisonous, although they are used in medicine. The bitter oil of wormwood is used in absinthe, and the berries of some species of juniper are a component of gin.

There are many plants in the garden and in the wild that contain drugs, which may be of great use in medicine, or of infinite danger to the ignorant. We cannot afford to exclude them – but equally we need to beware of them. ●

Hemlock, *Conium maculatum*. From *The Botanical Magazine*, 1787. The poison drunk by Socrates, and by the ancient philosophers who had grown weary of life. They came to their last repast as to a banquet, garlanded.

XIV
Plants of Love, Hate and Blood

Right: *Papaver rhoeas.* The deceptively frail-looking poppy seemed to well up from past battlefields like spreading blood. John Tradescant the Elder (died *c.* 1638), gardener to Charles I, accompanying the Duke of Buckingham on his unsuccessful expedition to the relief of La Rochelle, brought back to England the seeds of the first red poppy.

Far right: *Play scene in* Hamlet, by Daniel Maclise (1806–1870). The court watch as the murder of the king, Hamlet's father, is re-enacted.

> Thou mixture rank, of midnight weeds collected
> With Hecate's ban thrice blasted, thrice infected –
>
> *Hamlet*, III, 2, 260.

Love

Orchid

The reputation of the orchid as an aphrodisiac has lessened with the years. Once the most desired of the desirous, it is now regarded as a mink- and-cleavage flower, and no one would think of eating its roots. The old herbalists wrote of the plant and its properties with considerable frankness, and gave to the species then known, names that were rather more descriptive than elegant, such as Dog's Stones, Souldier's Cullions, Foolestones, Goatstones and Foxstones, from the double formation of their tubers. It was the satyrion orchis that was believed to be the most effective, and it was so called as a tribute to the well-known prowess of the satyrs, and because the tubers were said to be their favourite food. The name derives from the Greek *orchis*, meaning testicles.

According to legend, the orchid owes its origin to Orchis, the lascivious son of Patellanus, a satyr, and the nymph Acolasia, who presided at the feasts held in honour of Priapus, the fertility god. In an unbridled moment, the youth laid

violent hands on one of the priestesses of Bacchus, which so incensed the Bacchanals that they tore him to pieces. In answer to Patellanus' pleading, the gods transformed his mangled corpse into the flower that bears his name. An unfortunate background for any flower, let alone one that has the strange formation of the orchid – the imprint of a bee, a fly, a spider, a hornet or a wasp; and the shapes of butterflies, lizards, monkeys, frogs, slippers, soldiers, and little green men. All added to its mystery and fascination. Parkinson claimed that the flowers, distilled, were as effective an aphrodisiac as the roots. He also recommended the fresh flowers of the Mountaine-Handed Orchis as beneficial to the health.

The same author quotes the ancients, with further details.

Dioscorides saith of *Cynosorchis* (Dog Stones) that the roote thereof being boyled is eaten as other sorts of bulbes are, and that if men eate the greater, they shall beget men children, and if women eate the lesser they shall bring forth women children: And that the women in *Thessalye* give the

soft roote in Goates milk to procure lust, and the dry roote to restraine it, and that the vertue of the one is extinguished by the taking of the other. *Pliny* also writeth the same words out of *Dioscorides*, yet it is generally held, by almost all nowadayes, that the firme roote onely is effectuall for that purpose, and the loose or spongy roote to be either of no force or to hinder that effect: but most of our Apothecaries doe promiscuously take, not onely both of these rootes to use, but of all sorts of Orchides in generall.

Culpeper says of these tubers: 'They are hot and moist in operation; under the dominion of Venus, and provoke lust exceedingly, which, it is said, the dry and withered roots restrain again.'

It comes as no surprise that Shakespeare was well aware of the supposed properties of this remarkable wild flower. In *Hamlet*, when the Queen tells of Ophelia's death by drowning, she describes the scene:

There is a willow grows aslant a brook,
That shows his hoar leaves in the glassy stream;

There with fantastic garlands did she come,
Of crow-flowers, nettles, daisies, and long purples,
That liberal shepherds give a grosser name,
But our cold maids do dead men's fingers call them.

The grosser names we know, and 'dead men's fingers' refers to the pale palmate roots of *Orchis palmata*.

Beliefs die hard, especially where love is concerned, and when a nourishing drink that was made of these roots, and called Salep or Saloop, was imported from Turkey, many must have hoped that they were enjoying rather more than a comforting night-cap. Anne Pratt, in 1855, described salep as 'a favourite repast of porters, coal-heavers, and other hard-working men', and added that the saloop-house was a much-frequented place less than a hundred years before. The root was said to contain more nutritious matter, in proportion to its bulk, than any root known at the time. Most of the tubers for the manufacture of saloop were imported from Italy, although it was made from

Phalaenopsis amicabilis. From *The Botanical Magazine*, 1847. Because of the formation of the tubers and flowers of the orchis, it was frequently employed for aphrodisiac potions, and the flower was regarded as a symbol of sex in many works of art.

English plants as well. It was mixed with milk and flavoured with ginger.

One of the strangest habits of this strange plant is that, in the European species, of the two lobes of its root, one is found plump and vigorous, when the other is wrinkled and withering, but about to be succeeded by a new one on the opposite side. In consequence, the plants move about half an inch every year, not only loving but moving, it seems. All in all, it is not surprising that the wild orchid has become a rare plant. All this and Tulips too.

I have preserved the rootes of these Tulipas in Sugar, as I have done the rootes of Eryngus, Orchis, or any such like, and have found them to be almost as pleasant as Eryngus rootes, being firm and sound, fit to be presented to the curious, but for force of Venereous quality, I cannot say, either from my selfe, not having eaten many, or from any other, on whom I have bestowed them; but surely, if there be any special propertie in the rootes of Orchis, or some other tending to that purpose, I think this may as well have it as they.

So wrote Parkinson, and it is as well that men have lost faith in the aphrodisiac qualities of these plants, or Tulipomania might have taken a different turn.

Dog's Tooth Violet

Even more efficacious than the orchis, according to the same author, is the dog's tooth violet, *Erythronium*. There were only four varieties of this plant, however, so that it could in no way compare in popularity with the orchid.

The roote hereof is held to bee of more efficacy for venereous effects ... than any of the Orchides and Satyrions ... Wee have from Virginia a roote sente unto us that we might well judge, by the forme and colour thereof being dry, to be either the roote of this, or of an Orchis, which the naturall people hold not only to be singular to procure lust, but hold it as a secret, loth to reveale it.

Mandrake

As the oldest known narcotic plant in botanical history, the identity of the mandrake has never been in doubt, although for centuries the herb was shrouded in dark mystery and magic. Although not a native of Egypt, mandrake fruits were found in the tomb of Tut Ankh Amun, eleven of them being placed at regular intervals in the sixth row of his floral colarette, with what significance is not known.

Mandragora, the old Greek name, was also known as the Plant of Circe, who used it in the magic brews by which she turned men into swine. The name was at some time transferred to the enchanter's nightshade, an insignificant plant whose only function seemed to be to give the ingenious Dr Erasmus Darwin yet another opportunity of versifying.

> *Thrice round the grave Circaea prints her tread,*
> *And chants the numbers, which disturb the dead,*
> *Shakes o'er the holy earth her sable plume,*
> *Waves her dread wand and strikes the echoing tomb.*

There is a curious drawing from the Vienna manuscript of Dioscorides in the fifth century, and reproduced by Dr Daubeny in his *Roman Husbandry*, in which the Goddess of Discovery is presenting to Dioscorides the root of a mandrake, which she has just pulled up, while the unfortunate dog that has been employed for the purpose is portrayed in his death agonies. This was founded on the belief that 'he who would take up a plant thereof must tie a dog thereunto to pull it up, which will give a great shreeke at the digging up; otherwise if a man should do it, he should surely die in short space after'. It was said 'never or very seldome to be found growing naturally but under a gallowes, where the matter that hath fallen from the dead body hath given it the shape of a man; the matter of a woman, the substance of a female plant'. It should be dug up at midnight. Another hazard, according to Bartolomaeus Anglicus, whose book *De Proprietatibus Rerum* was published in 1495, was the state of the wind. 'They

that dig Mandragora be busy to beware of contrary winds while they dig, and make three circles about with a sword, and abide with the digging unto the sun going down, and trow so to have the herb with the chief virtues.' It is obvious that mandrake seekers, like Shakespeare's samphire gatherers, must have earned every penny they received in their dreadful trade.

As well as a narcotic and an emetic, it was used as an ingredient in love-philtres, and as such was mentioned in the Bible.

And when Rachel saw that she bare Jacob no children, Rachel envied her sister. And Reuben went in the days of wheat harvest, and found mandrakes in the field, and brought them unto his mother Leah. Then Rachel said unto Leah, Give me, I pray thee, of thy son's mandrakes ... At first Leah was disinclined. Is it a small matter that thou hast taken away my husband? and wouldest thou take away my son's mandrakes also? And Rachel said, Therefore he shall lie with thee tonight for thy son's mandrakes. And Jacob came out of the field in the evening, and Leah went out to meet him, and said, Thou must come in unto me; for surely I have hired thee with my son's mandrakes. And he lay with her that night.

This strange bargain between the two women had the desired results, for Leah bore a son, Jacob, and then 'God remembered Rachel ... and she conceived, and bare a son', Joseph, which shows the complete faith of the age in the mandrake as a fertility drug.

In the Middle Ages it was used as a pain-killer, and mandrake wine was given to patients undergoing surgery. Bartolomaeus Anglicus said that 'the rind thereof sodden with wine ... gene them to drink that shall be cut in their body for they should slepe and not fele the sore knitting', yet mandragora must be warily used. 'As soon as it be jerked up take it immediately and twist it and wring its ooze into a glass, that when need come upon thee to help therewith any man – thou hast it.'

Gerard, with regrettable reticence, comments on its reputation as an aphrodisiac, and mentions *en passant* 'many fables of loving matters, too full of scurrilities to set forth in print, which I forbear to speak of'.

The mandrake, like the hemlock, nightshade, aconite and other poisonous herbs, has reputation both for good and ill, and they were all collected by herbalists for their medicines, and yet used by witches in their deadly brews. In *The Masque of Queens*, there is a meeting of the twelve Hagges, Ignorance, Falshoode, Suspicion, Credulity, Murmur, Impudencie, Malice, Slaunder, Execration, Bitterness, Fury, and their Dame, Ate, goddess of Mischiefe, and leader of the Hagges. 'Fraught with spight', together they weave their evil spells.

> I, last night; lay all alone,
> O' the ground, to hear the Mandrake
>   grone:
> And pluck'd him up, though he grew full
>   low,
> And, as I had done, the Cock did crow.

Ben Jonson's notes to *The Masque of Queens* (c. 1605) make fascinating reading. He quotes Pliny, proving his knowledge of the ancient mandrake myth, and adds, 'But we have later tradition, that the forscing of it up is so fatallie dangerous, as the Grone kills, and therefore they do it with Doggs, which I thinke but borrowed from Josephus . . . Howsoever, it being so principall an Ingredient in their *Magick*, it was fit she should boast to be the plucker up of it herselfe'. Another Hagge tells of her night's adventures:

> And I ha' bene plucking, plants among,
> Hemlock, Henbane, Adders-tongue,
> Nightshade, Moone wort, Libbard's-
>   bane;
> And twice, by the Doggs was like to be
>   tane.

After giving the Latin names of the herbs, Jonson explains that they are 'the most common veneficall ingredients; remembred by Paracelsus, Porta, Agrippa, and others; which I make her

to have gath'red, as about a Castle, Church, or some such vast building (kept by Doggs) among ruines, and wild heapes'.

Shakespeare also was well aware of the properties and mystery of the mandrake. Juliet, in her terror of awakening in the tomb, 'where, as they say, At some hours in the night spirits resort', cries out:

> Alack, alack! is it not like that I
> So early waking, what with loathsome
>   smells,
> And shrieks like mandrakes torn out of
>   the earth,
> That living mortals hearing them run
>   mad:
> O! if I wake, shall I not be distraught,
> Environed with all these hideous fears?

Murder and malefaction were synonymous with this mysterious root, as when Suffolk in answer to Queen Margaret, in the Second Part of *Henry VI* cries:

> A plague upon them! Wherefore should I
>   curse them?
> Would curses kill, as doth the mandrake's
>   groan,
> I would invent as bitter-searching terms,
> As curst, as harsh, and horrible
>   to hear . . .
> As lean-fac'd Envy in her loathsome cave.

This, then, was a plant of hate as well as love.

The mandrake is frequently mentioned in plays of this period, in comedy as well as tragedy. In Thomas Dekker's ribald comedy, *The Honest Whore*, there is a passage between a brother and a sister, Fustigo and Viola:

VIOLA: I am married to a man that has wealth enough, and wit enough.
FUSTIGO: A linen-draper, I was told, sister.
VIOLA: Very true, a grave citizen, I want nothing that a wife can wish from a husband: but here's the spite, he has not all the things belonging to a man.

FUSTIGO: God's my life, he's a very mandrake.

Owing to the supposed difficulties and dangers of digging up these natural images, which grew in the form of miniature men and women, mandrakes were carved to render them more lifelike, by 'cheating Knaves and Quacksalvers that carry them about to be sold, therewith to deceive barren women'. Matthiolus was probably the first to expose the practice in 1567, when the fakers who sold the roots in Italy went a little too far in realism, by raising a crop of hair on the mandrake's head, rather like growing mustard and cress on a flannel. From then on, almost every herbalist wrote in protest. In 1568, William Turner said:

> The rootes whiche are counterfeited and made like little puppettes and mamettes, which come to be sold in England in boxes, with heir, and such forme as man hath, are nothyng elles but foolishe feined trifles, and not naturall. For they are so trymmed of crafty theves to mock the poore people with all, and to rob them both of theyre wit and theyre money. I have in my tyme at diverse tymes taken up the rootes of Mandrag out of the grounde, but I never saw any such thynge upon or in them, as are in and upon the peddlars rootes.

In 1629, John Parkinson wrote:

> The male is frequent in many gardens, but the female, in that it is more tender and rare, is noursed up but in a few . . . But many cunning counterfeit rootes have been shaped to such formes, and publickly exposed to the view of all that would see them, and have been tolerated by the Chiefe Magistrates of the Citie, notwithstanding that they have been informed that such practises were meere deceit, and insufferable; this happened through their overcreditie of the thing, or of the persons, or through an opinion that the information of the truth rose upon

envy, I know not, I leave that to the searcher of all hearts.

For the next hundred years misguided folk were buying, and herbalists and nature writers inveighing against, false mandrake images. Phillip Miller, in his *Gardener's Dictionary* (c. 1750), wrote: 'As to the feigned Resemblance of an human Form, which the Roots of this Plant are said to carry, 'tis all imposture, owing to the Cunning of Quacks and Mountebanks, who deceive the Populace, and the Ignorant, with fictitious Images shaped from the fresh roots of Bryony, and other Plants.'

So the mandrake trade was still going on, but the good times for quacks and mountebanks were nearly at an end. Phillip Miller declared that the root could be dug up without the assistance of dogs, and with neither groan nor shriek from the protesting plant. He also stated that, having established a mandrake in your garden, it was better left undisturbed, as the move would 'break their Fibres, and so stint the Plants, that they will not recover their former strength in two or three Years'. From the narcotic so desired by Cleopatra,

Give me to drink Mandragora . . .
That I might sleep out this great gap of time
My Antony is away,

this forked imposter shrank to a mere good-luck charm, as described by Richard Brook, in his *Cyclopaedia* (1800): 'As an amulet this root was deposited on the mantel-pieces to avert misfortune'. It is quite possible that we may yet see the revival of mandrake and womandrake in seaside gift-shops.

Meanwhile the mandrake has been transferred from the world of myth and fantasy to a sober place in the herbaceous border. Perhaps in the stillness of the night garden, like some retired diva, all passion spent, the mandrake strains to catch the far-off echo of those shrieks men thought they heard.

Cyclamen

In Gerard's time the cyclamen was also burdened with the unattractive name of Sow-bread; Pain-de-Porceau to the French. In spite of its name, it was considered, on the whole, harmful to pigs, but Linnaeus claims that it was the principal food for the wild boars of Sicily.

However that may be, Gerard recommends that 'being beaten and made up into trochisches, or little flat cakes, it is reported to be a good amorous medicine to make one in love, if it be inwardly taken'. But Parkinson, although he knew of ten different varieties, disagrees. 'But for any amorous effects, I hold it meere fabulous.'

Periwinkle

Readers of *The boke of secretes of Albartus Magnus of the vertues of Herbes, Stones and certain beasts* needed to be really seriously disposed if they were to follow his instructions regarding the periwinkle as an aphrodisiac. It would be easier, perhaps, to give up the whole idea? 'Perwynke when it is beate unto powder with wormes of ye earth wrapped aboute it and with an hearbe called houslyk it induceth love between man and wife if it be used in their meales.'

Seeds of rockets might be more palatable, or the corm of gladiolus, though Parkinson had little faith in its ability to 'stirre up Venerie', but a distillation of the sea holly, *Eryngium*, was found efficacious by the Italians, Spaniards, French, Germans and Dutch for the same purpose.

Stinkhorn

Richard Brook recommended the fungus called stinkhorn, or stinking morell, which, when dried in the open air, or smoked, and reduced to powder and taken in a glass of spirits, could be relied upon to have aphrodisiac qualities.

All in all, there was plenty to choose from. It therefore comes as a relief to find that, in case of an over-dose, or for patients in need of opposite treatment, there were draughts of tutsan, purslane, rue, chicory, lettuce, hellebore, woodbine, and even water lilies that were conducive to a more balanced existence.

Hate

Hebenon

Tree of many names, and under any of them, of ill repute, was the hebenon, hebona, hebenus, hebon or heben. At best, poets wrote of its narcotic effects. As early as 1386, John Gower wrote in *Confessio Amantis*, of 'Hebenus, that slepy tre'. To most, however, it was the source of a deadly poison. The ghost of Hamlet's father, appearing upon the battlements at Elsinore, speaks of 'murder most foul', and describes to his horror-stricken son his own hideous death.

Sleeping within mine orchard,
My custom always in the afternoon,
Upon my secure hour thy uncle stole,
With juice of cursed hebona in a vial
And in the porches of mine ears did pour
The leperous distilment; whose effect
Holds such an enmity with blood of man
That swift as quicksilver it courses
*   through*
The natural gates and alleys of the
*   body, ...*
O, horrible! O, horrible! most horrible!

Spenser writes in *The Fairy Queene* of 'trees of bitter gall and Heben sad', and Christopher Marlowe uses it as a curse in *The Jew of Malta*:

the blood of Hydra, Lerna's bane,
The juice of Hebon, and Cocytus breath,
And all the poison of the Stygian pool.

At first hebenon was considered another name for henbane, because the poison was poured into the ears of Hamlet's father, and according to Pliny this was the classical way of administering poison.

But henbane is not a tree, and a clue was found in another quotation from *The Fairy Queene*.

Fair Venus sonne . . .
Lay now thy deadly Heben bow apart.

It is now generally agreed that the yew tree is meant. Bows, as we know, were frequently made of its wood; also, the effects of yew-tree poisoning were similar to snake-poisoning, and

> 'Tis given out that, sleeping in mine
>   orchard,
> A serpent stung me; . . . but know, thou
>   noble youth,
> The serpent that did sting thy father's life
> Now wears his crown.

Henbane

Although the henbane is innocent of this particular crime, it still has a lot to answer for. Brewer believes it to be Shakespeare's 'insane root', when Macbeth and Banquo meet with the three witches on the heath, and Macbeth is accosted by the hags with 'All hail, Macbeth! that shall be king hereafter'. When the witches vanish, and Banquo doubts his own senses, 'Were such things here as we do speak about?' he says, 'Or have we eaten of the insane root That takes the reason prisoner?' It should be said here that other historians suppose the insane root to be the nightshade, which causes delirium and madness.

Bartolomaeus wrote on henbane in a book first printed in 1398: 'This herb is called insana wood, for the use thereof is perilous: for if it be eate or dranke, it bredeth woodenes, or slowe liknes of slepe; therefore the herb is commonly called *Morilindi*, for it taketh away wytte and reason.'

According to Gerard, 'The seed is used by mountibank tooth-drawers which run about the country, to cause worms to come out of the teeth, by burning it in a chafing dish of coles, the party holding his mouth over the fume thereof: but some crafty companions to gain mony convey small lute-strings into the water, presuading the patient, that these small creepers came out of his mouth, or other parts which he intended to ease.'

Hemlock

The death-drink of the Greeks, the suicide's last draught, and a sought-after herb for witches' brews. 'The great Hemlocke doubtless is not possessed of any one good facultie, as appeareth by his loathsome smell and other apparent signs' according to one ancient herbalist. Regarded in Russia and Ger-

many as the devil's own plant – with the lovely lacey flower-heads that are the gentle lady flower-presser's delight. Convulsions, paralysis and death to humans – and on which sheep may safely graze. So lethal, that even snakes wriggle away in revulsion, yet the song-thrush will make a meal on its seeds. Its botanical name is *Conium maculatum*. Hemlock adds largely to the beauty of our hedgerows and is reputed to have medicinal properties. Culpeper says that 'If the root is roasted in embers afterwards wrapt in double wet papers, and then applied to any part afflicted with the gout, it will speedily remove the pain thereof'.

Deadly Nightshade

An ominous name for a 'furious and deadly' plant. 'Not one of our British plants is so deadly as this', wrote Anne Pratt; and 'it will never be allowed to become really familiar, for the same reason that a man would not give his children prussic acid to "play shop" with, or let them have a loaded revolver to amuse them because it was too wet to go out', says Edward Hulme.

Children, it seems, stand in the greatest danger, because its luscious-looking black berries, sweet to the taste, might well have been especially designed by some wicked fairy to lure them to destruction.

Fortunately, it is rarely seen nowadays, except in some chalky localities, but it is a poisonous member of a poisonous family, which includes henbane, thorn-apple, mandrake, and last, but by no means least, we are told, tobacco. Like most families, it can boast of a few respectable characters, and among these we are pleased to be able to mention the potato and the tomato. Even these are possessed of base qualities; the potato, when it is allowed to turn green in the sun, and the deliciously aromatic leaves of the tomato, both contain poison. Also, like many other plebeian families, it includes one aristocrat; in this case, the Duke of Argyll's tea-plant. This aristocratic connection, as so often happens, is a trifle tenuous, inasmuch as the plant owes its name to a careless exchange of labels with a genuine tea-plant which

had been sent to the Duke. There are few opportunities for name-dropping in a botanical Who's-Who, so no opportunity should be missed.

This plant, *Atropa belladonna*, is of the Solanum family, and owes its name, *Atropa*, to Linnaeus, who called it after Atropos, daughter of Erebus and Night. She was one of the three Parcae, the Fates. Her office was to cut man's thread of life. *Belladonna* comes from the Italian ladies who used it as a cosmetic. Its now obsolete name of Dwale, a word of doom, is from the Latin *dolere*, to suffer. In Germany it is the *Tollkraut*, the frantic herb, and in France, *morelle mortelle*, the cherry of death. You have been warned.

Blood

The folk-lore of blood may be discovered in root and stem, leaf and flower of many plants, and country names such as Bloodwort, Bloodroot and Bloody-fingers are common. Sometimes the name has a religious origin, as the Blood-drops of Christ, given to the deep-coloured wallflower which was supposed to have been flowering under the Cross. In Palestine, the same name belongs to the scarlet anemone. A secular name for the wallflower was Bloody Warrior, and it was planted at cottage windows to defend the inmates from intruders. Bloody Mary was one of the many local names for herb robert, because its red stems made it a plant to staunch blood, in the Doctrine of Signatures; and the red sap of *Hypericum*, St John's wort, was a symbol of the blood of St John. Tormentil is called Blood-root because a red dye could be extracted from its root. The American Blood-root *Sanguinaria canadensis*, is so called for the same reason, although it bears no resemblance to the tormentil, and is unrelated. One of the loveliest of American wild flowers, it is related to the poppies and was used by the Indians for ceremonial painting.

It seems a little hard on the red valerian that it is known in Devonshire as Bloody Butcher, a regional name given by Geoffrey Grigson in *The Englishman's*

Flora, so little do its dark red lacy heads suggest either butchers or blood. The names of Bloody Man's Fingers, Bloody Fingers, or Bloody Bells seem inappropriate, too, for the soft and freckled pink of foxgloves, but these country names are listed in the same book. 'Bloody Man' probably referred to the Devil, for although the foxglove is a medicinal plant of great value, there is poison in its leaves.

The crimson clover, *Trifolium incarnatum*, has a splendid muster of military names: Bloody Triumph, Red Fingers, Soldiers and Napoleon (perhaps a rustic attempt at trifolium?). Most country names have their own logic behind them, although it is not always clear what it is.

In Oscar Wilde's play, *Salome*, it is the red rose that is the symbol of blood, and from the cool and dewy flower that is so familiar to us, it becomes a sultry exotic, wreathed round the head of Herod, and witness to a scene of lust and violence.

HEROD: Loosen my mantle. Quick! quick! loosen my mantle. Nay, but leave it. It is my garland that hurts me, my garland of roses. The flowers are like fire. They have burned my forehead. (*He tears the wreath from his head, and throws it on the table.*) Ah! I can breathe now. How red these petals are! They are like stains of blood on the cloth! That does not matter. It is not wise to find symbols in everything one sees. It makes life too full of terrors. It were better to say that stains of blood are as lovely as rose-petals. (*The slaves bring perfumes and the seven veils and take off the sandals of Salome.*) Ah, thou art to dance with naked feet! 'Tis well! 'Tis well! Thy little feet will be like white doves. They will be like little white flowers that dance upon the trees . . . No, no, she is going to

Illustration from *The Rubáiyát of Omar Kháyyám*, translated by Edward Fitzgerald, 1859. Omar Khayyám (*c.* 11th–12th century), was a Persian poet-astronomer who was one of eight learned men appointed to reform the calendar.

dance on blood! There is blood spilt on the ground. She must not dance on blood. It were an evil omen.

Salome, seeing that her step-father desires her, dances for him against the strenuous opposition of Herodias, her mother. In a frenzy of remorse and blood-lust, she kisses the severed head. Herod, in a spasm of jealousy orders his soldiers: 'Kill that woman!' and the red velvet curtains sweep down upon the red roses and the blood. 'I have heard that the Roses which grow in such plenty in Glover's field every yere the field is plowed, are none other than Corn Rose, that is, red Poppies, however our Author was informed', wrote Gerard. Perhaps Herod's red roses were poppies after all.

The ancient legend of St Leonard, who slew a 'mightie worm', or fire-drake, a kind of fiery dragon, in a dark forest in Sussex, since then known as St Leonard's Forest, is one of the earliest tales of flowers arising from a field of battle. Three long days St Leonard fought the dragon, although he was seriously wounded, and wherever his blood fell, lilies of the valley grew.

More than one of our wild flowers is said to grow from where the Danes were killed in battle on English soil. Defoe, in his *Tour through Great Britain*, wrote of a camp called Barrow Hill, near Daventry, which was supposed to have been built by the Danes. Here a weed called Dane-weed, Dane-wort, or Danes' Blood, grew in great profusion, and it was believed to bleed on a certain day, to commemorate the battle. The snake's head fritillary, *Fritillaria meleagris*, another plant of mystery, also springs from Danish blood, although there is little about its subdued and neatly-chequered flower that speaks of war to us.

The story of many a grim struggle is perpetuated in a wild flower that has taken the torn land, and itself made an emblem of some age-old victory. There is one recorded case, however, of flowers planted after a battle by fellow countrymen in memory of the slain, and

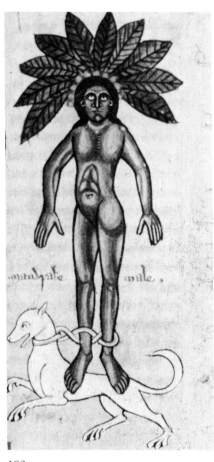

which were growing still after nearly four hundred years. The battle of Towton, in the West Riding of Yorkshire, was fought between the Yorkists and Lancastrians on 29 March 1461, when 36,000 Englishmen, White Rose against Red, were slaughtered in one of the bloodiest battles of English history. A paper, dated July 1846, was written by the Reverend G. F. Tounsend, and published in the *Memoirs Illustrative of the History and Antiquities of the County and City of York*.

It is reported that the soldiers were buried in one large mound on the field of battle, and that the Yorkists either in affection or in triumph, planted some rose-trees on the tombs of their countrymen. These mounds, through the lapse of four centuries, have worn nearly down to the level surface of the soil, but you may see a kind of circles in the field above the quarry which I have mentioned, and these circles are covered with patches and clusters of rose-trees. The rose is white, and now and then [on] the appearance of a pink spot on the flower traces the blood of Lancaster.

Marigolds are known in Mexico as 'death-flowers', from a legend that they grew on earth stained by 'the life-blood of those who fell victims to the love of gold and cruelty of the early Spanish settlers in America', and among the American Indians the story is told that the red clover grew from the blood of the redskins killed in battle.

Most sinister of all these legends is that of the 'bleeding tree', from which the Marquis of Argyll hanged thirty-six of his enemies. The tree was cut down, but a stream of blood ran from its stump, saturating the earth, and for several years after, blood flowed from its roots. The name of this tree of horror is forgotten; and the last Marquis of Argyll was put to death, and his marquisate became extinct, when Charles II was restored to the throne. Whether this was the man who perpetrated this violent deed, it is now too late to discover.

Long before the Flanders poppy grew to be the emblem of two world wars, the field of another battle was covered the following year by a scarlet stream of healing poppies. It was the battle of Neerwinden, or Landen, as it was sometimes called, after a small river that flowed nearby. It was fought on 29 July 1693, when Luxembourg defeated William III. Here is Macaulay's description of the protagonists.

At Landen two poor sickly beings, who, in a rude state of society, would have been regarded as too puny to bear any part in combats, were the souls of two great armies . . . It is probable that, among the hundred and twenty thousand soldiers who were marshalled round Neerwinden under all the standards of Western Europe, the two feeblest in body were the hunchbacked dwarf who urged forward the fiery onset of France, and the asthmatic skeleton who covered the slow retreat of England. . . . During many months the ground was strewn with skulls and bones of men and horses, and with fragments of hats and shoes, saddles and holsters. The next summer the soil, fertilised by twenty thousand corpses, broke forth into millions of poppies.

Macaulay quotes from a letter from Lord Perth to his sister, dated 17 June 1694.

The traveller who, on the road from Saint Tron to Tirlemont, saw that vast sheet of rich scarlet spreading from Landen to Neerwinden, could hardly help fancying that the figurative prediction of the Hebrew prophet was literally accomplished, that the earth was disclosing her blood, and refusing to cover the slain.

The year following the battle of Waterloo, the devastated fields were blue with forget-me-nots, forerunners of the message of the Flanders poppy – 'Lest we forget'. Colonel John McCrae was the author of the lines which are remembered each year on 11 November:

In Flanders' fields the poppies blow
Between the crosses, row on row,

That mark our place; and in the sky
The larks still bravely singing fly,
Scarce heard amid the guns below.

In May 1918, John McCrae died of wounds.

After the Armistice was signed, one man resolved to make a War Garden, a Corner of Remembrance, in his own garden. In the autumn of 1919, Newman Flower went out to the battlefields to gather seeds from the wild flowers that were already growing on the stricken battlefields.

He collected poppy seeds from Fricourt, where he found them growing round a patch of bandages, stained rust-red with last year's blood. He found the seeds of blue chicory flowers in what remained of Delville Wood, and on Vimy Ridge the antirrhinums had seeded, and these he took with the others, and labelled them, and brought them home. He collected chalk to add to the loam of his garden, and sowed his war seeds in the spring of 1920. Eventually an article appeared in a national newspaper telling the story of his Garden of Remembrance, and he received letters from relatives of men who had died in the war, and to these he sent small packets of seeds, so that these Gardens of Remembrance might be started in many parts of the world. Herb robert, traveller's joy, self-heal and forget-me-not were also homely symbols of the resilience of nature that soon covered the devastated areas of the Somme; a resilience that is perhaps best summed up in Edward Fitzgerald's words.

I sometimes think that never blows so red
The Rose as where some buried Caesar
  bled;
  That every Hyacinth the Garden wears
Dropt in its lap from some once lovely
  Head.

And this delightful Herb whose tender
  Green
Fledges the River's Lip on which we
  lean –
  Ah, lean upon it lightly! for who
  knows
From what once Lovely Lip it springs
  unseen!

Left: Mandrake, *Mandragora*. From an early English Herbal, 13th century. Bodleian Library, Oxford. Most ancient of the love-hate plants, the mandrake was endowed with mysterious powers against demoniacal possession.

Below: Vervain. Man stabbing a serpent. From a 13th-century English herbal. Bodleian Library, Oxford. A plant of both good and ill repute, sacred to the Romans and Druids, but Gerard says; 'Manie old wives fables are written of vervayne tending to witchcraft and sorcerie, which you may read elsewhere, for I am not willing to trouble your eare with such trifles.'

The Language of Flowers, through which the lover communicates his sentiments to his beloved through the symbolism of the tributes he offers her, is referred to by Lady Mary Wortley Montagu. On 16 March 1718 she wrote from Constantinople to a friend:

> I have got for you as you desire, a Turkish Love-letter, which I have put in a little box, and ordered the Captain of the Smyrniote to deliver it to you with this letter. The translation of it is literally as follows. The first piece you should pull out of the purse is a little Pearl, which is in Turkish called *ingi*, and should be understood in this manner.

Pearl.	Fairest of the young.
A clove	You are as slender as this clove;
	You are an unblown Rose;
	I have long lov'd you, and you have not known it,

and so on.

At the end of the list, which contains other objects as well as flowers, Lady Mary continues with enthusiasm, 'You see this letter is all verses, and I can assure you that there is as much fancy shewn in the choice of them as in the most study'd expressions of our Letters, there being (I believe) a million verses design'd for this use'.

Other writers of the time were more critical. Dumont describes a similar love-letter as 'nothing but bits of Charcoal, Scarlet Cloth, Saffron, Ashes and such-like trash, wrapt up in a Piece of Paper'. Not many flowers here.

Aubrey de la Mottraie, who introduced the flower language into France, wrote, 'Fruit, Flowers, and Gold and Silver Thread, or silk of divers Colours . . . have each of them their particular Meaning explain'd by certain Turkish verses, which the young Girls learn by Tradition of one another'. La Mottraie was the companion of Charles XII, King of Sweden, who invaded Denmark in 1700 and defeated the Russians at Narva in the same year. He was in turn

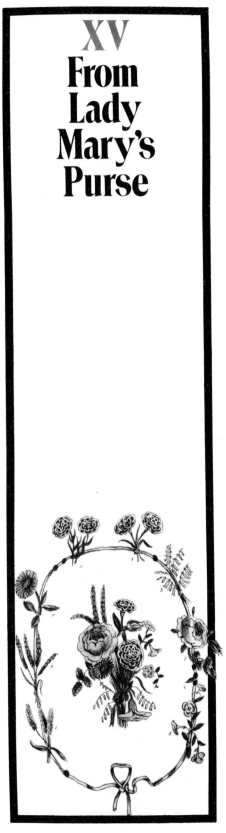

XV
From Lady Mary's Purse

defeated by Peter the Great in 1709. Charles escaped into Turkey, and it is likely that he and La Mottraie learnt there the Turkish Language of Flowers from which Aimé Martin, the well-known author of *Lettres à Sophie*, evolved the French version. Martin's *Langage des Fleurs* was published in 1830, and he also produced a similar version with different illustrations under the pseudonym of Madame Charlotte de la Tour. This was translated into the *Blumen-Sprache* of Germany, and thence found its way to many other parts of this cupid-dominated globe.

The German *Blumen-Sprache* differs a little from the English. To carry marjoram, *Dost*, which in English meant Blushes, in Germany was the sign of a light heart, and was then called *Wohlgemuth*, or happy minded. Camellia japonica meant Thou art my heart's sovereign, instead of Unpretending excellence, or sometimes Perfected loveliness, as it meant in England. But so long as the loved-one was pleased there would have been little chance of misunderstanding, and what is a Blush or two between friends? A rose is a rose is a rose be it German or English.

The German Iris, which meant Flame in both countries, came from the charming custom once common in the German countryside of growing irises on the roofs of the cottages. In an old copy of the *Blumen-Sprache* it says, 'when the sun gilds their petals, tinged with gold, purple and azure, it looks as if light flames were playing on the top of those rustic dwellings.'

The Turkish and Arabic flower language is formed, not by an idea or sentiment originating in the flower itself, but by its capacity for rhyming with another word. Again according to Lady Mary 'there is no flower without a verse belonging to it; and it is possible to quarrel, reproach, or send letters of passion, friendship, or civility, or even of news without even inking your fingers'.

It is believed that the Greeks understood the art of sending messages by a bouquet and it is evident from the old *Dream-book of Artimedorus*, who lived about AD 170. That every flower of which their garlands were composed had a particular meaning, but we have no certain knowledge of this ancient flower language. The Chinese, whose chronicles antedate the historic records of all other nations, used a simple but complete mode of communication by means of florigraphic signs. The Assyrians, Egyptians and Indians also used floral symbols.

The Sélam, the oriental flower language, had been brought to Turkey from Persia, where it was an ancient poetical art. In Pierre Zaccone's *Nouveau Langage des Fleurs* (1860) there is a story entitled 'The Sélam' which tells of a French artist, Georges de Raincy, who travels to the court of Rokneddin Karschah, sultan of Ispahan, and is commissioned to paint a series of portraits of the beautiful women of the harem. The inevitable happens, and Georges believes himself to be in love with the sultan's favourite, Kamil (chaste, like the other ladies of the harem!). One morning Kamil comes to the studio carrying a small bouquet, which Georges takes. Georges' young Persian assistant, Alkendi, offers to teach him the Language of Flowers.

The bouquet was composed of the most strange flowers, whose colours did not seem, at first glance, to combine very happily. It was a confused mixture, hastily put together, of violets, field lychnis, the leaves of the mountain ash, golden rod and bryony . . . Alkendi took the bouquet from the painter's hands, and taking the flowers that composed it one by one, 'This violet', he said, 'signifies "pure love"; the field lychnis says "invincible desire"; the mountain ash, "prudence"; the golden rod, "protect me", and the bryony, "I implore your help".'

Alkendi carries on the romantic *tête-à-tête*, delivering bouquets each day between Kamil and Georges. The final bouquet is sent by Kamil. It is composed of jonquils, yellow roses, veronica and morning glory. 'This was as much as saying, "I die for love. I desire to be your wife. I offer you my heart. Count on my devotion".' Kamil is making herself perfectly clear.

Then Fate steps in, and the Sultan discovers all. Georges has been deceived (to say nothing of the Sultan). Alkendi and Kamil have been carrying on their own private love affair by means of Georges' bouquets. Georges nobly steps in and saves Alkendi's head from being severed from his shoulders. 'Kamil and Alkendi departed happily, intoxicated with love and gratitude, and Georges returned to his studio with a new, but different, ardour. There he spent more than four years. It was a long time. What did he do there?' The story does not say precisely. Only, Kamil was not the only pretty woman shut up in the harem – and thanks to Alkendi, the young painter now understands the Language of Flowers.

No wonder Lady Mary was all for carrying on the tradition. On her return to England she introduced from Turkey the diverse practices of the innoculation of the small-pox, and the Language of Flowers. 'She took a delight in the idea that she was instructing the world at large and informing it of things which it could learn from nobody else', though there is little doubt that she found considerably more opposition to the startling medical innovation than to the romantic imagery that caused such flutterings in the hearts of the young ladies – and gentlemen – of her time. Leigh Hunt wrote a light-hearted verse on these floral love-letters:

An exquisite invention this,
Worthy of Love's most honied kiss.
This art of writing billet-doux
In buds, and odours, and bright hues, –
In saying all one feels and thinks
In clever daffodils and pinks,
Uttering (as well as silence may)
The sweetest words the sweetest way:
How fit, too, for a lady's bosom,
The place where billet-doux repose 'em!
How charming in some rural spot,
Combining love with garden plot,
At once to cultivate one's flowers,
And one's epistolary powers,
Growing one's own choice words and
*   fancies*
In orange tubs and beds of pansies;
One's sighs and passionate declarations
In odorous rhet'ric of carnations;

Left: 'I shall be at no. 33 after the Opera.' A concealed message from *The Floral Telegraph, or Affections Signals*, by 'the late Captain Marryat, R.N.', undated. The centre group represents the Flowers tied together as a bouquet; the surrounding circle as untied and laid open.

Forget-me-not, Myrtle, Anemone,
Laurestinus – 'Do not forget me,
love, for if forsaken I die'. An
imploring message from *The
Poetical Language of Flowers*, by
Thomas Miller, *c.* 1847.

Seeing how far one's stocks will reach;
Taking due care one's flowers of speech
To guard from blight as well as bathos,
And watering, every day, one's pathos!

The books were arranged usually in two sections; flowers first, followed by their meanings, then a second list with meanings first, so that if the message was imperative one had to beg, borrow or steal, or even buy the flowers. A cheaper and easier method was to go out into the garden and pick a nosegay, and see what the flowers meant afterwards.

Even when the meanings were committed to memory, great care must be taken in the presentation of the posy. One must follow the *Directions* or one risked giving altogether the wrong impression. For instance, 'If a flower is *reversed* its original signification is understood to be contradicted, and the opposite meaning to be implied'. Or, 'Place a marigold on the head, and it signifies "Mental anguish"; on the bosom, "Indifference".'

One now begins to grasp the full implications of embarking on this difficult subject. It would be advisable, therefore, to get a degree in the Language of Flowers before venturing abroad, posy in hand. How many wordless proposals may have been accepted or rejected because the participants hadn't done their homework properly, it is now too late to discover. When one learns that bladder senna was not a prescription to be taken before breakfast, but was indicative of 'Frivolous Amusements', and that meadow saffron meant 'My Best Days Are Past', or a sprig of laurestinus meant 'I Die If I'm Neglected', one can see that this was no undertaking for the amateur.

It must have been therefore not a moment too soon, that is, about 1847, that Thomas Miller came to the rescue with a little book which he dedicated to 'The Rosebud of England, The Princess Royal': *The Poetical Language of Flowers; or, The Pilgrimage of Love*, in which, with the accompaniment of some charming hand-coloured plates, he guided his pilgrims along paths which, even at the best of times, are fraught with peril. 'All the books which have hitherto treated on the Language of Flowers are', wrote Mr Miller in his preface, 'with the exception of a few slight alterations and additions, mere translations from the French work of Aimé Martin; nor am I aware of any production in the English language on this subject which professes to be original, saving the present . . . This task I have attempted, taking for my guides no less authorities than Chaucer, Spenser, Shakespeare and Milton'. With such mentors at his elbow, Mr Miller was on firm ground, and one wonders whether there was already a Mrs Miller, won unassisted at an earlier period of his life; or whether his book was compiled with some suitable damsel in view. If the latter was the case, what a triumph was hers! Thomas Miller must have been a rare catch for a romantic young lady. One of his most ingenious suggestions to the young and fair was divination by the lines on pansies.

If the petal they plucked was pencilled with four lines it signified hope; if from the centre line started a branch, when the streaks numbered five, it was still hope, springing out of fear; and when the lines were thickly branched, and leaned towards the left, they foretold a life of trouble; but if they bent towards the right, they were then supposed to denote prosperity unto the end: seven streaks they interpreted into constancy in love, and if the centre one was longest, they prophesied that Sunday would be their wedding-day; eight denoted fickleness; nine, a changing heart; and eleven – the most ominous number of all – disappointment in love, and an early grave.

Thomas Miller must have been an interesting character as well as a prolific writer. Born in 1807, he worked as a basket-maker in Sailor's Alley, Gainsborough. Being an ambitious lad, he decided to go to London, where he worked at his trade while writing poetry. He sent some verses in a basket to the Countess of Blessington, a writer herself, and editress of the famous *Books of Beauty*. After this, his success was assured. In 1841, with the help of a fellow poet, Samuel Rogers, he commenced business as a bookseller, and during this time he wrote upwards of forty-five books; novels and histories, as well as works on country life and flowers. One evening at Lady Blessington's he met Disraeli, who was instrumental in getting the Basket-Maker, as he was still called, a grant of £100 from the Royal Bounty Fund, but in this same year, 1874, Thomas Miller died. How many love affairs might have been still-born, but for the little books of Thomas Miller, we shall never know.

About the time of Miller's death, Captain Marryat, author of *Peter Simple*, *Midshipman Easy*, and other classic sea stories, must have been working on his own completely original method of communication by flowers. This he called *The Floral Telegraph*, and it was a most sophisticated version of a hitherto artless means of correspondence. The vocabulary contains emblems that would take the reader to the Strand Theatre, Vauxhall, St James's Park, the British Museum, the National Gallery, and for those with fewer cultural pretensions, the Fancy Fair or the Bazaar. For country dwellers there is a further list which includes the Soirée, the Fête Champêtre, the Conversazione and the Oratorio. The flowers are tied together on a knotted cord or ribbon, and when this is unrolled, the initiated may read quite complicated messages, in which the knots, as well as the flowers, have significance.

TO MY FAIR FRIENDS

In Part II of the Vocabulary, you will find several numbers without any corresponding words attached to them. The blanks you may fill up at your option with a crowquill, either with words or sentences that may be most useful to you and your friends. In Part III of the Vocabulary, which consists wholly of sentences, or names of places in general request, you will find most of the phrases used affirmatively. If you wish to use them interrogatively, a blade of grass bound up with any of the numbers will cause them so to be understood; if negatively, any small leafless and flowerless twig – for example, 256, 'There is occasion for concealment'. If the Flowers forming that number be bound up with a blade of grass, it will be understood, 'Is there occasion for concealment?' if with a leafless twig, 'There is no occasion for concealment'.

Vocabulary III seems to have a message to cover any eventuality: 'My little brother may be trusted', 'Mama always goes to sleep before dinner', 'En avant, or we are ruined', 'Where was your discretion last night?' are a few examples gathered from many equally indispensable.

Frederick Marryat was a man of many facets. Born in 1792, he sailed as a midshipman under Lord Cochrane in 1806. He commanded a sloop cruising off St Helena, to guard against Napoleon's escape from the island in 1820–1, and was there when Napoleon died. He chased smugglers in the Channel, and saw some hand-fighting in the Burmese rivers; and then, in 1830, this extraordinary man retired to start an entirely new career, that of a man of letters. He wrote at least eleven novels, some of them still best-sellers, and edited *The Metropolitan Magazine* from 1832 to 1835. He died in 1848, and his *Floral Telegraph* was published posthumously.

Many of the compilers of these books of floral emblems and flower language were botanists, as well as literary men, and first-class flower painters, such as James Andrews, were employed as illustrators. All over Europe, it would seem, men and women were sending to each other messages that they dared not put into words. The language barrier was crossed, and lovers could communicate in a sort of floral Esperanto. In the New World, too, the self-same declarations of love were shyly proffered. Nearly all of these amorous text-books contained flower verses as well as meanings.

In *Flora's Interpreter* (1852), Mrs Sarah Josepha Hale has a few sharp words to say in her Introduction. After acknowledging her debt to her own countrymen for 'the choicest and best specimens of American poetry', she goes on, 'We feel quite at liberty to select what-

ever is best and brightest from the productions of British genius for this work [she quotes Shakespeare, Drayton, Dryden, Southey, Scott, Keats, *et al.*, but only mentions the American poets in her Index], because *Flora's Interpreter* has been republished in London, and, under the title of *The Book of Flowers*, sold largely without any remuneration to the author.

It is quite probable this new and enlarged work may have the same honour.' Those were naughty days in the publishing world, on both sides of the Atlantic. There are many of Sarah Josepha's own verses in the book, and most, though not all, are included as 'anonymous'. A footnote gives us an endearing portrait of her struggle with her own modesty. 'It may be best to state that all the poetic selections here designated "anonymous", were written by Mrs. Hale, expressly for *Flora's Interpreter*. Those who use these will know from whom they borrow'. Sarah Josepha has gone where fame must be her only remuneration, but rather than make an international incident of the injustice that was done, let us, good floraphiles that we are, let bygones be bygones with a spray of rosemary, for remembrance.

These Language of Flowers books were not only intended for the use of sentimental young women. Men, too, not only presented these dictionaries of love to their wives or to their 'intendeds', but were not ashamed to own their own reference copies. Indeed, how else could such communication take place? One such book, dated July 1874, was once the property of John Henry Smith, who, far from hiding under a pseudonym, as might be supposed, was not ashamed to write his address on the flyleaf – 16, St Saviorgate, York. That John Henry made frequent use of his floral lexicon is obvious, not only from the signs of wear, but from the *Bouquets as Examples* ticked off to avoid repetition. For instance, he had started with a modest bouquet of moss, bearded crepis, primrose, daisy and wood sorrel, which meant, 'May maternal love protect your early youth in innocence and joy'. This he followed up, a little later in the season, with 'Your

humility and amiability have won my love', exemplified in a nosegay of broom, white jasmine, parsley and myrtle.

It is reassuring to think that, even if John Henry's addresses were rejected, at least the parsley need not be wasted. Indeed, there were signs of clouds on the horizon, for in the *Vocabulary* the next flower to be underlined is 'Acacia, Elegance', followed by '*Achillea Millefolia*, War'. Is this a sign of a quarrel, perhaps, because his loved one is showing signs of extravagance – or has he gone for a soldier, seeking anonymity as Private Smith?

There is one disquieting portent. In the section headed 'Modifications of the Flower Language', the sentence 'If a flower be given *reversed*, its original signification is understood *to be contradicted*, and the opposite meaning to be implied' is heavily underlined, which leaves one wondering. What is quite clear, however, is that it is essential that the nosegay be proffered in person. It is useless to hire a younger brother as a messenger, or all kinds of misunderstandings may ensue. However, in the case of John Henry Smith, we may presume a happy ending to the story, for the last marked flower, *Camellia japonica*, white, brings a message of 'Perfected Loveliness'.

But suppose it was for a mistress that the fond message was to be composed? Surely it would be wrong for a wife or fiancée to be subject to the same intimate language of Love? Was there then a special edition for the unacknowledged she? An under-the-table Language of Love?

In Warne's *Language and Sentiment of Flowers* (c. 1874), claims are made that they have added about thirty new significant blossoms to the old ones, 'and our fair readers will thus find "a tongue" for the flowers which bloom in the conservatory and greenhouse, as well as for our old garden favourites, and will not be condemned during the long winter months to floral silence', which must have been a great relief to them.

Both John Ingram and Robert Tyas produced a number of scholarly, if sentimental, books on floral emblems and the Language of Flowers, each of which

THE LANGUAGE OF THE FLOWERS

SUITE DE BALLET

BY

Nº 1	DAISY	(Innocence)		Nº 4	COLUMBINE	(Folly)
	2 LILAC	(First Emotions of love)		5	YELLOW JASMINE	(Elegance & Grace)
	3 FERN	(Fascination)		6	LILY OF THE VALLEY	(Return of Happiness)

Play it with Flowers, or Love in the safety of the Victorian Drawing-room. Daisy – Innocence; Lilac – First emotions of love; Fern – Sincerity; Columbine – Folly; Yellow Jasmine – Grace and elegance; Lily of the Valley – Return of happiness.

included an anthology of flower verses. These books are larger and more comprehensive than the average pretty little parlour gift books, and contain chapters with headings such as Typical Bouquets, Emblematic Garlands, The Dial of Flowers, Holy Flowers, and so on. One includes a game called The Flower Oracle, which claims that 'This oracle cannot fail to excite much harmless mirth; but some kinds of floral divinations, as these pages testify, have oft produced deeper thoughts and more serious consequences'.

There followed *The Bible Language of Flowers*, with plentiful and charming

coloured illustrations, and each flower with its meaning more or less unchanged, accompanied by a suitable text.

In his introduction to one of these little books, the compiler writes: 'The most charming of all gifts is one of flowers. A Queen may (and we rejoice to say our own beloved Sovereign Victoria often does) give them to her subjects; and the poorest subject may offer them to a monarch.' The inference being that the second most charming gift would be a copy of his *Language of Flowers*.

One of the prettiest and most sought-after of these books is illustrated by Kate

Greenaway. It is a slightly abridged version and some of the more exotic plants such as Syphocampylos, 'Resolved to be Noticed', and Stephanotis, 'Will You Accompany Me to the Far East?', are excluded, possibly as being unsuited to the charming simplicity of the illustrations. The meaning of nightshade is given as 'Truth', whereas most other books give 'Falsehood', 'Sorcery', 'Scepticism', 'Witchcraft' or 'Dark Thoughts'. The verses do not follow the exact pattern of the others of the period, although they are all familiar. One of the best is Carew's 'Red and White Roses':

Read in these the sad story
Of my hard fate, and your own glory;
In the white you may discover
The paleness of the fainting lover:
In the red the flames still feeding
On my heart with fresh wounds bleeding.
The white will tell you how I languish,
And the red express my anguish.
The white my innocence displaying,
The red my martyrdom betraying;
The frowns that on your brow resided,
Have these roses thus divided.
   Oh! let your smiles but clear the
      weather,
   And then they both shall grow together.

Birthday books of the period often made use of floral emblems. In a Floral Birthday Book of 1880, the turnip is made the emblem of Charity; faintly Dickensian, but entirely suitable. Cards of all kinds, some with hand-coloured and detachable flowers and a message hidden behind each one, others containing perfumed sachets, and all of them bearing words of love, were sent for St Valentine's Day.

If perfume may be considered the Language of Flowers, it can be no surprise that Eugene Rimmel, the celebrated perfumer, also specialized in valentines. From his sweetly-scented emporium in London in the 1860s and 70s, hearts and darts, and loves and doves, encircled with gilt and paper lace and secured with satin bows, were dispatched to all parts of Britain's far-flung and complaisantly acknowledged Empire. It would be pleasant to think that in

this perfumed and highly commercial bower, only the Language of Flowers was spoken.

That same language was certainly known to my grandfather, who for many years, and long after his Valentine had become his wife, had never failed to paint a card for her birthday, at Christmas, and for St Valentine's Day. These cards usually took the form of a spray of flowers, or a single flower, cut to hold a tiny card which carried his message in microscopic writing, the ink now faded, but the flowers as fresh as on the day they were folded inside the envelope bearing her name.

That this floral communication carried on into the Edwardian era is proved by a series of picture postcards, two bearing legible postmarks of 1905 and 1907. Lilac, 'The First Emotions of Love', shows a couple balanced insecurely on a five-barred gate; the gentleman, though obviously with the most honourable intentions, has ventured an inexperienced arm around the shoulders of his lady-love. More than this is clearly out of the question, if only for the reason of their precarious position. Marigold, 'Grief', shows a couple in a Gothic library, the lady having given way to an abandonment of tears, although not, regrettably, having first placed a marigold on her head, as advised in her floral guidebook. Chinese primrose, 'Welcome', shows a lady giving a hearty English greeting to her admirer at what can only be the back gate.

The reasoning behind this floral meaning is abstruse. Monkshood, which purports to stand for 'Knight Errantry', shows a gentleman in a cloth cap stooping to lace a lady's boots. Knowing the nature of this plant, I wouldn't have trusted him an inch. Most pleasing of all is sainfoin, 'Agitation', depicting a moustachioed gentleman bearing a strong resemblance to Mr Smith, of the Brides in the Bath case, standing in a wood, knee-deep in bracken, and anxiously consulting his watch, while his charmer peeps from behind a tree. No good can come of this one either.

There was a Language of Flowers card in the form of a fan, which opened to show convolvulus, 'Humility'; forget-

me-not, 'True Love'; pansy, 'Thoughts'; bluebell, 'Constancy'; cowslip, 'Winning Grace'; china aster, 'Mutual Love'; and on the reverse side, pink, 'Pure Affection'; lily, 'Purity'; lilac, 'First Love'; geranium, 'Preference'; honeysuckle, 'Constancy'; jonquil, 'Mutual Affection', and daisy, 'Cheerfulness'.

Language of Flower compositions were tinkled on the pianoforte, and Carl Bohm obliged with *Six Morceaux Mélodiques; La Rose; La Violette; Fleurs de Mai; Le Lis; Le Myrte* and *Le Réséda*; with a charmingly evocative cover. A popular song entitled 'Blue Bell' commemorated the heroes of the Boer War, and two picture postcards were issued, the first depicting a soldier saying farewell to his girl,

Sweetheart, your tears are falling;
  Blue Bell, we two must part,

and the second even more heart-rending, showing the same lad, now wounded and delirious, with an inset of his visionary loved one,

There on the hillside lying,
  There mid the guns loud roar,
Blue Bell, your true love's dying;
  Calling for you once more.

Remembering that Blue Bell is the emblem of Constancy, one can only hope that the poor fellow recovered after all. Flower language was likewise seized upon by the authors of improving tales for Victorian misses, and its meaning directed from matters of the heart to things of higher purpose, as in an unsigned story, believed to be the work of Charlotte Yonge, entitled 'Look Up'. The story opens with a group of girls choosing, as a game, the flower each one would like to resemble. The handsome Laura Bennet predictably chooses the rose, her sister Helen, the rhododendron, because, she says, if roughly shaken it scatters honey drops and immediately begins to fill its cups again. One girl chooses the bindweed, a flower that augers ill for her future husband, and another, the laurel – 'That's because you write verses and think yourself clever', remarks Laura uncharitably. The last girl chooses a daisy because it is always looking upward.

The rate of mortality in this small period piece is satisfactorily high, and the atmosphere of gloom maintained. '"Our flower wreath is beginning to fail", said Florence, "and who knows which will be the next taken?" Mrs. Delmont thought it would in all probability be the meek, drooping daisy, [the author had by this time forgotten its reputation for looking upwards] and something whispered to the awakened heart of the anxious mother, as she gazed upon the pale, worn cheek of her child, that the laurel herself was not immortal.' The doctor pops in and out of the pages delivering words of doom with satisfaction. 'There is nothing to be done,' said he, 'human aid is of no avail!'

The story ends symbolically. 'We have seen the rose wither; the rhododendron striving to stand alone; the convolvulus clinging to the cross; the laurel yearning after the palm; and the meek-eyed daisy, with its upward glance of love and faith. Reader, choose you also among the flowers.'

What a relief it is to turn from these wan countenances to the *Nonsense Botany* of Edward Lear, with its *Manypeeplia upsidownia*, gracefully hanging like a bleeding heart; its *Piggiwiggia pyramidalis*, a muster of little pigs decreasing in size, and the horrific *Nasticreechia krorluppia*.

In 1889 Walter Crane charmed a receptive world with his *Flora's Feast, A Masque of Flowers*, followed in 1909 by *Flowers From Shakespeare's Garden*; two of the most delightful flower books ever designed. There is something of the same fantasy in Crane's women-flowers as in those of Albert Grandville, whose work appeared on the Continent some fifty years earlier. Grandville, a pseudonym of Jean Ignace Gérard, was a French political caricaturist, whose illustrations for *Les Fleurs Animées*, the strange, sad, at times amusing stories of Taxile Delord, have become classics. Neither Grandville nor Crane was a botanist, but each saw the character within a flower.

Life at this time seemed burgeoning with flowers, paper flowers; and to paraphrase a popular song that came later, 'Every little blossom had a meaning of its own'. These meaningful blossoms are a vivid memory of my childhood. In the top right-hand drawer of the chest-of-drawers in my mother's bedroom was a small tissue-wrapped parcel which she allowed me to open on special occasions. It contained a number of odd-shaped pieces of silk and satin and velvet, on each of which was painted or embroidered a spray of flowers. There was a single rose, worked in bright pink floss; a spray of forget-me-nots painted on white watered silk, and two painted violets lurking modestly, as violets are expected to lurk, behind a crumpled dead leaf. The dead leaf worried me. Why couldn't she, the artist, have given two perfectly fresh violets a perfectly fresh leaf? I did not know much about Art in those days, but I knew what I liked.

Each of these little scraps of materials was signed – Minnie, Maudie, Amy, Trissie and Edith, and others that I cannot now recall. My mother told me that they were for a 'friendship cloth', and that when she had enough pieces she would sew them together. I loved those little pieces very much, and waited until the wonderful day when the friendship cloth would appear in all its glory. Now my mother's friends are all of them gone, and so is she, and even the flowers for the friendship cloth are gone, lost in one of her vigorous and often disastrous forays at spring-cleaning time, no doubt. I wish it had been completed, for it too in its way, was part of the Language of Flowers.

Perhaps, after all, the Language of Flowers will never die. When the postal strike of 1971 blocked the path of true love on St Valentine's day, an article in one of the evening papers suggested the sending of flowers instead of valentines. It even gave an abbreviated dictionary of meanings, although neglecting to warn readers of the implications of a marigold upon the head. What came out of this stimulating article was this – that a single red rose in a ribbon-tied box was the best buy. The message was clear, and success practically guaranteed.

Top: *Dielytra spectablis*, a botanical specimen from *The Floricultural Cabinet*, 1853. *Not* by Edward Lear.

Lower: *Manypeeplia upsidownia*. From the *Nonsense Botany* of Edward Lear, *c.* 1872.

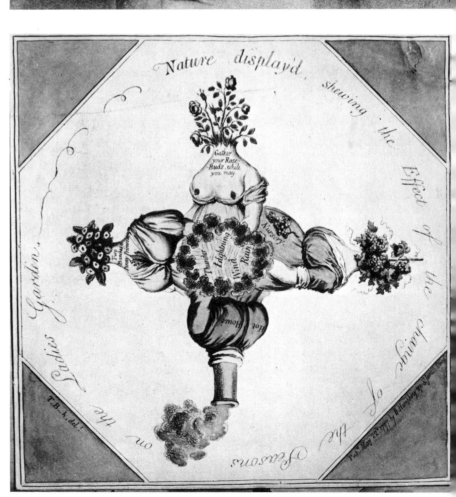

Clinton's Edition of

CHARLES CZERNY'S
MUSICAL GREENHOUSE,

Containing

Choice *MELODIOUS* Flowers Culled to adorn the

Piano Forte.

And presented to The Beau Monde by the Arranger,

J. CLINTON.

COPYRIGHT

Top far left and top centre: The Language of Flowers was still employed in the Edwardian era. It was the age of the picture postcard, and messages could thus be sent on both sides of the card. Though its message is commonplace, the Chinese primrose was unusual (right) in the Language of Flowers. Lilac, however, was very common (left).

Bottom left: Nature display'd, shewing the Effect of the change of the Seasons on the Ladies Garden. A rare floral emblem *not* to be found in The Language of Flowers. Published at Mrs Hannah Humphrey's famous printshop in St James's St, London, over which Gillray had his lodgings. 1797.

Left: A young Victorian pianist in exotic surroundings renders Choice Melodious Flowers Culled to Adorn the Pianoforte, arranged from the works of Charles Czerny. Love blossoms in The Musical Greenhouse.

For dwellers in green places every season has its own perfume; a bouquet as subtle as the bouquet of wine.

Spring has the sappy smell of working bulbs, piercing sword leaves, and swelling buds. Smell a daffodil and you know the entire fragrance of spring. During high summer the golden liquid of a thousand scent bottles changes unnoticed into a pot-pourri of fallen petals. The smell of autumn, perhaps the most nostalgic of all scents, of rotting leaves, wood-smoke and mushrooms, hangs motionless between the trees – until one day we realize that it has gone, who knows where, and the chill of splintered mirrors in frozen ditches gives out the faintest perfume of the year.

Translate these scents of the seasons into colour, and you have for spring the sap green of students' paint-boxes, always the first to be used up, such are the heavy demands made on it. Summer's scent is a deep rose-pink, and autumn's orange-red, fading to brown and then to grey, as the season dies. Winter's cold, faint perfume is ice-blue.

Barren as our language is when we are describing colours, at least we have a range of well-understood names to draw from. We have red, blue, green, orange, and so on, any of which may be harnessed to another to give a more precise impression – seal-red, sea-blue, nut-brown, burnt-orange, etc., and with these we may manage fairly well. But for scents we have only a few poor adjectives – spicy, heavy, faint, sweet or 'heady', and with these we are left to flounder. The inevitable result is that a flower or a leaf or a root is described as rose-, or vanilla-, or almond-scented, which does little but send us back to the rose, the vanilla, and the almond, and how are we to describe these? A whiff of honey does nothing for the man in whose country there are no bees. Eleanour Sinclair Rohde describes the scent of apple-blossom as 'soft', and that of Solomon's Seal as 'thick', and that will have to serve. The tools at our disposal are poor, but we must do what we can with them.

In the ancient world plant perfumes were enjoyed and made use of in religious ceremonies, as a disinfectant in the sickroom, and for embalming. Hebrew women wore perfume balls suspended by a chain from the neck or the waist, like the later pomanders. Distilling was unknown, and perfumes were first made by boiling vegetable substances in fat to make a fragrant ointment. It is said that the mortar used in the building of some ancient temples was partly mixed with musk, and for many years the walls continued to give out a powerful scent. The Greeks cov-

XVI
Remembered Perfumes

ered their sacrificial victims with garlands of scented flowers, herbs and sweet-smelling ointments. They also loved the scent of beanfields after rain and worshipped a god of the beans, and a Bean Feast was held every year. Bay leaves were chewed by the Romans to keep off deadly plagues.

The art of distilling is said to have originated in Arabia, when the favourite wife of Jehan-Geer was walking in her garden through which ran a canal kept constantly flowing with rose-water. She noticed some oily particles floating on the water, and when these were collected they were found to be so sweetly perfumed that means were devised to collect this first attar of roses.

By the twelfth century perfume-makers in France had their own charter, but in England women depended on garden and still-room for perfumes, ointments and pomanders, and their recipes for elderflower water, lily water, and violet and rose syrups are to be found in ancient still-room books. Little bags of dried leaves and petals were made to hang on chairs, or to take to bed, and pillows filled with hops were used to encourage sleep.

In the Middle Ages, the strewing of public places with aromatic flowers and leaves to ward off fevers was widespread. Tansy, *Tanacetum vulgare*, with its

Almanack of the Language of Flowers, by Eugene Rimmel, 1863. Burrel Collection. A splendidly evocative almanac, full of sentiment and Victorian clutter, in a world-wide language of flowers and love. *Book of Perfumes*, 1865.

strong camphor-smell, was often used to disinfect public places in the days of the plague, and so was the spicy marjoram, *Origanum vulgare*. In the nineteenth century church pews were still strewn with lavender, rosemary, woodruff and balm, and a sprig of southernwood was worn on the Sunday smocks of the farm folk. Other worshippers might carry a Sunday posy, with stems decently wrapped in a clean pocket handkerchief, which would usually include a sprig of fennel.

> *And here on Sabbath mornings*
> *The goodman comes to get*
> *His Sunday nosegay – Moss rose buds,*
> *White pink, and Mignonette.*

In America, too, Sabbath-day posies of fennel, dill, caraway and southernwood were carried, and their seeds, known as Meetin' Seeds, were given to the young and fidgetty to chew. 'A sprig of Fennel', said Peter Parley, that prolific author of improving books for children, 'was the theological smelling-bottle of the tender sex and not unfrequently of the men, who from long sitting in the sanctuary, after a work of labour in the field, found themselves tempted to sleep, would sometimes borrow a sprig of Fennel, to exorcise the fiend that threatened their spiritual welfare'.

Scented teas were made for medicinal purposes or purely as a pleasant beverage, from an infusion or *tisane* of the leaves of sage, or balm, basil, mint, catmint, marjoram, camomile, wormwood or bergamot. The latter is known in the United States as Oswego tea. Agrimony, *Agrimonia odorata*, was also used by our grandmothers to add to their expensive tea to make it go further. Wormwood, *Artemisia absinthium*, had other uses, as we find in Thomas Tusser's *Five Hundred Points of Good Husbandrie*.

> While Wormwood hath seed get a
>   handful or twaine
> To save against March, to make flea to
>   refrain,

while clothes-moths refrained at the first sniff of southernwood, which was known as Garde-robe in France. Michael Drayton's 'breathful camomile' was believed to keep surrounding plants healthy. Camomile was known in England as Stinking Mayweed, but the Greeks considered that it smelled of apples, and so called it Ground Apple. Betony, *Stachys officinalis*, and melilot, *Melilotus officinalis*, were sometimes used in the making of herbal snuff and smoking mixtures.

The mossy scent of fennel, unpleasant to some people, was evidently enjoyed by the Serpent in the Garden of Eden, for, as he said to Adam, the scent of the apple tree 'more pleased my sense than smell of sweetest fennel'. Linen was not only kept sweet with lavender, but with woodruff, rosemary, costmary, marjoram, rue, iris roots and the roots of avens, *Geum urbanum*, whose botanical name of *Geum* comes from a Greek word meaning 'giving perfume'.

Perfumes come and go with the rising or setting of the sun, or with the changing seasons. They may be carried on breezes or they may linger after rain. With box, *Buxus sempervirens*, however, there is a 'fragrance of eternity; for this is one of the odours which carry us out of time into the abysses of the unbeginning past'. In the autumn the aromatic earth-smell of chrysanthemum leaves brings comfort to our short days. Chrysanthemums, after they are dead, if thrown on to an open fire, will fill the room with an agreeable incense.

Few, but for that reason most precious, are our winter perfumes. One of the earliest of the year is wintersweet, *Chimonanthus fragrans*, blooming before the leaves appear. Accompanied by winter heliotrope, *Petasites fragrans*, both have quietly unassuming flowers and a sweet scent, like a plain woman with a charming smile. Spicy witch hazel, *Hamamelis*, and the 'fragrant, pleasant sweet smell' of *Daphne odora*, the freshness of lemon verbena, *Lippia citriodora*, and the faint velvet-sweetness of winter pansies lead us gently on to spring.

Some flowers, like woodruff, are scentless when growing, but for several years after being dried a strong fragrance lingers. The perfume of sweet vernal grass, *Anthoxanthum odoratum*, and of melilot increases when they are dried. Henry King, Bishop of Chichester, drew a lesson from the fragrance of flowers:

You fragrant flowers! then teach me, that my breath
Like yours may sweeten and perfume my death.

Perfumes may come from massed flowers in the distance, when a single bloom seems almost scentless. Scents may fade entirely that once were strong, like that of the musk, once a popular scented plant in Victorian conservatories and cottage windows, which today has entirely lost its fragrance. It was discovered in British Columbia in 1824 when it was even then in some places without scent, but in areas around river banks was deliciously scented. By 1880 the scent was diminishing in whichever part of the world it was cultivated, and it has now gone completely. We can only hope that since, as Francis Bacon says, the scent of flowers 'comes and goes like the warbling of music', as far as musk is concerned we are perhaps only experiencing an extended interval.

At all events, it is the faintest flower scents that we love best, and heady exotic perfumes at times becomes unbearable. *Lilium candidum*, narcissus of the Poeticus group, hyacinths and philadelphus, with its heavy fruit-like scent,

can be enjoyed for short periods only. Gerard, in his *Herbal*, describes the White Pipe tree, by which he means the philadelphus, as 'of a pleasant sweet smell; but in my judgment they are too sweet, troubling and molesting the head in a very strange manner. I once gathered the floures and layed them in my chamber window, which smelled more strongly after they had lien together a few houres, with such an unacquainted savor that they awaked me out of sleepe, so that I could not rest till I had cast them out of my chamber'. We smile across the years at the rumpled figure of Gerard, night-cap awry, with his arms full of mock orange, irritably throwing them out of his chamber door and shuffling back to his bed.

There may be fragrance in root, leaf, flower or seed, but in herbs the storage of essential oils lies most frequently in the leaves. Some plants, like bay and rosemary, as Francis Bacon says, 'hold fast of their perfumes', and one needs to crush their leaves in passing. Plants with strongly aromatic leaves often have small and insignificant flowers. Some have great variations in their smells, and seem to have stolen the scents of other plants. Thus mint can smell like apples, ginger, peppermint, lemons and eau-de-cologne; some geraniums or pelargoniums have borrowed the scents of nutmeg, oranges, lemons, almonds, roses, filberts and pinewood, and there are night-scented varieties also. 'Sweete Cranesbill – it is often called Geranium *noctu olens*, because of its excellent sweet smell in the night only, and Geranium Triste, because it rejoyceth not in the day . . . a pott of it in flower will perfume a room sufficiently in the night time', wrote Thomas Hanmer in his *Garden Book*. There are varieties of basil, also, that smell of lemon, cloves, tarragon and fennel.

Oliver Wendell Holmes, the Autocrat of the Breakfast Table, remembers a cupboard in the house where he was born in 1809. 'On its shelves used to be bundles of sweet-marjoram and pennyroyal and lavender and mint and catnip . . . The odorous echoes of a score of dead summers linger yet in those dim recesses.'
And now the fragrance of herbs, so loved

by our grandmothers, is returning to our pine-panelled kitchens once again, and it is pleasant to re-read Dion Clayton Calthrop's memorial to his lavender bush:

Here lies
Imprisoned in this grey bush
the scent of
LAVENDER
It is renowned for a simple purity
A sweet fragrance and a subtle
strength it is the odour of
the domestic virtues and the
symbolic perfume of a quiet life
Rain
Shall weep over this bush
Sun
Shall give it warm kisses
Wind
Shall stir the tall spikes
Until such a time as is required
When it shall flower and so
Yield to us its secret.

There is a subtle difference between the scents of wild and garden flowers. The faint smell of Yellow Bedstraw; a field of clover in the hot sun; hawthorn-scented bluebells in a damp wood; the fragrance of primroses, gentle and restrained, and the stronger sweetness of cowslips, hiding the secret of their aniseed-smelling roots beneath the soil – all carry the freshness of the countryside.

George Meredith describes the scent of heather as 'nutty, gold-like and warm', but just as surely as heather rhymes with leather, so heather smells like leather, and the tough and resilient heather stems have an unmistakable leatheriness in their composition.

Many wild flowers have the bitter-sweet smell of almonds; bindweed, hawthorn and meadowsweet among them. 'A little plant of which I am very fond is the restharrow', wrote George Gissing.

When the sun is hot upon it, the flower gives forth a strangely aromatic scent, very delightful to me. I know the cause of this peculiar pleasure. The restharrow sometimes grows in sandy ground above the seashore. In my childhood I have many a time lain in such a spot under

the glowing sky, and, though I scarce thought of it, perceived the odour of the little rose-pink flower when it touched my face. Now I have but to smell it, and those hours come back again.

Garden flowers frequently have a richness of perfume that seems to have been gained by care and cultivation – a richness, and yet a sort of simplicity, like that of pinks, and lilacs, and 'Sweet William, with his homely cottage smell'. Wallflowers, too, have a strong and simple fragrance that is 'very delightful to be set under a parlour or lower chamber window', as Francis Bacon wrote. Some scents are powdery, like that of buddleia, telling of hot days and a quiver of butterflies; and mignonette, once a popular plant for balconies. 'We have frequently found the perfume of the Mignonette so powerful in some of the better streets that we have considered it sufficient to protect the inhabitants from those effluvia which bring disorders with them in the air', wrote Henry Phillips.

According to Reginald Farrer, the perfume of clove-scented pinks, or gilliflowers as they once were called, is 'decadent', but this was the opinion of William Lawson in *The Country Housewife's Garden* (1618):

July flowers, commonly called Gillyflowers or Clove July-flowers (I call them so, because they flower in July) they have the name of Cloves of their sent. I may well call them the King of Flowers (except the Rose) and the best sort of them are called Queene-July-flowers. I have of them nine or ten severall colours, and divers of them as bigge as Roses. Of all the flowers (save the Damaske Rose) they are the most pleasant to sight and smell. Their use is much in ornament and comforting the spirites by the sence of smelling.

Some garden perfumes are of such a pure sweetness and strength that they seem to rise in the air like a boy's clear treble – lilies of the valley, jasmine and honeysuckle, although honeysuckle be-

longs equally with the wild scents.

Oh how sweete and pleasant is Woodbinde, in Woodes or Arbours, after a tender soft rayne: and how friendly doth this herbe if I may so name it, imbrace the bodies, armes, and braunches of trees, wyth his long winding stalkes and tender leaves, opening or spreading forth his sweete Lillies, like ladies fingers, among the thornes or bushes.

Thus Bullein's *Bulwarke of Defence* (1562).

The perfume of violets, too, was once common in our countryside, but now the scentless dog violet seems to have taken over. Mary Russell Mitford wrote of 'violetting' on those pleasant expeditions of long ago.

I must go violetting – it is a necessity – I shall go quite alone with my little basket, twisted like a beehive, that I love so well . . . I smell them already – their exquisite perfume steams and lingers in this moist, heavy air. Through this little gate, and along the green south bank of this green wheat-field, and they burst upon me, the lovely violets, in tenfold loveliness. The ground is covered with them white and purple, enamelling the short dewy grass, looking but the more vividly coloured under the dull, leaden sky.

Most common and most loved is the scent of roses, their perfume the distillation of high summer. In Persia, wine was brought to the table with a rose in the bottle instead of a cork – one bouquet complementing another. It is said that when Saladin entered Jerusalem in 1187, he had the floors and walls of Omar's Mosque entirely washed with rosewater. An eminent rosarian once described seventeen different kinds of rose scent, including Sweet Briar scent, Musk Rose scent, Sweet Tea scent, and, somewhat unfortunately, Old Cabbage scent. He claimed that the petals of highly scented varieties have on their inner surfaces minute perfume glands containing highly volatile essence, those of Sweet Briar and Moss Rose almost visible to the naked eye.

Many experiments have been attempted to change, or to improve upon the scent of flowers. As early as 1577 Thomas Hyll wrote in *The Gardener's Labyrinth*:

> If you will have your Gilliflowers of divers smels or odours, you may also with great ease, as thus for example: if you will take two or three great Cloves, steepe them for foure and twenty houres in Damaske Rosewater. Then take them out and bruise them and put them into a fine Cambrick ragge and so bind them about the heart roote of the gilliflower near to the setting of the Stalk, and so plant it in a fine, soft, and fertile mould, and the flower which springeth from the same will have so delicate a mixt smell of the clove and the Rose water that it will breed both delight and wonder.

Gervase Markham repeated the same experiment in *The English Husbandman* (1613), and one wonders whether he actually tried it out for himself, or was content to quote from *The Gardener's Labyrinth* without question. Stephen Blake, in *The Complete Gardener's Practice* (1664), was evidently familiar with this theory also.

> Now for altering the sent of these flowers [Carnation Gilliflowers], there be divers things they say will cause this effect, which I think altogether needlesse, because it hath a passing smell of its self; therefore if you have any desire to make use of what Authors have said for altering of the sent of flowers, make trial upon such as have little or no sent as Flowerdeluces, Scarlet Beans or Tulips, because they are flowers that Ladies love to have so nigh their noses, which have little or no sent.

Francis Bacon sought to gild refined gold, to paint the lily, and literally to throw a perfume on the violet, when he wrote in his *Natural History*: 'Take a common briar and set it among violets

An elegant perfume box from Eugene Rimmel's famous perfumery in London. Mid-late 19th century. It has a scene of people gathering flowers, and a distillery may be seen in the background. The box contains three bottles of different fragrances.

or wall-flowers, and see whether it will not make the violets or wall-flowers sweeter and less earthy in smell'.

Ruskin, describing the grape hyacinths growing in the south of France, said that 'it was as if a cluster of grapes and a hive of honey had been distilled and pressed together into one small boss of celled and beaded blue', but two hundred years earlier Parkinson had noticed that the scent was 'very like unto starch when it is new made and hott'.

Not all garden flowers smell sweet. The glossy petals of the poppy and of the common peony have a sort of rankness, and the smell of the marigold is challenging rather than entirely pleasant. It brought back memories to Oliver Wendell Holmes.

> When I was of smallest dimensions, and wont to ride impacted between the knees of fond parental pair, we would sometimes cross the bridge to the next village-town and stop opposite a low, brown, 'gambrel-roofed' cottage. Out of it would come one Sally, sister of its swarthy tenant, swarthy herself, shady-lipped, sad-voiced, and, bending over her flower-bed, would gather a 'posy', as she called it, for the little boy. Sally lies in the church-yard with a slab of blue slate at her head, lichen-crusted, and leaning a little within the last few years. Cottage, garden-beds, posies, grenadier-like rows of seedling onions – stateliest of vegetables – all are gone, but the breath of a marigold brings them all back to me.

Many flower scents have been firmly labelled 'stinking'. There is the Stinking Iris, *Iris foetidissima* (the 'issima' would seem to be the final insult), which is allowed a place in our gardens only because of its decorative scarlet-berried seed-heads; nor would the Stinking Hellebore, *Helleborus foetidus*, be admitted were it not for its handsome glossy leaves and green flowers edged with purple. But handsome is as handsome does, and we keep Stinking Cranesbill and Stinking Mayweed firmly outside the garden gate. Many strongly aromatic wild plants have similar unflattering folk-

names. Feverfew is known as Stink Daisies in Somerset; Stinking Willie is given
to ragwort in the USA and tansy in the
north of England. Figwort is Stinking
Roger, and water betony, Stinking
Christopher. Horehound was Stynking
Horehound to the herbalist Turner in
1548. Herb robert was known as Stinker
Bobs, short for Stinking Robert. In
Cumberland, Stinking Weed is the red
deadnettle. The beautiful but garlic-
scented ramsons are called Stinking
Lilies in Yorkshire, while restharrow,
is known in Northumberland as Stinking Tam.

Even the aristocratic tulip was described by Thomas Fuller, chaplain to
Charles II, as 'a well-complexion'd
stink, an ill favour wrapt up in pleasant
colours', yet nearly two hundred years
later J. C. Squire wrote that 'the scent of
them stings me with a youthful joy'.

Shakespeare has Arviragus say to Cymbeline,

And let the stinking elder, grief, untwine
His perishing root with the increasing
vine.

The wild arum, or Cuckoo Pint, is
known in some places as Dragons, and it
smells, as no doubt all dragons do, de-
cidedly unpleasant. The lovely green
and white bells of the triangulated leek
reek like the stockpots of a Welsh kitchen, and otherwise attractive flowers
give off odours that have been variously
described as rank, offensive, something
like a horse, and reminiscent of mangy
dogs, foxes, and dirty hen-houses.

Some poisonous plants, such as henbane, that 'pencill'd flower of sickly
scent', give off a warning odour, and this

odour itself was believed to be injurious.
Henry Phillips, describing the aconite
or monkshood, says: 'we find that some
persons only by taking in the effluvia of
the herb in full flower by the nostrils,
have been seized with swooning fits, and
have lost their sight for two or three
days', while it was believed that the
juice and smell of lovage injured the
eyes.

Not for us, though we may share them if
we will, but for the silent night-flying
moths come the evening perfumes.
Plants that wake while others sleep,
slowly unfolding pale luminous petals;
flower-trumpets, twisted and drooping
by day, mysteriously expanding, sending wave upon wave of fragrance out
into the still air. Evening primroses
making a sudden faint explosion as they
open to shed their light scent, of cowslips, lemons or far-away honeysuckle.
Dittany, or *Fraxinella*, on a still night
gives out a perfumed gas that will ignite
if a match is applied to it.

Strongest of all is the night-perfume of
the tobacco plant, *Nicotiana affinis*, a rich
balsam rising from the dim white stars.
The undistinguished flowers of the
night-scented stock, *Matthiola bicornis*,
give out a compelling sweetness, and
lupins, sweetly peppery by day, grow
stronger in their fragrance as darkness
falls. We catch a whiff of scented cigar-
ette smoke from the cottage-garden
phloxes, and night makes it clear to us
why sweet rocket, *Hesperis matronalis*,
should have become known as Dame's
Violet.

In July 1653, Dorothy Osborne wrote to
Sit William Temple: 'Last night I was in
the garden till eleven o'clock. It was the
sweetest night that e'er I saw. The gar-

'La Dame à la Licorne'. Millefleurs tapestry. End of the 15th century. The lady, guarded by a lion and a unicorn, symbolizes the sense of smell.

den looked so well and the jasmine smelt beyond all perfume'.

As it grows late, and the wavering moths disappear, we think of Keats in the darkness of his garden.

> I cannot see what flowers are at my feet,
>   Nor what soft incense hangs upon the
>   boughs,
> But, in embalméd darkness, guess each
>   sweet
>   Wherewith the seasonable month
>   endows
> The grass, the thicket, and the fruit-tree
>   wild;
> White hawthorn, and the pastoral
>   eglantine;
>   Fast-fading violets cover'd up in
>   leaves;
>   And mid-May's eldest child,
> The coming musk-rose, full of dewy
>   wine,
>   The murmurous haunt of flies on
>   summer eves.

At the end of the summer the fragrant flowers of day and night have a second gift for us – the rising blue plume of aromatic smoke from autumn bonfires. Finally, the story of a lady of such extreme sensibility that she is said to have lived upon no other nourishment than the smell of flowers. Her name was Eve Fliegen, or Vliegen, and she was a native of the Duchy of Cleve in Germany.

This is her story in her own simple words:

> 'Twas I that prayed I never might eat
>   more,
> 'Cause my step-mother grutched me my
>   food;

> Whether on flowers I fed, as I had store
> Or on a dew that every morning stood
> Like honey on my lips, full seventeen year.
> This is a truth, if you the truth will hear.

Eve was by no means the first to have lived on a diet of honey-dew. William Coles, in 1656, wrote of a Doctor Hackwill, who 'in his Apology for the World's not Decaying, tells a story of a German gentleman who lived fourteen years without receiving any nourishment downe his throat, but only walked frequently in a spacious Garden full of Odoriferous Herbes and Flowers'.

That Abraham Cowley was in wholehearted agreement is certain.

> Who, that hath Reason, and his Smell,
> Would not among Roses and Jasmin
>   dwell,
> Rather than all his spirits choak
> With exhalations of Durt and Smoak,

although there is nothing to prove that he carried his enthusiasm for the perfume of flowers quite so far as Eve and the unknown German gentleman; or even as the prophet Esdras, who lived for fourteen years on flowers themselves, admittedly a more nourishing diet. At all events, Eve's fame spread, although her nationality seems to have become confused with the passing of time; for in *Love's Cure, or The Martial Maid*, a play by Beaumont and Fletcher, a rather more earthy character, Aurelia, enquires of Frank Plotwell,

> What would you have me do?
> D'ye think I'm a Dutch virgin that could
>   live
> By th' scent of flowers?

●

Shakespeare wrote of flowers as he wrote of everything else – as if seen in the clear light of morning, and for the first time. Garden flowers then were few, but wild flowers were many, and as a small boy in Stratford-on-Avon he was probably aware of the herbs that were an essential part of every Elizabethan garden, and of the blossoming fruit trees in the Warwickshire orchards. Like any small boy of that, or any other period, he would have been a good deal more interested in the fruit than in the blossoms of those orchard trees, and it was the fruit rather than the flower that one hears of most frequently in his plays. Crab-apples in particular are often mentioned, for they were held in far greater esteem in the sixteenth century than they are today. Roasted crab-apples were a favourite dish, and they were served in hot ale at Christmas.

When roasted Crabs hiss in the bowl,
Then nightly sings the staring owl,

and in *A Midsummer Night's Dream*, Puck says,

And sometimes lurk I in a gossip's bowl
In very likeness of a roasted Crab;
And when she drinks, against her lips I
*   bob,*
And on her wither'd dewlap pour the ale.

Out of twenty-four references to apples in Shakespeare's plays and sonnets, there is not one mention of apple-blossom, although the lanes must have been pink and white with its petals when the boy Shakespeare was growing to manhood there.

England's emblem, the rose, is mentioned by England's first poet more than seventy times, and he has given two of the most familiar lines in our language to Juliet – the symbol of youthful and ill-fated love. This poor little unwilling-Capulet laments the family names that keep true lovers apart.

What's in a name? That which we call a
*   Rose*
By any other name would smell as sweet.

From the earliest times the rose has been

XVII
A Few Flowers from Shakespeare

regarded as the flower of love, but it has also been used for many hundreds of years as an historical emblem, as Queen Elizabeth was at that time employing the Tudor rose. Shakespeare gives the origin of the red and white roses of the houses of York and Lancaster in the famous quarrel scene, set in the hitherto peaceful Temple Gardens.

PLANTAGENET: *Let him that is a true*
*   born gentleman,*
And stands upon the
*   honour of his birth,*
If he suppose that I have
*   pleaded truth,*
From off this Brier pluck
*   a White Rose with*
*   me.*
SOMERSET: *Let him that is no coward*
*   nor no flatterer,*
But dare maintain the
*   party of the truth,*
Pluck a Red Rose from off
*   this thorn with me.*

No one is likely to forget Warwick's conclusion:

This brawl today,
Grown to this faction in the Temple
*   Garden,*
Shall send, between the Red Rose and the
*   White,*
A thousand souls to death and deadly
*   night.*

But the few simple ordinary roses, growing in the gardens of the people Shakespeare knew, also blossom in his plays; the musk rose, the Provence rose, the damask, the variegated and the sweet briar, roses that are being grown with renewed interest in gardens today.

When the king and queen make their exit in guilty horror after witnessing Hamlet's play, the prince turns to Horatio and says, 'Would not this, sir, and a forest of feathers, if the rest of my fortunes turn Turk with me, with two Provincial roses on my razed shoes, get me a fellowship in a cry of players, sir?', he is describing two large artificial roses worn upon slashed theatrical shoes. Whether by 'Provincial' he means the Provins Rose, or the Rose of Provence, is not clear, as the Latin word *provincialis* –

of the Province – could have applied to either. The Provins Rose, *R. Gallica*, is the old Apothecary's Rose, which from medieval times was used for medical purposes. It was grown in Provins, the centre of a great rose industry near Paris, and it was this rose that was supposed to be the red Rose of Lancaster. It is more probable that Hamlet was alluding to the Provence Rose, *R. centifolia*, for cabbage roses would make a more splendid decoration for an actor's shoe. This rose, one of the oldest and most sweetly scented, was also familiar to Chaucer.

We can find the musk rose in that quiet bank, sweet with country flowers, that Oberon speaks of to Puck, in *A Midsummer Night's Dream*.

> I know a bank whereon the wild Thyme
> grows,
> Where Oxlips and the Nodding Violet
> grows;
> Quite over-canopied with luscious
> Woodbine,
> With sweet Musk-Roses, and with
> Eglantine.

Sweet-briar, known as eglantine to many of the old English poets, mingled its sharp country perfume, stronger after rain, with the softer sweetness of the musk roses in Shakespeare's flowery tale. Musk roses, *R. moschata*, were brought from Italy in the reign of Henry VIII, so one would not expect them to be found growing wild in the English countryside, but this is fairyland. The sweet-briar, however, is a true native, belonging to the south of England. Gerard says that 'the fruit when it is ripe maketh most pleasant meats and banqueting dishes, as tarts and such like, the making whereof I commit to the cunning cooke, and teeth to eat them in the rich man's mouth'.

The roses mentioned in Sonnet XCIX are the variegated roses, which were known at that time.

> The Roses fearfully in thorns did stand,
> One blushing shame, another white
> despair;
> A third, nor red nor white, had stol'n of
> both

> And to his robbery had annex'd thy
> breath.

These would have been either York and Lancaster, a damask, with each petal blotched with white, or pink, or both; or Rosa Mundi, a gallica, with red and white striped petals.

The canker-rose, so frequently mentioned, is the wild rose.

> The Rose is fair, but fairer we it deem
> For that sweet odour that doth in it live.
> The canker-blooms have full as deep a
> dye
> As the perfumed tincture of the Roses,
> Hang on such thorns, and play as
> wantonly
> When summer's breath their masked buds
> discloses;
> But, for their virtue only is their show,
> They live unwoo'd and unrespected fade;
> Die to themselves; sweet Roses do not so;
> Of their sweet deaths are sweetest odours
> made.

It is likely that it was called canker-rose because of the curious red-green mossy rose-galls, made by a small insect, *Cynip rosae*, for a nursery for its grub. This is common in wild roses, but scarcely ever seen in gardens.

We think of daisies pied, with freckled cowslips and pale primroses, particularly as Shakespeare's flowers. 'Pied', meaning parti-coloured, refers to the daisy's pink tips, and the 'crimson drops i' the bottom of a Cowslip' are its freckles. The pale cleanliness of the primrose is of a tint unmatched by any other flower, and may be compared only to the wings of the brimstone butterfly, itself a wavering primrose on wings.

There is sadness in the colour, and evanescence in the perfume of Shakespeare's violets, and they are to him, and through him to us, flowers of vanishing youth and death. But when Laertes follows the body of his sister, Ophelia, to her burial, he says,

> Lay her i' the earth;
> And from her fair and unpolluted flesh
> May violets spring,

and we realize that perhaps, after all, he

wants us to read in the violet a message of hope.

Ophelia earlier gives the meaning of pansies, 'And there is Pansies – that's for thoughts', many years before the Language of Flowers was brought to England. Since another medieval name was Pawnce, it seems clear that both names must have come from the French, *penseés*; why, we do not know. Love-in-idleness was the popular country name, and it is used by Oberon in his instructions to Puck about its magic qualities:

> Yet mark'd I where the bolt of Cupid fell:
> It fell upon a little western flower,
> Before milk-white, now purple with love's
> wound,
> And maidens call it, Love-in-idleness.
> Fetch me that flower; the herb I show'd
> thee once:
> The juice of it on sleeping eyelids laid
> Will make a man or woman madly dote
> Upon the next live creature that it sees.

That a rudimentary flower language existed, and that Shakespeare was aware of it, is made clear in the following extract, taken from *A Handful of Pleasant Delights* (1584).

The poem is believed to have been written by Hunnis, and it is entitled 'A Nosegay always sweet, for lovers to send for tokens of love at New Year's Tide, or for fairings'.

> Rosemary is for remembrance
> Between us day and night;
> Wishing that I might always have
> You present in my sight.
> And when I cannot have
> As I have said before,
> Then Cupid with his deadly dart
> Doth wound my heart full sore.

> Violet is for faithfulness
> Which in me shall abide;
> Hoping likewise that from your heart
> You will not let it slide;
> And will continue in the same
> As you have now begun
> And then forever to abide
> Then you my heart have won.

> Roses is to rule me
> With reason as you will,

For to be still obedient
  Your mind for to fulfil;
And thereto will not disagree
  In nothing that you say,
But will content your mind truly
  In all things that I may.

Carnations *is for graciousness,*
  Mark that now by the way,
Have no regard to flatterers,
  Nor pass not what they say:
For they will come with lying tales
  Your ears for to fulfil:
In any case do you consent
  Nothing unto their will.

Marigold *is for marriage,*
  That would our minds suffice,
Lest that suspicion of us twain
  By any means should rise:
As for my part, I do not care,
  Myself I will still use
That all the women of the world
  For you I will refuse.

Cowslips *is for counsel,*
  For secrets us between,
That none but you and I alone
  Should know the thing we mean:
And if you will thus wisely do,
  As I think to be best,
Then have you surely won the field
  And set my heart at rest.

There are also verses for *Lavender, Sage,
Fennel, Thyme,* and so on.
Most of the references to the lily in the
plays and sonnets make use of it in its
emblematic sense, as the symbol of
purity, a sense that has remained unchanged through the centuries – as in 'a
most unspotted Lily shall she pass'. In
Venus and Adonis, when the Queen of
Love seeks to ensnare the unwilling
youth, whiteness of lily and purity of
snow are a world apart.

*Full gently now she takes him by the
    hand,*
A lily prison'd in a gaol of snow,
Or ivory in an alabaster band;
So white a friend engirts so white a foe:
  *This beauteous combat, wilful and
    unwilling,*
  *Show'd like two silver doves that sit a-
    billing.*

The lily of Adonis's unwilling hand is
imprisoned in a gaol of snow that must
surely melt with the fever of her unre-
quited love, as in a later verse Venus
pleads,

*Who is so faint, that dare not be so bold
To touch the fire, the weather being cold?*

The marigold, *Calendula officinalis,* was
grown in most monastery and convent
gardens, for its healing properties and its
value in cooking. It was called Marygold or Marybud because it was in
bloom and in use at the times of all the
festivals of the Virgin, and its other
name of *Calendula* was given for a similar
reason, that it blooms in nearly every
month, even through the winter. Shakespeare was aware of its habit of opening
and closing with the rising and setting
sun. In *The Winter's Tale,* Perdita calls it

*The marigold, that goes to bed wi' the
    sun,*
And with him rises weeping.

In *Cymbeline* there is the song,

*Hark! hark! the lark at heaven's gate
    sings,*
  And Phoebus 'gins arise,
*His steeds to water at those springs
  On chalic'd flowers that lies;*
*And winking Mary-buds begin
  To ope their golden eyes,*

– a happy marriage of pagan and religious symbolism.
By the time Shakespeare had left London and the theatre for good, and returned to the Stratford of his boyhood,
the varying kinds of cloves, carnations,
pinks and picotees that were to lead to
the status of 'florists' flowers' were so
many that Gerard wrote, 'A great and
large volume would not suffice to write
of every one at large in particular, considering how infinite they are, and how
every yeare, every clymate and coun-
trey bringeth forth new sorts, and such
as have not heretofore bin written of'.
The Elizabethans delighted in the fantastic and bizarre, and the striped and
streaked gillivors, as they were sometimes spelt, were eagerly sought after.

Whether Shakespeare shared in this
enthusiasm we do not know, but
his shepherdess, Perdita, shows hearty
disapproval.

        *Sir, the year
        growing ancient,
        Not yet on summer's death,
          nor on the birth
        Of trembling winter, the
          fairest flowers o' the season
        Are our carnations, and
          streak'd gillyvors,
        Which some call nature's
          bastards: of that kind
        Our rustic garden's barren,
          and I care not to get slips
          of them.*
POLIXENES: *Wherefore, gentle maiden,
        Do you neglect them?*
PERDITA: *For I have heard it said
        There is an art which in
          their piedness shares
        With great creating nature.*
POLIXENES: *Say there be;
        Yet nature is made better by
          no mean
        But nature makes that
          mean: so, over that art,
        Which you say adds to
          nature, is an art
        That nature makes. You
          see, sweet maid, we marry
        A gentler scion to the
          wildest stock,
        And make conceive a bark of
          baser kind
        By bud of nobler race: this
          is an art
        Which does mend nature,
          change it rather, but
        The art itself is nature.*
PERDITA: *So it is.*
POLIXENES: *Then make your garden
        rich in gillyvors,
        And do not call them
          bastards.*
PERDITA: *I'll not put
        The dibble in earth to set
          one slip of them;*
        *No more than, were I
          painted, I would wish
        This youth should say,
        'twere well', and only
          therefore
        Desire to breed by me.*

The *Winter's Tale* is winter in name only, for it is full of flowers, and Perdita, Titania not excepted, is the most flower-loving of all Shakespearean heroines.

> *O Proserpina!*
> *For the flowers now that*
> *frighted thou let'st fall*
> *From Dis's waggon! daffodils,*
> *That come before the*
> *swallow dares, and take*
> *The winds of March with*
> *beauty; violets dim,*
> *But sweeter than the lids of*
> *Juno's eyes*
> *Or Cytherea's breath; pale*
> *prime-roses,*
> *That die unmarried, ere*
> *they can behold*
> *Bright Phoebus in his*
> *strength, a malady*
> *Most incident to maids;*
> *bold oxlips and*
> *The crown imperial; lilies*
> *of all kinds,*
> *The flower-de-luce being*
> *one. O! these I lack*
> *To make you garlands of,*
> *and my sweet friend,*
> *To strew him o'er and o'er!*

> FLORIZEL: *What! like a corse?*
> PERDITA: *No, like a bank for love to*
> *lie and play on;*
> *Not like a corse; or if, – not*
> *to be buried,*
> *But quick and in mine*
> *arms. Come, take your*
> *flowers.*

Under his spell, and 'adding this to that, and so to so', we are left with the totally undeserved impression that we know as much about flowers as he does.

Page 122: Quite over-canopied with
luscious woodbine,
With sweet musk-roses, and
with eglantine.
A Midsummer Night's Dream, II, 2, 192. From Walter Crane, *Flowers from Shakespeare's Garden*, 1906. Eglantine was then considered to be symbolic of pleasure mixed with pain.

Overleaf: *Ophelia*, by Arthur Hughes, 1852.
City of Manchester Art Gallery.
There with fantastic garlands did
she come,
Of crow-flowers, nettles, daisies
Hamlet, IV, 7, 169.
The crow-flowers of Ophelia's garlands were probably the ragged robin, *Lychnis flos-cuculi*. Gerard says that the flowers 'serve for garlands and crowns and to deck up gardens'.

FLOWERS · FROM · SHAKESPEARE'S · GARDEN:
a Posy from the Plays, pictured by Walter Crane

Cassell & Co: Ltd 1906

There was no child in the first garden, unless Adam and Eve in their innocence may be regarded as children; but the happiness of a child in a garden has the same quality of freshness.

Children who love flowers, and that is by no means every child, may examine them singly with absorbed interest; they may gather them into posies, or balls, or chains; pull off their petals and arrange them in patterns, and finally discard them, leaving them to wither in the sun, or blow away in the wind, with never a second thought. When childhood is past, how often we remember a certain field of buttercups, a daisied lawn, or the day we looked, we really looked, at a worried pansy, or a crumpled poppy petal. The texture of a petal can awaken memories and remind us of other textures. Rose-petals for velvet, poppies for silk, peonies for satin, buttercups for glazed cotton. What superb drapers' shops we found in field and garden.

Nothing could be more common than my first flower, and nothing more romantic. My father and mother were house-hunting in a suburb of Birmingham, and I, an only child six years of age, made a somewhat unwilling third on this expedition. How many houses we visited I do not now remember, but towards the end of the afternoon we came to an utterly undistinguished terraced house, which must have been empty for some time. The garden, which was long and narrow, with mercifully high wooden fences, had almost disappeared under the summer grasses that had taken possession; but there, lifting tall spires of deep blue above the yellowing green, was the most wonderful flower, I thought, that I had ever seen. I remember how its green leaves, like tapered fingers, were joined in the centre by a single glittering dewdrop, like a diamond on the slender hand of a princess, and I longed for my parents to take the house, so that this beautiful flower could be ours. I never saw it again, and for some years did not know that this beautiful blue spire that might have been ours was a common lupin.

Barbara Castle, a child in the West Riding of Yorkshire, remembers the market

XVIII
A Child Among Flowers

gardens of Pontefract, where the liquorice root grew, and her visits with her mother to the liquorice works to buy 'those sticky black treasures'. Not every child is given the tremendous luck of seeing her own sweets growing.

At times a strange and pungent smell will bring back memories of the marigolds that bordered the path to grandma's cottage. A jonquil revives the first awareness of sin, as Ruth Duthrie, the garden historian, recalls.

One spring day when I was maybe, six years old, I could not resist picking a very sweet-scented, deep-yellow jonquil. My father had planted just a few bulbs of these and this was the first to flower. I recall walking up the kitchen stairs holding the flower behind my back, and encountering my mother, who asked me what I was hiding. When she saw it was one of these precious miniature daffodils, she was angry with me. I said, 'I picked it for you', and indeed I had meant to give it to her. I was upset by her lack of understanding but yet I knew I had picked it because of an overwhelming desire to do so. Thus for the first time I knew the agony of realizing the mixed motives for an action. Nevertheless the jonquil remains as a vision of beauty, so delicate, so neat with its glowing colour and its wonderful scent.

Oliver Wendell Holmes found the scent of a little box hedge to be suggestive of eternity – 'the incalculable remote time of childhood' – because he had smelt it when he was on the level of its fresh leaves. Even the memory of the smell of mildewed paste, coming from the sheepskin covers of a little Latin book, brought summer back to Edmund Gosse. 'The windows would be open in summer, and my seat was close to it. Outside, a bee was shaking the clematis blossom, or a red-admiral butterfly was opening and shutting his wings on the hot concrete of the verandah.'

The most exciting smell of all, delicious, heady, and to be renewed each year, was the scent of the Christmas tree. Could one ever, to the last moment of recorded time, forget that bathroom-cupboard, furniture-polishy smell, so full of promise?

On occasion it may be a name that catches our youthful fancy, Butter-and-Eggs, Jack-by-the-hedge, Lords and Ladies – lords for the dark ones, ladies for the light. 'There are splendid lords and ladies in the hedges of Mary's Meadow. I can never make up my mind when I like them best. In April and May, when they have smooth plum-coloured coats and pale green cowls, and push up out of last year's dry leaves, or in August and September, when their hoods have fallen away, and their red berries shine through the dusty grass and nettles that have been growing up round them all the summer out of the ditch', said Mary, of Mrs Ewings' classic.

Richard Jefferies first met with Butter-and-Eggs under the name of bird's-foot lotus (birds foot trefoil).

The boy must have seen it, must have trodden on it in the bare woodland pastures, certainly run about on it, with wet naked feet from the bathing; but the boy was not conscious of it. This was the first, when the desire was to identify it and to know, fixing upon it by means of a pale and feeble picture . . . In the mind all things were written in pictures – there is no alphabetical combination of letters and words; all things are pictures and symbols. The birds-foot lotus is the picture to me of sunshine and summer, and of that summer in the heart which is known only in youth, and then not alone. No words could write

that feeling: the bird's-foot trefoil writes it.

But the alphabetical combination of letters and words was soon to come. 'The first conscious thought about wild flowers was to find out their names – the first conscious pleasure – and then I began to see so many that I had not previously noticed. Once you wish to identify them there is nothing escapes, down to the little white chickweed of the path and the moss of the wall.' Hundreds of comic and outrageous names our wild flowers have been given; Fat Hen, Brandy Bottles, Codlins and Cream, Wet-a-bed, Ringing-all-the-bells-in-London – elderly country folk can remember them still.

Bright warm colours attract us in childhood too. 'It was the reflected glow of your blazing line along the terrace, O geraniums, and yours, O foxgloves, sprung up amid the coppice, that gave my childish cheeks their rosy warmth', wrote Colette; and Percy Lubbock loved the nasturtiums that rioted along the wall, bright yellow, bright red – 'very few plants of the earth are as clean in negligent ease as a yellow nasturtium'. We remember the jam-jars of wild flowers on sunny kindergarten window-sills, and being taught to paint our first flower at school; a disheartening experience, that could be, for seldom did our picture turn out as well as we had hoped. Yellow tulips have been hateful ever since we were told to paint a straight-up yellow tulip in a straight-up vase at school.

But William Hazlitt, peering through the gates of distance, looks through rosier

ve cast them at your feet;

d about your life to wind.

K.G.

Page 127: Some worried pansy faces from *The Floricultural Cabinet*, 1837. Their expressions, ranging through agitation and vexation to extreme irritability, have fascinated generations of children.

Left: Victorian Christmas card by Kate Greenaway. Victoria and Albert Museum. Kate Greenaway invented a style of children's dress that is timeless. Derived from the late eighteenth century, it was copied by fond mothers for their little girls, who wore them with satisfaction, as little girls still wear them today. Even small boys may be thrust protesting into Kate Greenaway suits for weddings.

Buttercups and Daisies. A vocal waltz for children. Undated.

spectacles. 'My sensations are all glossy, spruce, voluptuous, and fine: they wear a candied coat, and are in holiday trim. I see the beds of larkspurs with purple eyes; tall hollyhocks, red and yellow; the broad sunflowers, caked in gold, with bees buzzing round them; wildernesses of pinks, and hot-glowing peonies; poppies run to seed; the sugared lily, and faint mignionette, all ranged in order, and as thick as they can grow.' Colours, brighter and more various than the best box of crayons could ever reproduce – small wonder that most of us retain something of the summer days of childhood.

Heine writes in *Reisebilder* of the days of his youth, spent in the court garden of Dusseldorf, and his intimacy with the flowers – 'the rouged tulips, proud as beggars, condescendingly greeted me, the nervous sick lilies nodded with melancholy tenderness, the drunken red roses laughed at me from afar, the night-violets sighed – with the myrtle and laurels I was not then acquainted, for they did not entice me with a shining bloom, but the mignonette, with whom I now stand so badly, was very intimate.'

'Do you like butter?' The old childish game, when we held a buttercup under another child's chin, and peered beneath to see the golden reflection which was supposed to supply the answer, is now outmoded. Buttercups, 'the little children's dower', will soon go the way of the golden sovereigns of the prosperous Victorian grown-up world. As motorways rip up their creeping root we turn to daisies, small and deceptively frail-looking, still maintaining obstinate tenure. As long as we have grass, it seems, we shall have daisies. But shall we have daisy-chains? The making of daisy chains is an occupation of some skill and precision. We might almost regard it as a minor country craft. The pin must be inserted in the narrow stem with accuacy. It must be drawn down just far enough to allow room for the head of the next flower – a fraction too far, and all you have is a daisy with two legs. Katharine Mansfield remembered playing 'ladies and gentlemen', an introductory course to 'mothers and fathers', no doubt. This involved being married in a daisy-chain, with the wedding service read from a seed catalogue. She wrote later to her sister, Chaddie, 'Oh, how I love flowers! People always say it must be because I spent my childhood among all those gorgeous tropical trees and blossoms. But I don't seem to remember us making daisy-chains out of magnolias – do you?'

The northern name of Bairnswort, Childing or Childling Daisy, confirms the daisy as the children's own particular flower and even that indomitable character, Sylvia Pankhurst, recalls 'the great lawn of daisies, the dearest of childhood's flowers, and the lawn of white clover, frequented by the humblebees', of her parents' home. German children, too, had pet names for the daisy; *das Gänselblumchen*, little goose flower, and *Tausendschönchen*, that is, a thousand prettinesses. *Marienblumchen* made it Mary's little flower, and *Massliebchen*, love's measure, showed it to be the flower of he-loves-me, he-loves-me-not, the prophetic flower, as it was in France and Italy also. The star-flower or aster was sometimes used for the same purpose. Gowans, another northern name, could be applied to either buttercups or daisies. Charles Dickens, by no means a country writer, was aware of this, and introduces them, by way of Mr Micawber. Recalling earlier days with nostalgia, Mr Micawber remarks,

'I may say, of myself and Copperfield, in words we have sung together before now, that "We twa hae run about the braes And pu'ed the gowans fine', in a figurative point of view, on several occasions. I am not exactly aware', said Mr Micawber, with the old roll in his voice and the old indescribable air of saying something genteel, 'what gowans may be, but I have no doubt that Copperfield and myself would frequently have taken a pull at them, if it had been feasible'.

Gowans or Bairnswort, or by whatever other name we may know them, may they never be mown or chemicalized out of existence, and may poor John Clare be proved right when he wrote,

Trampled under foot,
The daisy lives and strikes its root
Into the lap of time: centuries may come
And pass away into the silent tomb,
And still the child, hid in the womb of
*   time,*
Shall smile and pluck them, when this
*   simple rhyme*
Shall be forgotten, like a churchyard
*   stone,*
Or lingering lie, unnoticed and alone.

Were it not for the invaluable time-telling properties of the dandelion clock, and the fascinating way the downy seeds sail against the blue sky, their tiny parachutes turning from silver to gold in the sunshine, perhaps the flower might not have held our hearts so firmly as the daisy; but to Countess Russell, better known as the author of *Elizabeth and Her German Garden*, published in 1898, dandelions and daisies are linked together, as buttercups and daisies are to the rest of us.

I was too little to do lessons and was turned out with sugar on my eleven o'clock bread and butter on to a lawn closely strewn with dandelions and daisies. The sugar on the bread and butter has lost its charm, but I love the dandelions and daisies even more passionately now than then, and never would endure to see them all mown away if I were not certain that in a day or two they would be pushing up their little faces again as jauntily as ever.

'Too true', says the disgruntled gardener, 'they will.' But still, for most of us, buttercups, daisies and dandelions remain the gold and white symbols of childhood.

Matthew Arnold, in a letter to his sister in April 1879, said, 'I have had some happy gatherings of white violets, though the cottage children are apt to be before me, and they spoil as much as they gather.' Children, 'as such forgive them', as Arnold wrote in one of his poems, would be lucky to go white violetting now. It was not only picking for picking's sake that made flowering such an absorbing occupation for yesterday's children. Sometimes small bunches might be collected for the old or sick or housebound; sometimes to sell by the wayside, or to be 'cried' in the city streets. W. H. Hudson writes that

on Easter Saturday the roadsides and copses by the little river Nadder were full of children gathering primroses; they might have filled a thousand baskets without the flowers being missed, so abundant were they in that place. Cold though it was, the whole air was laden with delicious fragrance. It was pleasant to see and talk with the little people occupied with the task they loved so well, and I made up my mind to see the result of all this flower-gathering next day in some of the village churches in the neighbourhood.

Often children were sent cowslipping by their parents, for the cowslip 'peeps' were made into wine, and an excellent wine it was.

Folks tell me that the May's in flower,
The cowslips-peeps are fit to pull,
And I've got leave to spend an hour
To get this little basket full.

But cowslips are fast disappearing to make way for neat ranks of houses, and primroses and violets are in full retreat. And what of the town child? More than a hundred and fifty years ago, Louisa Anne Twamley, who wrote some charmingly 'moral' flower books, used to carry her basket along the dull, dusty turnpike road close to the town, 'to pick a smoky-faced daisy from the bank, or look for skeleton-leaves under the hedge'. – And today?

Charlotte Yonge remembered bluebell picking in her youth. 'A long walk round Kitley Point, with the sea sparkling on one side and the wood sloping up filled with bluebells. We gathered them in the ecstasy of childhood, exchanged our finest clustering stems of blue, and felt our hearts go out to one another'. May still brings its fleets of energetic young cyclists bearing away bundles of bluebells, which, rapidly turning a dank grey, lean over the handlebars like seasick passengers over the ship's side.

A handful of windflowers, withered as soon as touched; a forlorn tangle of vetch and potentilla, dropped like a symbol where turf meets asphalt; it is not only a robin redbreast in a cage that puts all Heaven in a rage!

Quite the best of the prizes we hunted for were the wild strawberries, equally satisfactory to dolls and children. They grew at their best on the chalk downs, rather hard, hairy and seedy and with short stems in the exposed places, but lower down, in sheltered nooks which harboured, maybe, little pockets of good soil, the plants grew taller, and the scarlet fruit hung down, clear and red, like lanterns. Garden strawberries were quite different, of course. You had to have permission to pick them, and it wasn't given very easily. The trouble was, you couldn't wait until there were lots of strawberries before you asked. You always asked too soon. Dean Hole once asked a boy what a garden was for. 'Strawberries!' he said.

If you were lucky enough to know some-one with a mulberry tree, it was truly wonderful. Grown-ups don't mind how many mulberries you eat, because they don't much like picking them up out of the long wet grass. But, and this is vital, you must be sure to wipe your feet when you go indoors, or the consequences will be *dire*. I was one of the lucky ones, for an immensely old and twisted tree grew in our school garden. Every year, as soon as the time and the mulberry tree were ripe, we made mulberry pie in cookery class, and although the pastry may not have been of *cordon bleu* quality, the berries with their rich purple juice were good enough to get drunk on. Percy Lubbock remembered such a tree, in the garden at Earlham.

To a few of us it is revealed that the mulberry is paragon and nonsuch among the fruits of the garden; it is what all the rest of them would be if they could . . . There is this about mulberries, that you can only attain to them on their own ground; you must go to them, search them out where they be; they are too precious and tender, with their bursting purple juices to be handled and transported to meet you. A ripe black mulberry is a gift to you direct from the opulent tree; and I cannot help it if I pass on my way, after an interval, plentifully stained with noble dyes.

Here we come gathering nuts and may,
Nuts and may, nuts and may;
Here we come gathering nuts and may
On a cold and frosty morning.

We knew well enough that we couldn't go gathering nuts and may in the same season, nor could we find nuts in May, especially on a cold and frosty morning. Nobody had told us that 'nuts' was probably a corruption of 'knots' and referred to the old custom of gathering knots of flowers on May Day. So we still sang the nonsense cheerfully at Christmas parties, trooping back and forth, and tugging an unwilling victim chosen for nuts and may to our side across the great divide of a borrowed handkerchief. When it came to nutting on a sharp autumn day, we forgot about the may, though we weren't averse to a blackberry or two. After the 10th of October, they said, you shouldn't eat blackberries, because the Devil had spat on them; and indeed, they did taste a bit watery.

There is a fascinating assortment of seeds and berries that may not be eaten but, laid out in matchbox trays, make tempting bargains for dolls' greengrocer shops. Mahonia berries, with the blue bloom of grapes; shining black privet berries; sweet-pea pods for marrowfats; hips and haws dubiously edible and tempting; the delicate and bright pink yewberries, so poisonous and so pretty. Doubtless God could have made a prettier berry, but doubtless He never did; and yet, He very nearly did when he made the spindle-berry. The snowberry, too, so hard to believe in. This exotic, however, made an excellent substitute for the homely dumplings on the dolls' dinner table.

Among other seasonal desirables were acorns, beech nuts, and shining horse chestnuts, all suitable for furniture and equipment, and eagerly sought after by do-it-yourself dolls' house owners. Baskets, rings and bracelets could be woven of rushes, burrs could be stuck together for cradles and birds' nests. The silver seeds of honesty were all the money needed in our Garden of Eden. Honey lurked in the horns of the honeysuckle, clover and nasturtium, and sunflower seeds and mallow cheeses were the week's free offer. John Clare wrote of

The sitting down, when school was o'er
Upon the threshold of the door,
Picking from mallows, sport to please,
The crumpled seed we called a cheese.

A few years ago the most charming sight was to be seen in a wide avenue on the outskirts of Cambridge, where three children were building a snowman. Already its rotund figure had reached their shoulders' height, and the children were laughing and calling to each other in their excitement, for it was May, and their snowman was made of the fallen white blossoms of the cherry trees that lined the avenue.

Victorian Christmas card. Victoria and Albert Museum. A solemn Victorian child, ready perhaps for a Christmas party. 'The daisy's for simplicity and unaffected air', as Burns wrote in 'The Posie', but this is an ox-eyed child dressed as an ox-eyed daisy.

Right: *Children picking blackberries,*
by William Bromley (1835–1888).
That long arched prickly
    streamer, which bent o'er,
Down from the hedge's top, its
    garland rough,
Bearing the loved Blackberries.
Louisa Twamley (1812–1895),
Romance of Nature, 1836.

Fantasies could be lived out of doors as well as in. Little Sam Coleridge, who never played except by himself, and then only acting over what he had been reading, spent long hours acting to the docks and nettles, and the rank grass, slashing at the weeds with a long stick, as one of the seven champions of Christendom. In Japan boys fight bloodless duels with iris leaves.

To convince oneself that an iris leaf is a sword, or to translate one's every-day garden into a tropical forest is a simple thing, but a boy who invents a flower is no ordinary boy. In the early part of the nineteenth century lived such a boy, Hugh Miller by name, and he grew to be no ordinary man, as his position as President of the Royal Physical Society of Edinburgh proves. At the age of three, he says in his autobiography, 'I remember, for instance, getting out unobserved one day to my father's little garden, and seeing there a minute duckling covered with soft yellow hair, growing out of the soil by its feet, and beside it a plant that bore as its flowers a crop of little mussel-shells of a deep red colour.

I know not what prodigy of the vegetable kingdom produced the little duckling; but the plant with the shells must, I think, have been a scarlet-runner, and the shells themselves the papilionaceous blossoms.' It is probable that these plant fantasies had their origin in Gerard's *Herbal* or Parkinson's *Theatrum Botanicum*, and that little Hugh had seen plates of the Goose Barnacle tree, or the Vegetable Lamb of Tartary, or some other strange growth that our ancestors described, for it is not only children who imagine rather more than they see.

Young Charles Darwin, when at school, told another little boy that he could produce variously-coloured polyanthuses and primroses by watering them with certain coloured fluids. He also brought a flower to school and said that his mother had taught him that by looking at the inside the name of the plant could be discovered. Perhaps he had learnt from his learned grandfather, Erasmus Darwin, about the Doctrine of Signatures, and imagined each flower to be signed at the bottom of its petals like

a limited edition of a botanical print. It was this same streak of fantasy that caused an otherwise well-balanced gentleman past, one would have thought, the first age of childhood, and not yet eligible for the second, to go out into his front garden after dark one Saturday night, to decorate the monkey puzzle tree that was the fashionable centre-piece of his, as it was of so many other, Victorian lawns, with large pink flowers from the rhododendron bushes which grew in the shrubbery at the back of the house. Morning dawned, and the neighbours in twos and threes on their way to divine service, or to their Sunday morning constitutional, paused in astonishment to admire the exotic tree so suddenly ablaze with bloom on Mr Statham's lawn. It was well worth the efforts of the night before, which must have been fraught with considerable discomfort and not a little danger, poised as he was on a step-ladder in the darkness, amid the prickly architecture of the monkey-puzzle. But that was typical of my grandfather.

The child's acceptance of flowers is quite different from that of the adult. To an adult, a flower may be a miracle of colour and form and texture, with perhaps the added wonder of perfume. If we are gardeners we may value it for its ease, or even its difficulty, of growing. We value it for what it *is*. A child examines a flower not so much for what it is, as for what, with a little ingenuity, it might be. The furry leaves of the *Stachys lanata* are rabbit's ears; antirrhinums are bunny's mouths; foxgloves are thimbles. And foxgloves *are* thimbles if thinking makes them so, and a pastel-coloured hollyhock bloom, with a poppy-seed head and silver honesty-seed wings, a fairy queen. That sweetpeas are babies' bonnets must be obvious to anyone, but it is no longer certain that the large white flowers of *Convolvulus major* are used for grannies' nightcaps as they once were – today's grannies being an altogether different breed from yesterday, and nightcaps an outmoded form of millinery.

It is not quite clear why hawthorn leaves should be bread and cheese, but custom says they are and it must be accepted.

Seaweed and pimpernels are still our faithful weather prophets, and marguerite and poppy petals are as reliable fortune tellers as those ladies of black velvet and mystery who make their seasonal appearance on seaside piers.

Resist as one may the long-term promise of a patch of soil, I believe there to be no child, of either sex or any age, who can be blind to the delights of the garden-of-an-hour that lurks in the bottom of a rockpool. Those shining brown purses, empty of mermaid's housekeeping money, but none the less highly satisfactory to pop between the fingers; the beckoning antennae of the sea-anemones that turn into sulky jujubes if poked with a stick; and most exciting of all, the small shell, motionless on its sandy bed, that suddenly and without warning takes off and scuttles away on the borrowed legs of a hermit crab, are a between-tides performance of infinite variety. The slippery, seaweedy progress from one rock pool to another; always the next pool is full of even greater promise.

It contains perhaps a tropical forest of gently-moving red and ferny trees; or the translucent, cast-off shell of a minute crab – had he outgrown it, leaving it carelessly where he had dropped it, instead of tidily hiding it under a rock? Or had he, poor innocent, met with an untimely end too horrible to contemplate? Most sought after, but not to be found on every occasion, a starfish – surely dropped from yesterday evening's pale sky with only the smallest splash.

Perhaps young Edmund Gosse, collecting specimens with his father, who later published a *History of the British Sea-Anemones and Corals*, hardly belongs among the happy, carefree children absorbed with their sea-gardens.

These pools were our mirrors, in which, reflected in the dark hyaline and framed by the sleek and shining fronds of oar-weed there used to appear the shapes of a middle-aged man and a funny little boy, equally eager, and, I almost find the presumption to say, equally well prepared for business. They were living flower-beds, so exquisite in their per-

fection, that my Father, in spite of his scientific requirements, used not seldom to pause before he began to rifle them, ejaculating that it was indeed a pity to disturb such congregated beauty . . . the great prawns gliding like transparent launches, anthea waving in the twilight its thick white tentacles, and the fronds of the dulse faintly streaming on the water, like huge red banners in some reverted atmosphere.

Rock pools and sea-gardens inevitably lead us to *The Water Babies*, and Charles Kingsley's little Tom, the chimney sweep, starting on his watery journey, in company with the tall Irishwoman. He sees his first wild flowers – 'and a stream large enough to turn a mill; among blue geranium, and golden globe-flower, and wild raspberry, and the bird-cherry with its tassels of snow', he sees starwort, and milfoil, and water-crowfoot – but there is no end to the wonder of what he sees. In Kingsley's sea-gardens 'there were water-flowers there, too, in thousands; and Tom tried to pick them: but as soon as he touched them, they drew themselves in and turned into knots of jelly; and then Tom saw that they were all alive – bells, and stars, and wheels, and flowers, of all beautiful shapes and colours; and all alive and busy, just as Tom was', and just as little, earnest Edmund Gosse was more than a hundred years ago.

But the colours have faded, and in 1907, Edmund Gosse, now a grown man, wrote sadly,

All this is long over, and done with. The ring of living beauty drawn about our shores was a very thin and fragile one. It had existed all those centuries solely in consequence of the indifference, the blissful ignorance of man. These rock-basins, fringed by corallines, filled with still water almost as pellucid as the upper air itself, thronged with beautiful sensitive forms of life – they exist no longer, they are all profaned, and emptied, and vulgarized. An army of 'collectors' has passed over them, and ravaged every corner of them. The

fairy paradise has been violated, the exquisite product of centuries of natural selection has been crushed under the rough paw of well-meaning, idle-minded curiosity. That my Father himself so reverent, so conservative, had by the popularity of his book acquired the direct responsibility for a calamity that he had never anticipated became clear enough to himself before many years had passed and cost him great chagrin. No one will see again on the shore of England what I saw in my early childhood, the submarine vision of dark rocks, speckled and starred with an infinite variety of colour, and streamed over by silken flags of royal crimson and purple.

Children who are lucky enough to have a garden of their own know, without doubt, that flowers need to be helped. If you plant a row of sweetpea seeds on Saturday, and they haven't appeared by Monday, then of course you must turn over the soil to see what has happened to them. If your peony has a nice fat bud on it, well, naturally, it needs a little assistance. A borrowed hairpin makes an excellent reluctant-bud opener. And those bare twigs that you planted after breakfast, if it is bedtime and there isn't so much as one single little leaf to be seen, you had better pull them up.

Which just goes to show that little Edmund Gosse was not like other children, for he once carried his small red watering can, full of water, to the top of the village, and then all the way down Petitor Lane in a drought, to water a corn field, 'hoping by this act to improve the prospects of the harvest'. Perhaps, after all, Edmund was like other children and it was the little red watering can that was the cause of his altruistic gesture. For isn't a watering can of one's own the most satisfying of all implements? Any kind of a small and entirely personal tool is a pleasure to own, but a watering can, and a red one too! No doubt young Edmund hoped that the villagers would come out to their garden gates to admire the vessel.

Few children have the patience to car-

or their gardens throughout the year, but those that do, are gardeners for life. William Cobbett was one of these. 'From my very infancy, from the age of six years, when I climbed up the side of a steep sand rock, and there scooped me out a plot four feet square to make me a garden, and the soil for which I carried up in the bosom of my little blue smock-frock, I have never lost one particle of my passion for these healthy and rational and heart-cheering pursuits.'

But to the normal child, the patch of earth should be his own; the tools not borrowed grown-up tools, but a trowel and a fork, that red watering can, and, almost as important, a wheel-barrow, that are entirely his. The seeds he sows must be bought with his own pocket money, and although he may admit a few marigolds and pansies, ready-grown, and donated by well-wishers, he will never think so highly of them as of the three double daisies that he saved his pennies for.

And those seed-packets, envelopes of promise they are, far too large for the salt-spoonful of seeds they contain, and yet scarcely large enough for the wonders they hold. Seeds with such black and shiny carapaces that one might expect them to grow into beetles rather than flowers; dry, wrinkled seeds looking old before their time; crescent-shaped seeds that might have been brought to earth by some moon-traveller; flattened seeds like tiny brown pennies; some as fine as pepper and others feathered at one end like miniature paint-brushes. The luggage of next summer's garden party, packed into a tiny space.

Dean Hole, a gardener-for-life, remembered 'the first plant which I could call my own, the salvia, which I bought for sixpence from the nurseries near to our school. I have grown and shown a multitude of specimens in the greenhouse and the stove since then; I have won prizes of gold and cups of silver, but have never exhibited anything half so precious as that tiny pet, no colour which could compare with its splendid flowers.'

But the path of the young gardener is not always a primrose one, and perhaps it is no bad thing if, like Oliver Wendell Holmes, he learns the horticultural facts of life at an early age.

Like other boys in the country, I had my patch of ground, to which in the spring-time, I intrusted the seeds furnished me, with a confident trust in their resurrection and glorification in the better world of summer. But I soon found that my lines had fallen in a place where a vegetable growth had to run the gauntlet of as many foes and trials as a Christian pilgrim. Flowers would not blow; daffodils perished like criminals in their condemned caps, without their petals ever seeing daylight; roses were disfigured with monstrous protrusions through their very centres . . . radishes knotted themselves until they looked like centenarians' fingers; and on every stem, on every leaf, and both sides of it, and at the root of everything that grew, was a professional specialist in the shape of grub, caterpillar, aphis, or other expert, whose business it was to devour that particular part.

But after all, one can't learn too young that a gardener's life is not necessarily a bed of roses, nor is it, like the beautiful Zephrine Drouhin, entirely without thorns.

A child's world is small and private. It is preoccupied and all-absorbing. Not so much gardens, or fields of flowers, but a single flower will hold his interest; not landscape, but a single stone engages his attention. William Allingham wrote in his diary:

From my own experience, I judge that a child's little camera obscura, however sensitive to the picturesque, cannot include it on a large scale. There were mountains in daily sight, where I lived, and a large cataract in the river close by; I must also have seen the ocean sometimes, which was but three miles distant, yet it was none of these that impressed me with a sense of beauty and mystery, but the water-tub and the well, flowers and leaves, and, very particularly, a heap of grey rocks, touched with moss and in one part laced with briars, in a certain green field to which the nurse often used to bring us.

And because of this nearness to the ground, it is the small flowers they love the best – stitchwort and speedwell, eyebright and wild pansies with funny faces, tiny toadstools and grasses. They leave traces of the day's activities in small pebble-edged gardens, whose neat rows of decapitated flowers have withered in the afternoon sunshine. Underneath the bushes, a few berries show where a miniature greengrocer's stall recently stood, and the curling petals that were, only this morning, the stock-in-trade of a dolls' draper's shop. In hollows between gnarled tree-roots there are signs that flower battles have been fought – violets turned into soldiers by interlocking their heads and having a tug-of-war with their stems. In autumn, beneath the horse-chestnut trees, we walk on other battlefields, where recent conker wars have been fought.

Headless grasses are signs that Grandmother-grandmother-hop-out-of-bed has been played, and the poor old lady flicked ruthlessly into the ditch; snapdragons and foxglove bells have served a turn for Fly-away-Peter, Fly-away-Paul. Threaded phlox and lilac blossoms are necklaces fit for princesses, and fallen fuchsia flowers lie spent upon the ground like the exhausted ballerinas they are. Split stems of dandelions, warmed for a moment in the mouth, make splendid curls for an afternoon's wearing; poppy petals can squeak, and grasses, if manipulated with sufficient skill, make the most pleasing noises. Pink and blue larkspurs, woven into wreaths, may be pressed between the pages of a book, where they keep their secret until in after years, and perhaps in alien places, the pages are opened, and their still-pink, still-blue petals are revealed.

Dorothy Wordsworth wrote in her journal of two beggar boys. 'I saw two beggar boys before me, one about 10, the other about 8 years old, at play chasing a butterfly. They were wild figures, not very ragged but without shoes and stockings. The hat of the elder was wreathed round with yellow flowers, the younger, whose hat was a rimless crown, had stuck it round with laurel leaves', like some junior member of the Lakeland poets.

Another budding poet, Mistral, fell in love with a colony of yellow irises, which grew in a ditch in the Provence of his childhood. Twice, within one fateful half-hour, he fell into its muddy depths in vain endeavour to reach the blossoms. Twice he was whipped and his clothes changed, but 'his hands still itched so to clutch some of these beautiful bouquets of gold' that he went back to the forbidden spot for the third time; for the third time he fell in, after which he was sentenced to bed.

> And what do you think I dreamed? Of my yellow irises, of course . . . Dragonflies with blue silk wings alighted on them, and I swam about nude in the laughing water. I seized the fair-haired fleur-de-lis by handsful, by double handsful, and by armsful, but the faster I plucked them the faster they grew.

The joy of discovery of a simple coltsfoot may be as vivid to a child as the mysterious night-blooming cereus or the gigantic Victoria Regina water lily to an explorer. The pictures are endless. Little Carl Linnaeus, whose toys were flowers. The young Hans Christian Andersen, standing silently studying a gooseberry bush, and wondering, perhaps, whether this was the one under which he had been born. Katharine Mansfield stealing out into the garden at dead of night with a blanket to cover a snowdrop that had bloomed the day before; and her struggles, with her friend Marion, to compose an Ode to that flower.

'All of you with little children,' said Richard Jefferies, 'and have no need to count expense, or even if you have such need, take them by hills and streams, if you wish their highest education . . . they will forget their books – they will never forget the grassy fields'. If that were true more than a hundred years ago, how much, how very much more true it is today.

Below: The frontispiece from Kate Greenaway's *Language of Flowers.* Undated. The charming evergreen world of Kate Greenaway was, and still is, loved by adults and children alike.

Opposite: Orange Blossom, as symbolized by Grandville. *Les Fleurs Animées.* The wearing of orange blossom by brides is a comparatively modern custom, drawn from the Language of Flowers. The white blossom symbolizes purity, but the fruit, did she but know it, is an emblem of fecundity.

XIX
Ceremonial Flowers

Flowers have been used in festival and ceremony since the earliest times, on every conceivable occasion, in simplicity or with extravagance. Customs have been handed on through the centuries, turning on the way from pagan to religious with little noticeable change. Altars have been decorated for false gods and true. Indeed, to the believer there are no false gods. That which we call a rose would smell as sweet for Juno as for Mary.

The Roman festival of Floralia, in honour of the reappearance of spring, was renewed in our May Day celebrations, until these in turn were put down by the Puritans. The setting up of a maypole with its garlands of flowers was prohibited in 1644.

> *Alas, poore May Poles; what should be*
>   *the cause*
> *That you were almost banish't from the*
>   *earth?*
> *Who never were rebellious to the Lawes;*
> *Your greatest crime was harmlesse, honest*
>   *mirth.*

After the Restoration they were once again permitted, although many of the clergy continued to preach against them as a remnant of pagan superstition. There can be no doubt that the Queen of the May was the legitimate descendant of the goddess Flora of the Roman festival.

Even the smallest villages had their May festivals, and Richard Jefferies described one in *Field and Hedgerow.*

> The children have been round with the May garland, which takes the place of the May-pole, and is carried slung on a stick, and covered with a white cloth, between two little girls. The cloth is to keep the dust and sun from spoiling the flowers – the rich golden kingcups and the pale anemones trained about two hoops, one within the other. They take the cloth off to show you the garland, and surely you must pay them a penny for the thought of old England. Yet there are some who would like to spoil this innocent festival. I have heard of some wealthy people living in a vil-

lage who do their utmost to break up the old custom by giving presents of money to all the poor children who will go to school on that day instead of a-Maying. A very pitiful thing truly! Give them the money, and let them go a-Maying as well.

Richard Jefferies was the champion of young children and old customs alike. The Roman Fontanalia, when wells and fountains were crowned, and the people gave thanks for the blessing of water, has survived to the present in certain parts of England. Wells are decorated with elaborate structures of leaves, petals, rice, straw, beans, cones and anything else that grows, pressed into wet clay and arranged in patterns and pictures, interwoven with symbols and texts. The mother-place of well-dressing was Tissington in Derbyshire, where the date of its beginning is a little vague – some give it as 1350, and others 1615, but what do two or three hundred years matter in a tradition which is carried on to this day? A comparable propitiatory offering is that of the fishermen of Weymouth, who

on 1st May put out to sea, leaving garlands of flowers on the waves.

The Festival of the Rose takes place on the fourth Sunday in Lent, when the Pope blesses the Golden Rose. He dips it in balsam, sprinkles it with holy water and incenses it, pronouncing over it several prayers in which Jesus is called the Eternal Rose, that has gladdened and embalmed the heart of the world. The Rose is then presented by the Pope to some distinguished person he wishes to honour.

The Rose was also part of the celeb-

Left: *The May Day Polkas*. Victorian sheet music cover. Victoria and Albert Museum. A lively depiction of May Day revels. The traditional green man or Jack-in-the-green, usually a chimney-sweep, dances, preceded by blackamoors ringing bells and banging shovels.

Below: *Philo Day – Mourning Day*. Artist unidentified. 1825. Ink on silk. The tomb, its pensive mourner, the drooping plants, withering oak and weeping willow are all reminders of the transitory nature of earthly life.

rations at St Paul's, on St Paul's day, when the Dean and Chapter of the Cathedral were 'apparelled in coaps and vestments with garlands of roses on their heads'; 'a probable relic of this custom', as John Stow says, 'may be traced in the fact that the Judges, the Lord Mayor, the Aldermen, Sheriffs, and Common Councillors, when they attend Service at the Cathedral on the Sunday after Easter, and on Trinity Sunday, with many of the Clergy, carry each of them a bouquet of flowers in their hands, which they either leave

behind after the service, or give to the Choristers or female members of the congregation'.

On 12 July, the Vintners' procession took place. The Master, Wardens, and members of the Worshipful Company of Vintners went in state to a service at the church of St James, Garlickhithe, in the City of London. They were preceded by two wine porters sweeping the street with besoms. Then followed the beadle, the stavesmen, the swan-marker, and the barge-man. The officers carried bunches of scented flowers, which, with the sweeping of the besoms, were reminders of the filthy state of the streets at the time of Edward III, in whose reign the company received its charter.

In the changing state of society most of these old customs are discontinued – some survive, like the Lord Mayor's Show, others may be revived, and so it is impossible to state with certainty whether or not some ceremony may be seen in its time-honoured setting.

In the city of Exeter, for example, on the third Tuesday in July, a huge white stuffed glove, decorated with flowers, was hung on the front of the Guildhall. This was to signify that the Lammas Fair was on. Lammas or Loaf-mass Day, on 1 August, was the day of first-fruit offerings, the harvest festival, when a loaf made from the first ripe corn was given to the priests in lieu of the first-fruits. A Lammas apple was an early apple, ripened by Lammas day. Harvest festivals are still held in churches, and sometimes in the village pub, but the Lammas Fair has long been discontinued, and the decorated Glove outlived and recorded the vanished delights of the Fair. It was tied on the end of a long pole, and carried to the site of each of the four city gates. Afterwards it was hoisted on to the Guildhall where it remained for three days.

In farms and gardens the Romans grew beds of hyacinths, narcissi, violets and roses, especially to weave into chaplets and garlands for religious ceremonies. Sometime flowers were grown in window boxes, and all would be sold in the flower-markets. The Greek and Roman marriage custom of strewing flowers before the bridal pair was taken over by

Top left: *The Path of Roses*, by W. F. Yeames. A young couple exchanging the primrose path of dalliance for the path of roses which lies invitingly before them.

Far left: Well-dressing at Hope, Derbyshire, England. There are two distinct schools of well-dressing; some are designed entirely with petals, others with flowers, mosses, bark, dried peas and beans, shells and stones.

Above: Herb-woman and her six maids strewing herbs. The Coronation of his Sacred Majesty King George IV solemnized in the Collegiate Church of Saint Peter, Westminster, upon the nineteenth day of July, 1821. Sir George Naylor, 1837.

Left: *The Milkmaids' Garland or the Humours of May Day*, by Francis Hayman (1708–1776). On the first of May, and the five or six days following, the milkmaids, finely dressed, carrying on their heads a number of vases and silver vessels in a pyramid with ribbons and flowers, danced to the music of a fiddle from door to door.

143

the Christians. The strewing of herbs and flowers, and sometimes rushes, by young girls, from the homes of the betrothed couple up to the church door, has been mentioned in many an old verse or play, such as this scene from *Ram Alley, or Merry Tricks*, an anonymous play of 1636.

(Enter Adriana, and another, strewing herbs.)
ADRIANA: *Come straw apace, Lord shall*
                            I never live
To walke to Church on flowers? O 'tis fine,
To see a bride trip it to Church so lightly,
As if to see her new Choppines would scorne
     to bruze
A silly flower.

Or another by Braithwaite, of 1615.

   All haile to Hymen and his Marriage day,
   Strew rushes and quickly come away;
   Strew rushes, Maides, and ever as you
        strew,
   Think one day, Maides, the like will be
        done for you.

After the ceremony, the showering of the bride and bridegroom with flower petals gave place to the shower of rice to denote plenty, and this in turn to paper rose petals and confetti, the latter custom much deprecated by the clergy.

The small posy carried by the bride was once of simple country flowers with often a slip of gorse included, alluding to the saying that 'when furze is out of bloom, kissing is out of season'. Victorian wedding bouquets were more elaborate, and usually included orange blossom, an emblem of chastity formerly denied to undeserving cases.

When Aphrodite rose from the waves, the Hours preceded her with a garland of myrtle, and thus the myrtle became a necessary part of a bride's bouquet, as an emblem of fertility. This was seldom mentioned by mama and papa. Bridesmaids carried flowers too, as they still do. The bride would often plant her symbolic sprig of myrtle, believing that if it took root it foretold long life and happiness. German brides wore a myrtle wreath, and were often presented with a wreath of vervain, because

it was formerly used as a love-philtre. In England flowers were worn by betrothed couples.

The strewing of herbs in public places was a part of medieval life, not necessarily connected with festivals. In church and in the theatre the floors were strewn for reasons of health, and in *The Gull's Horn Book* the stage was strewn. 'Let our gallant . . . advance himself up to the Throne of the stage; I mean not into the lord's room, which is now but the stage's suburbs; no, . . . but on the very rushes where the comedy is to dance.'

From ancient civilizations until the present time, funeral rites have been accompanied by flowers. Greeks and Romans wore flowers to accompany their dead to the burial. The Egyptians placed wreaths, particularly of mignonette, on the heads of mummies, and these flowers have been found in a good state of preservation. At one period short-lived flowers were replaced by holly, rosemary and other evergreens, and later by everlastings and immortelles. In some countries herbs were planted, basil, sage and rosemary to sweeten the journey of death. Flowers were dropped into open coffins. When, in *Cymbeline*, Arviragus weeps over the body of his sister Imogen, who, disguised as the youth Fidele, he believes dead, he says,

   With fairest flowers
Whilst summer lasts, and I live here,
     Fidele,
I'll sweeten thy sad grave: thou shalt not
     lack
The flower that's like thy face, pale
     primrose, nor
The azured harebell, like thy veins; no,
     nor
The leaf of eglantine, whom not to
     slander
Out-sweeten not thy breath; the ruddock
     would
With charitable bill, O bill, sore-
     shaming
Those rich-left heirs that let thy fathers
     lie
Without a monument! bring thee all this;
Yes, and furr'd moss besides, when
     flowers are none
To winter-ground thy corse.

In some country towns and villages the death of an unmarried girl was marked by a procession which preceded the coffin. One young woman wore a garland of flowers and herbs from which hung two black ribbons signifying our mortal state, and two white ones as an emblem of innocence and purity. The ends of these were held by four girls, while two more strewed their path with yet other flowers and herbs.

A somewhat similar custom was noted by Washington Irving in his *Sketch Book*. A chaplet of white flowers was carried by a girl nearest in age and size to the dead girl, and this chaplet, after the service, was hung up in the church.

In some parts of Derbyshire these chaplets, made of white paper instead of perishable flowers, and sometimes carrying a pair of white gloves, or a handkerchief or collar on which was written the dead girl's name, were kept permanently hung up in the church, or at least until dust and decay necessitated their removal.

Like the Greeks, the Romans valued the rose as a funeral flower. As an emblem of renewed or reborn life, men and women would leave directions for a rose to be planted on their graves. To them red roses represented a life source. In some parts of Germany a pink was used in season, and forget-me-nots were usually grown on childrens' graves. In Italy it was the periwinkle, death's flower, that was scattered over the small graves, and in France roses and orange blossoms were dropped in their coffins. The homely wallflower was loved as a grave flower by English country folk, who liked to think that they would be greeted at the end of their journey into the unknown by the face, or rather the petals, of an old friend.

No one should ever take a flower from a grave, only perhaps the smallest sprig or leaf, to press and keep in memory of a loved one.

Throughout the year, in times of sorrow and of rejoicing, flowers still play their part. Even at birth, a new baby may be brought a miniature cradle full of tiny flowers. In great national celebrations and in our own small family rites, flowers still mark the milestones of our lives.

A crown of a particular leaf or flower, each with its own symbolism, was the highest award at the athletic games of ancient Greece and Rome. A winner in the Olympic Games was crowned with olive; in the Isthmian Games with pine. In the Pythian Games it might be beech, laurel or palm, and the Nemaean victor wore a crown of parsley. Fashions change. Parsley was held in the highest esteem by the Greeks. At feasts they wreathed their brows with it because they believed that it had the effect of increasing their cheerfulness. Crowns of parsley and of hyacinths were worn by bridesmaids at Greek weddings, when the brides wore crowns of hawthorn blossom. Parsley was also strewn over the dead, and used to decorate their graves. Doubtless the victorious athlete, parsley-crowned head held high above the shouting populace, was a noble sight. Today's hero, similarly adorned, would feel a fool. It is indeed a plant of varied fortune, for not so long ago the parsley bed, as well as the gooseberry bush, was the euphemistic breeding-ground of babies.

In connection with the wearing of hawthorn blossom wreaths by Greek and Roman brides, it is interesting to read in one of the Floral Language books that 'The Romans accounted it [the hawthorn] a symbol of marriage because it was carried at the rape of the Sabines; it was ever after considered propitious', though not, one would imagine, by the Sabine women. The author goes on to say, 'The Turks regard the presentation of a branch of hawthorn as denoting the donor's desire to receive from the object of his affections that token of love denominated a kiss'. Perhaps the hawthorn should be regarded as the poor man's mistletoe.

It has been the strange fate of the myrtle not only to be made the emblem of love and peace, but also to become an emblem of war and death. It was used by the Greeks as a burial plant, together with amaranth. It was also worn by the magistrates of Athens as a symbol of their office, and such was the demand for crowns and garlands of myrtle in Athens, that one quarter of the market-place was devoted to the garland makers

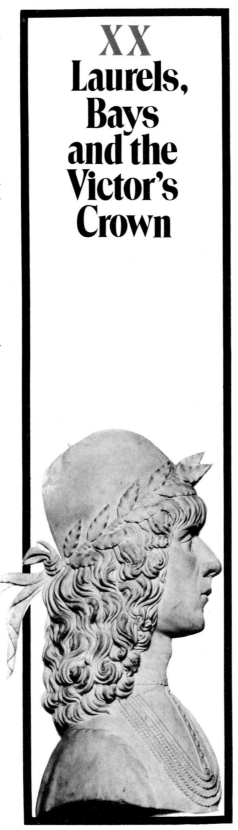

XX
Laurels, Bays and the Victor's Crown

and their wares. It was known as the Murrinae, or myrtle market.

Myrtle boughs were steeped in wine to improve the flavour and bouquet, and so it also became the emblem of festivity. But it was the hardness of its wood, making it suitable for the manufacture of weapons, which finally caused it to symbolize war; and a general who had gained a victory without bloodshed was always crowned with myrtle. The Romans and the Sabines, when at last they were reconciled, laid down their arms under a myrtle bush, and purified themselves with its boughs. Papirius Cursor, who erected the first sundial in Rome, made the myrtle the symbol of the Roman Empire. According to the Arabs, myrtle was one of the three growing things taken by Adam when he was driven out of Paradise: an ear of wheat, the most valuable of all food; dates, the finest fruit; and myrtle, the sweetest-scented flower in the world.

The laurel, or more properly the bay, was sacred to Apollo, the giver of victory, as the olive was the symbol of peace. Both trees played their part in the Daphnephoria, the Feast of the Laurel-bearing, a Greek festival to celebrate Peace and Victory. The procession was led by a youthful priest called the Daphnephorus, the Laurel-bearer, and before him a boy carried a piece of olive-wood made into a standard adorned with the sun, moon and stars, with garlands representing the days. These were followed by a crowd of Theban maidens, crowned with laurel and each carrying a laurel branch, singing hymns to Apollo. 'You may read the history of half the earth in one of those green oval leaves – the things that the sun and the rivers have made out of dry ground . . . There is nothing so constantly noble as the pure leaf of the laurel', wrote Ruskin in *Proserpina*. A laurel wreath was modelled on a Roman coin of 342 BC.

In France, young doctors of physic were crowned with laurel berries (*Bacca lauri*), whence are derived the words 'bachelor' and 'laureate'. Students who have taken their degrees at the University are called bachelors, from the French *bachelier*, which is in turn derived from the Latin *baccalaureus*, a laurel-berry. These students were not allowed to marry, lest their duties as husband and father should take them from their literary pursuits, and so in time all single men were called bachelors.

Roman poets were crowned with bay leaves, Petrarch among them. And if Petrarch, why not Mrs Lennox? There is a charming story of this Mrs Lennox, a minor poet of the eighteenth century, who on the publication of her first novel, *The Female Quixote*, was regaled at a supper given in her honour, with 'a magnificent hot apple pye' stuck with bay-leaves, while no less a person than Samuel Johnson encircled her brow with a laurel wreath prepared by himself.

At one time the laurel must have symbolized virginity. A traditional verse tells of a young man:

> *I had not been in the garden,*
> *Not passing half an hour,*

> *Before I saw two virgins*
> *Sat in a pleasant bower.*
> *The one was lovely Nancy*
> *So beautiful and fair,*
> *The other was a virgin*
> *Who did the laurel wear.*

> *I boldly stepped up to them,*
> *These words to her did say,*
> *'Are you engaged to any young man,*
> *Come tell to me I pray.'*
> *'I'm not engaged to any young man,*
> *I solemnly declare,*
> *I mean to be a virgin*
> *And still the laurel wear.'*

Eliza Cook, Victorian poet and editor of *Eliza Cook's Journal*, was a great one for arboreal symbolism. Her *Complete Poetical Works*, all edges gilt, are generously sprinkled with bays, laurels and cypresses, especially bays.

> *Oh, beautiful Bay, I worship thee –*

Page 145: Francesco Cynthio, Poet Laureate of Ancone. Florentine, 15th century. He wears the laureate's wreath.

Right: Portrait of an unknown lady representing Petrarch's Laura, against a background of laurels, symbolizing glory. Giorgine, *c.* 1506. The Laura of Petrarch's sonnets was believed to be the wife of Hugues de Sade of Avignon, although the poet may have used a fictitious name around which to write of the incidents of his life and love.

Far right: *The Rape of the Sabine Women*, by Peter Paul Rubens (1547–1640). A notable incident in the legendary history of early Rome. Romulus, requiring wives for the men of his new city, invited neighbouring tribes to a celebration of games, and the Roman youths carried off a number of Sabine virgins.

I homage thy wreath, I cherish thy tree.
And of all the chaplets Fame may deal
'Tis only to this one I would kneel.

It is pleasant to think that Eliza achieved her bays, for she was a close runner-up in popularity with Mrs Hemans of 'Casabianca' fame. And if today her chaplet is a little dusty, in her time she gave, as she hoped to give, pleasure to hundreds of fluttering hearts.

But the withering of bay trees was an omen of death. ''Tis thought the king is dead; we will not stay, The bay trees in our country are all withered', says the Captain of a band of Welshmen in answer to Salisbury's invitation to 'stay yet another day', in *King Richard II*. The superstition that the bay trees in a country withered just before the fall or death of the king had been current in the days of the Roman Empire. In the year 1399, when Richard was deposed, the bay trees withered and grew again.

A chaplet of oak leaves was awarded to the Roman soldier who saved the life of another. They considered it the greatest of all awards, but in order to attain it, the candidate must be a citizen, and must have killed an enemy or saved a Roman life. It was awarded to Cicero for his detection of Catiline's conspiracy. Scipio Africanus refused the offer after having saved his father's life on the field of Trebia, because he considered the action its own reward. Oak leaves were also worn at the festival of Ceres, because acorns were man's food before corn was cultivated. Montesquieu said that it was with two or three hundred crowns of oak that Rome conquered the world. In *Coriolanus* Shakespeare says, 'To a cruel war I sent him, from where he returned his brows crowned with oak'. So said Volumnia of her gallant son. The helmet of the Black Prince had a coronet of oak leaves.

Trials of intellectual skills were held for many years in medieval France, in the Floral Games of Toulouse, so called because the prizes competed for were the Golden Violet, for the best song, the Silver Eglantine, for the best pastoral poem, and the Yellow Acacia for the best ballad. These symbolic flowers, more than a foot high, were set upon silver-gilt pedestals upon which the arms of the city were engraved. These splendid trophies were the gift of Clemence Isauré, a poetess who died in 1540, having bequeathed the bulk of her fortune to the civic authorities to be expended in prizes for poetry in fêtes to be held on the 1st and 3rd of May.

It is said that in her youth Clemence had been imprisoned, and had lightened the weary hours by sending her chosen flower, the violet, to her knight Raymond, to wear in her honour. Clemence was buried in the church of La Daurade, and her gold and silver flowers were

preserved on the high altar. The competitions were known to have taken place at least two hundred years before Clemence Isaure revived them, and they continued until 1694 when the Jeux Floreaux merged with the Academie des Belles Lettres.

Tennyson mentions the symbolic violet in his play, *Becket*, when Eleanor of Aquitaine, now divorced from Louis of France and married to Henry II, speaks in jealousy of Henry's mistress, Rosamund de Clifford, Fair Rosamund.

True, one rose will outblossom the rest, one rose in a bower [here she refers to Rosamund's Bower], I speak after my own fancies, for I am a Troubadour, you know, and won the violet at Toulouse; but my voice is harsh here, not in tune, a nightingale out of season; for marriage, rose or no rose, has killed the golden violet.

The Floral Games were discontinued during the French Revolution, and revived in 1808.

Troubadours wore an emblematic flower, often a wallflower, as they travelled from place to place.

A golden gilliflower today
I wore upon my helm alway,
And won the prize of this tourney,
Hah! ! la belle jaune giroflee.

Geoffrey de Rudel, a twelfth-century troubadour from Provence, in love with the Countess of Tripoli, a lady whom he had never seen, travelled in search of this beauty, bearing the sunflower as his cognizance; for the sunflower was believed to turn its face always towards the sun, as he, Rudel, turned his towards his beloved. After many adventures Rudel fell ill, and on reaching Tripoli he died, but not before seeing the face of his unknown love. Browning told his story in *Rudel to the Lady of Tripoli*, and describes the sunflower in Rudel's dying words:

. . . in the lost endeavour
To live his life, has parted, one by one,
With all a flower's true graces, for the
grace
Of being but a foolish mimic sun,

148

With ray-like florets round a disk-like
face –
. . . I, French Rudel, chose for my device
A sunflower outspread like a sacrifice
Before its idol . . .
Say, men feed
On songs I sing, and therefore bask the
bees
On my flower's breast as on a platform
broad . . .

The wearing of wreaths was not only a sign of joyous celebration, for the willow, cypress and yew were tokens of mourning. Disappointed lovers in Elizabethan times, it seems, wore wreaths of willow. Fuller, in his *Worthies* says, 'A sad tree whereof such as have lost their love make them mourning garlands', and in Massinger's *Maid of Honour* Sylli says,

If you forsake me,
Send me word, that I may provide a
willow garland
To wear when I drown myself.

Another of the love-lorn receives a willow garland sent for a New Year's gift.

A willow garland thou didst send,
Last day perfum'd to me,
Which did but only this portend,
I was forsook of thee.

Since that it is I'll tell thee what,
Tomorrow thou shalt see
Me wear the willow, after that
To die upon the tree.

As beasts unto the altar go,
With garlands, so I
Will wear my willow wreath also
Come forth and sweetly die.

The traditional song says,

It's all round my hat, I will wear a green
willow,
It's all round my hat for a twelvemonth
and a day;
If anyone should ask you for the reason
why I wear it,
O tell them I've been slighted by my own
true love.

The reader of the Elizabethan poets,

therefore, must reluctantly be convinced that the willow is an emblem of self-pity, although the Language of Flowers gives it as mourning. Apparently about one third of the population of that age was jilted or unloved, and instead of taking practical steps to remedy the situation, they seemed to spend their time weaving willow garlands, decorating their hats with its leaves, singing sad songs about it, or hanging their harps on its branches. It was obviously a valuable outlet for those with nothing better to do, of whatever rank in society; for Desdemona, telling of her mother's love-sick maid, Barbara, says,

She had a song of 'willow',
An old thing 'twas, but it expressed her
fortune,
And she died singing it.

Sir Philip Sidney's sister wrote a touching verse in memory of her beloved brother.

Break now your garlands, oh ye shepherd
lasses,
Since the fair flower that them adorned
is gone;
The flower that them adorned is gone to
ashes;
Never again let lass put garland on!
Instead of garland, wear sad cypress now
And bitter elder, broken from the bough.

One more sad shepherd must suffice. He is Aeglamour, Ben Jonson's Sad Shepherd, who tells of how Earine the Beautifull had been 'strip'd of her garments, to make Maudlin's daughter Douce, the Proud, appear fine'. Earine had been shut up in a tree as Maudlin's son's prize, 'if he could winne her; or his prey if he would force her'. But now the wretched Earine was reported drowned in passing over the Trent some days before.

AEGLAMOUR: *A Spring, now she is*
dead: of what, of
thornes?
Briars and Brambles?
Thistles? Burs and
Docks?

Cold Hemlock? Yewgh?
the Mandrake, or the
Boxe?
These may grow still;
but what can Spring
beside?
Did not the whole Earth
sicken when she died?

To wear a green chaplet may be a sign of mourning, but if a girl is 'given a green gown', all it signifies is a romp in the hay; a romp, however, that might possibly go beyond the bounds of innocent playfulness. Peter Pindar wrote in *Old Simon* of a really nice girl, Narcissa.

Had any dared to give her a green gown,
The fair had petrified him with a frown –
Pure as the snow was she, and cold as ice.

(Narcissa, as I said, was really nice.) Guests at Roman feasts wore garlands of flowers tied with the bark of linden or lime, to prevent intoxication. The image of Bacchus, the wine god, which presided over their feasts was ivy-crowned – not as a symbol of drunkenness as might appear, but because ivy was believed to be an antidote. But although the making of crowns and garlands was such a thriving business in ancient civilizations, it was only during festivals and sacred rites, or when setting out for battle, that they might be worn. Romans went bare-headed on all other occasions, and indeed, were liable to punishment if they appeared in public garlanded at other times. It was, however, the custom to throw garlands to actors on the stage when their performance pleased the public, a custom which has come down to the present time, for ballet dancers and opera singers, at least.

The eighteenth century clung to its sad cypress until the emblem of the urn with its drooping female supported by over-developed cherubs has come to be regarded as the symbol of the period. The gaiety of the garland withered and died earlier, leaving death itself with its cypress and willow to remain green for a few more years. But even death must die, and with it, the ceremonial garland – a matter for regret or celebration?

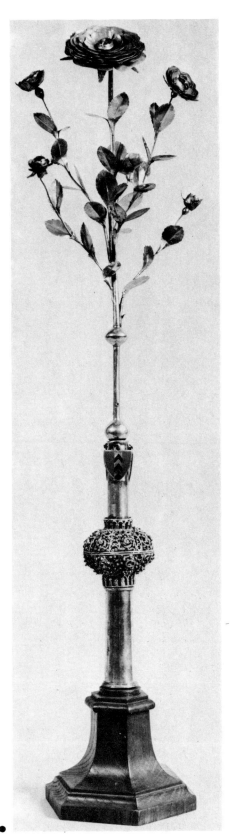

The Golden Rose of the Treasury of Basle. At Easter the Pope presented a golden rose tree to high-ranking persons whom he wished to honour. This is the oldest known rose, possibly given by Clement V (1305–1314) to the Bishop of Basle, and made by an Italian goldsmith in Avignon.

already adopted the white rose as her emblem. In due course it was inherited by her son, who became Edward I and had as badge 'a rose with stalk green, and petals gold'. It first appeared on the great seal of England in the reign of Edward IV, and it is to be found on all the great seals of all the succeeding monarchs down to James II. It appeared on coinage as the rose-noble of Henry VI. Of Edward IV it was said, 'He rent the crown from the vanquished Henry's head, Raised the white rose, and trampled on the red'. The white rose became the badge of the unhappy house of Stuart, and the 10th of June was celebrated as White Rose Day, that being the birthday of the Old Pretender, James Francis Edward, son of James II.

As an example of the bitter feelings aroused by the display of these political flowers, there is an interesting passage in the diary of Michael Kelly, a famous opera singer. In 1789 he and his leading lady, Mrs Crouch, who was for a short time a favourite of George IV, when he was Prince of Wales, were engaged to sing in Paris, where they visited the Opera on their arrival.

> The first night we went to the Grand Opera, Mrs. Crouch, who was seated in a box in a conspicuous part of the house, had the eyes of the parterre turned on her, the audience seemingly staring at her with displeasure and whispering to one another. A gentleman in the box with us explained the cause; poor Mrs. Crouch, quite unconscious of the impropriety, wore a white rose in her hair, which was the royalist colour. She was on thorns until she had quitted the box, but met with no insult, which was singular considering how completely the dominion of anarchy and tumult had brutalized the people.

The most ancient of all emblems, the thistle, was used as a badge and name of an order of knighthood instituted by King Achaius, when he obtained a victory over Athelstan, the grandson of Alfred the Great. The earliest known mention of the thistle as the national emblem of Scotland, however, is in the inventory

of the effects of James III, who probably adopted it as an appropriate illustration of the royal motto, 'In Defence'. Thistles occur on the coins of James IV, Mary, James V and James VI. On those of James VI they are for the first time accompanied by the motto, *Nemo me impune lacesset*, 'No one injures me with impunity'. A collar of thistles appeared on the bonnet pieces of James V in 1539, and the royal ensigns were also surrounded by golden thistles.

This 'very wasp of flowers', so legend has it, was chosen for Scotland's emblem because the Danes, stealing by night into the camp of the sleeping Scottish soldiers, were defeated when one of their number, having trodden with bare foot on the sharp spines of a thistle, cried out, and so warned the sleepers of their danger.

Queen Anne revived the Order of the Thistle in 1703. The star consists of a St Andrew's cross formed of silver embroidery, in the middle of which is a gold and green thistle. The collar is formed of thistles, intermingled with sprigs of rue – the one full of prickles and not to be touched, the other 'good against serpents and poyson'.

The 'green immortal shamrock' is worn throughout the world, wherever Irish feet may wander, on 17 March, St Patrick's Day, in commemoration of his landing at Wicklow at the beginning of the fourth century; although no one, least of all the Irish, can agree which of the trefoils is the true Irish shamrock. Only St Patrick could answer that, for it was when he first preached the Gospel to the heathen Irish that he stooped and picked up the little three-leaved plant at his feet, to demonstrate the mysteries of the doctrine of the Trinity, the Three-in-one. The four-leaved clover was believed to represent the Cross, and so was supposed to guard against evil. Thus it grew to be a lucky mascot. The Order of St Patrick was instituted by George III in 1783. On the jewel of the order is a wreath of shamrocks.

The earliest reason given for the Welsh having been saddled with the unlikely emblem of the leek is that when the Saxons invaded Wales in the sixth century, the men fighting under King Cad-

wallader were ordered by St David to wear leeks on their caps, to distinguish them from the enemy. They conquered the invaders, and so celebrate each anniversary on 1 March, dedicating the day to St David. Shakespeare knew of this emblem, and in *Henry V*, Act IV, Scene 7, Fluellen says to the king, 'If your majesties is remembered of it, the Welshmen did good service in a garden where leeks did grow, wearing leeks in their Monmouth caps; which, your majesty know, to this hour is an honourable badge of the service; and I do believe your majesty takes no scorn to wear the leek upon St. Tavey's day.'

Green and white are the Welsh colours, and we find in an ancient manuscript in the British Museum,

> I like the leeke above all herbes and
>   floures;
> When first we wore the same, the field
>   was ours,
> The leeke is white and green, whereby is
>   meant
> That Britaines are both stout and
>   eminente.
> Next to the lion and the unicorne
> The leeke the fairest emblym that is
>   worn.

However, the more socially acceptable daffodil was officially adopted as the national flower of Wales at the investiture of Edward, Prince of Wales, in 1911.

The iris symbol appeared on the crown of Charlemagne, and of Edward the Confessor. It was also one of the devices embroidered on the border of the Bayeux tapestry. It was adopted for the French by Louis VII, during his second Crusade, which commenced in 1145. Louis IX took it over in 1226. It then became known as the *fleur de Louis*, with its corruptions *fleur de luce* and *fleur de lys*. In *Henry VI*, Part I, Joan of Arc cries,

> Here is my keen-edged sword
> Deck'd with fine flower-de-luces on each
>   side.

'I cannot describe them more than they have been by others, as to the preheminence of them', wrote Stephen Blake in

Right: L'unique pensée de la France'. Bibliothèque Nationale, Paris. This and other violet cards concealing Napoleon's profile, with that of the Empress Louise and the King of Rome, were circulated in France about 1815. After his exile in Elba he was known as Caporal Violette, or Papa la Violette.

Below: *Portrait of the artist with a sunflower*, by Sir Anthony van Dyck (1599–1641). A great artist and a handsome flower – a flower that was said always to turn its face to the sun. After van Dyck's death, Charles I, awaiting his execution, wrote from his prison,
  The sunflower obeys the sun
  More than my subjects me have done.

The Complete Gardener's Practice (1664), 'the King of France's Arms is a witnesse, and our English Quoin is a testimony that this flower is or was in great estimation: Farther consider, that no inferior person dare put this flower in his Coat of Arms, though he may put it in his garden.' When the iris was placed on the sceptre of the French kings, the three large petals represented faith, wisdom and valour. The Bourbon lilies were interchangeable with the fleur-de-lys, and a sort of lily–iris symbol was employed. The violet was to Greece what the rose became to England and the fleur-de-lys to France. Macaulay wrote of Athens as 'the city of the violet crown', and in all seasons violets were sold in the marketplace, even when the ground was covered with snow, it is said. Ruskin, however, mentions in a letter, 'It is one of my little pet discoveries that Homer means the blue iris by the word translated violet'.

Napoleon adopted the violet as his emblem, and he was known affectionately as 'Corporal Violet'. When he was banished to Elba he promised to 'return with the violets'. Byron wrote of Napoleon's taking leave of his adopted country,

> *Farewell to thee, France! but when*
>   *liberty rallies*
>   *Once more in thy regions, remember me*
>   *then;*
> *The violet grows in the depths of thy*
>   *valleys,*
> *Though withered, thy tears will unfold*
>   *it again.*

This Bonapartist emblem was worn on rings and watchchains, and as a buttonhole, even while 'the flowers spoke words too dangerous to say'. They were still the political symbol of the Second Empire when, in 1852, an edict was passed making it 'unlawful to introduce upon any jewel, bracelet, cabinet work or tapestry any representation of the deposed fleur-de-lys', but twenty-two years later, such is the fate of political flowers, the violet itself, and any representation of violets or bees, the emblem of the Bonapartes, was forbidden by decree of the Third Republic – a decree,

as a writer of the time remarks, 'almost as difficult to enforce as to forbid bees to fly or violets to bloom'.

The cornflower, *die Kornblume*, was the favourite flower of Kaiser Wilhelm I of Germany. When his mother, Queen Louise of Prussia, was forced by Napoleon to leave Berlin, she took refuge in a cornfield, and in order to amuse her young children, she made them wreaths and crowns of cornflowers. In memory of that day her son, Wilhelm, the first Emperor of a united Germany, chose the cornflower as his emblem. It was also known to the country people as *Flockenblume*, or flake flower.

Alphonse Karr, one-time editor of *Figaro*, also wrote of the changing fortunes of the innocent political flower:

> The lilies have not escaped the fate of other political flowers, such as the violet, the imperial (the crown imperial), and the red pink; all have been, by turns, proscribed and recalled, multiplied to excess or pitilessly rooted up, in the flower-beds of the Tuileries, and generally placed under the watchful care of the police, considered as suspicious, hostile to power, and mixed up with several conspiracies. The parties and the men who planted and proscribed them are long since dead, and almost forgotten. And yet, every spring, these poor flowers, returned to private life, continue to bloom again in their proper seasons.

Alphonse Karr was referring to the Bourbon lily, but it was an orange lily that became a political symbol in Holland, some time before the French Revolution. So bitter became the feeling against the House of Orange in the eighteenth century, that normally sane burgomasters tore up lilies and marigolds from their gardens, and even prohibited the sale of oranges and carrots and the bulbs of the offending orange lilies in the markets. In Ireland, too, these same unfortunate flowers became a challenge when worn by the Irish Protestants, who had been christened the Orangemen owing to their adherence to William III; and many a broken head

resulted from the flaunting of an orange lily. There was a time when Catholics planted white lilies in their gardens and Protestants orange-coloured ones. If only battles might be fought with flowers in that unhappy country –

> *Unhappy! shall we never more*
> *That sweet militia restore,*
> *When gardens only had their towers,*
> *And all the garrisons were flowers;*

But today, in the Irish Republic, it still might be wiser to suppress this political flower.

Few people now would feel very strongly about the wearing of an oak apple, or a sprig of oak leaves, on Oak Apple Day. When Charles II returned from exile on his birthday, the Royalists displayed branches of oak to commemorate the battle of Worcester, when the young Prince Charles had lain concealed in an oak tree at Boscobel. From his insecure hiding-place, Charles, and Colonel William Carlo with whom he hid, could watch the soldiers searching for him below, and overhear the curses heaped upon him for giving them so much trouble. The battle was fought on 3 September 1651, but Oak Apple Day was celebrated on Charles's birthday, 29 May.

If flowers could feel surprise, the tulip might well have been a little astonished to find herself in company with a lord of the manor of Wimbledon, by name General Lambert, featured as the Eight of Hearts in a pack of satirical playing cards. This most able general of the Commonwealth and Protectorate, having become estranged from Cromwell, withdrew from political life, and spent his time rather more happily in his garden where, it was said, he grew the finest tulips and gilliflowers for miles around. It was to his unwonted passion for the sequestered life that he owed his full-length portrait, holding a tulip in his right hand, with the title, 'Lambert, Kt. of ye Golden Tulip', beneath.

It is a forgotten fact that the lotus, that most mystic of all flowers, became a messenger during the Indian Mutiny in 1857. The lotus flower was passed from hand to hand among the conspirators to spread news of the revolt, and to rally the Indians to take part in the rebellion. A late arrival on the political scene is the primrose, the Tory emblem, a somewhat simple and unsophisticated flower to be associated with Disraeli of the spit-curls. Was it really his favourite flower, or did he think the choice would go down well with Her Majesty? A zinnia would have better fitted the man, though not, perhaps, the party.

And here, is it an impertinence to allow one small, elusive scarlet flower to find a place among these historic figures with their legendary hawthorn and broom, their emblematic roses and proud fleur-de-lys? I refer, of course, to the inimitable Scarlet Pimpernel. Fictional character though Sir Percy Blakeney may be, he was tall and brave and handsome. There was a time when I wouldn't have swapped him for half a dozen of those Frenchies – the Bourbons with their lilies; the Sun King, with his symbolic sunflower; the Little Corporal with his violet – the Scarlet Pimpernel outshone them all in at least one pair of eyes. ●

The gateway of Christ's College, Cambridge, showing the Tudor Rose, adopted as the national badge of England by Henry VII in 1486.

Frozen flowers – flowers frozen in metal, in wood, in glass, in paper, miracles of art and craft, with the life strained out; each and every one of them having less of the essential flower than the smallest chickweed.

To make a flower is beyond our powers, although we can help and encourage flowers to grow. Even given the ingredients of earth and air, sunshine and the moon's influence, and using all the elements at nature's disposal we still could not make so much as a petal. To create a flower in metal or wood, in porcelain or in glass, in paper, or wax, or feathers, or shells, is to make not a flower, but the pattern of a flower. The green magic is missing. Yet men have never ceased to try, and their attempts have added another dimension that a living flower has not. A craftsman's flower, probably of greater perfection than the living model, is frozen in time – a sleeping beauty never to be awakened.

The jewelled flowers of Peter Carl Fabergé, goldsmith and jeweller to the Russian Imperial Court, have a delicacy that had never been equalled. A spray of cornflowers and some buttercups; a sprig of philadelphus; two rosebuds; or a single poppy with its bud, each negligently aslant in their rock-crystal vases, have a deceptive simplicity. The forms are naturalistic, the flower apparently carelessly dropped into a small pot, but there nature and Fabergé part, and the rest is pure fantasy. The golden stems twist and turn, the nephrite leaves curl, and the petals, each one enamelled in translucent blue, in yellow and mauve and pink, or carved in rhodonite or chalcedony according to their kind, are centred with diamonds or rose diamonds. Fabergé, it is said, could choose from 150 shades of enamel.

A spray of gypsophila in rose diamonds, green enamel and gold is so delicately made that it moves in the slightest current of air. We see a dandelion puffball, made of strands of asbestos fibre, spun platinum and rose diamonds, and we are afraid to breathe. They are, what Fabergé intended most of them to be, flowers for queens.

During the First World War, Fabergé's workshops were given over to the mak-

XXII
Flowers and the Craftsmen

ing of small arms and copper and aluminium parts for projectiles, and medical supplies. When the Bolsheviks took over in September 1918, Fabergé left Russia. He died on 24 September 1920, in Lausanne.

It is a long step from the enamelled fantasies of Fabergé to the scientific models of flowering plants, some of them with their attendant pollinating insects, made in glass by Leopold and Rudolph Blaschka for the Botanical Museum of Harvard University.

Leopold Blaschka, founder of the highly skilled art of representing natural history objects in coloured glass, was born in northern Bohemia in 1822. Workmanship in decorative glass was a tradition of the Blaschka family, who originally came from Venice. During a voyage in a sailing ship to the United States in 1853, Leopold made many drawings of the marine invertebrates which he collected, and from these he constructed glass models for the Natural History Museum in Dresden. His son Rudolph became his only assistant.

Father and son were working together in their studio near Dresden on models of extreme delicacy, made in glass and representing jelly-fish and other marine subjects, when they were approached by Professor Goodale of Harvard University, who persuaded them, not without difficulty, to embark on the incredible collection of several thousand models of flowers, each one scientifically accurate, and artistically beautiful. Perhaps this series of glass models comes nearer to the living flowers than we shall find in any other medium.

The entire collection was a gift to the University from Mrs Elizabeth Ware and her daughter, as a memorial to Dr Charles Eliot Ware, and although glass models of the Blaschkas' marine forms are to be seen in a large number of museums, their models of flowers and plants are only to be found in the Botanical Museum of Harvard University. The Ware collection is unique in that it contains specimens illustrating 164 families of flowering plants, a selected group of cryptograms illustrating complicated life histories, a group of models showing the relation of insects to the transference of pollen, and a group of rosaceous fruits illustrating the effect of fungus diseases. The glass flowers of Leopold and Rudolph Blaschka, made by father and son over a period lasting from 1887 to 1936, are a fascinating marriage of science and art.

It may be that glass, however skilfully contrived, is not the most sympathetic medium for the flower-craftsman to use. Perhaps in man's failure to make a flower, he comes nearest to his aim in the craft of wood-carving, for his material once possessed the green life that now evades him. From the medieval carvings of vine and oak and berry in our churches and cathedrals, to the delicate flowery garlands of Grinling Gibbons, something of the tree lies captured, like a hamadryad, in the convolutions of its grain, and life comes a little nearer. The wood-carver certainly retained a close relationship with one herb, the *herbe aux charpentier*, carpenter's wort, which is the old name for yarrow, or *Achillea*. The wounds of all wood-carvers and carpenters may be healed by the *Achillea*, which grew from the rust scraped from the spear of Achilles, which he used to heal the wounds of Telephus, King Priam's son-in-law.

Mrs Delany was what might be described as a 'late flowerer', for her collection of paper-mosaic flower pictures, which started in 1773, when she was already seventy-three, continued until her eighty-second year. According to Horace Walpole, Mrs Delany invented this art, in which coloured papers were cut to the shape of the many parts, arranged and superimposed, with often a transparent layer over a part to give a softness to the whole. Pasted on to a black background, they were only seldom touched up with paint. Neatly and accurately labelled, following the recently published nomenclature of Linnaeus, Mrs Delany's paper herbal was said by Sir Joseph Banks to be the only imitations of nature that he had ever seen from which he could venture to describe botanically any plant without the least fear of committing an error.

The idea which was to grow into the Flora Delanica had started with a glimpse of scarlet. Some red Chinese paper lay on her table, and Mrs Delany, catching sight of a geranium of the same shade, picked up her scissors, cut out some paper petals, and laid them on a black ground. Pleased with the effect, she cut the calyx, stalks and leaves in different shades of green, and pasted them down, and the new work started from that moment. Dr Erasmus Darwin viewed the mosaics with approval.

So now Delany forms her mimic bowers,
Her paper foliage and her silken flowers;
Her virgin train the tender scissors ply,
Vein the green leaf, the purple petals dye.

Poetic licence must, of course, be acknowledged, but the thought will obtrude, that Mrs Delany would have required her scissors to be good and sharp, rather than tender.

There are ten folios of these sensitively composed paper-mosaics in the Print Room of the British Museum, and a few other examples in the Library at Windsor Castle. Mrs Delany has been described as 'an artist between the coolings of her tea'. She collected shells and arranged them in plaster ceilings and in the grottoes which were fashionable in her day. She painted miniature playing cards, and made wonderful hangings for four-poster beds. She copied 'the masters' with skill, and embroidered with taste and patience, and she had a husband who adored her. What more could woman desire? But by 1782 her eyesight began to fail, and the volumes of the Flora Delanica were regretfully closed. She wrote sadly,

The time is come! I can no more
The vegetable world explore –

but the Flora contained 980 specimens, and the exploration could be regarded as one of the triumphs of the period.

The day of the 'accomplished female' was at hand, when the study of botany was expected, a modest repertoire of pieces for the harp or the piano required, songs must be practised, needles prettily employed, and above all, a young lady must be taught to paint; and the most suitable subjects for her brush, or hair-pencil as it was then called,

Left: Buttercup by Fabergé, St Petersburg, *c.* **1900. There is something touching in Fabergé's choice of familiar wild flowers instead of rare exotics for the gifts of royalty. The contrast between the sophisticated workmanship and the simplicity of the flower gives an added dimension.**

Below: *The Myrianthea, or Numberless Groups of Changeable Flowers*, by John Burgis, *c.* 1823. Collection of Mary Hillier. An unfinished arrangement. The flowers on the left are ready to slip into slits which may be seen in the background outline.

Right: Panel of tiles. Dutch, *c.* 1700. Victoria and Albert Museum, London. Dutch flower tiles, like the flower paintings of the same period, are unequalled in European art.

158

were, of course, flowers. The earnest endeavours of the young ladies may have proved almost as ephemeral as the flowers themselves, but a few of their painting instruction books remain, memorials of great charm. John Burgis, who was an instructor of this delicate art, was the inventor and publisher of an ingenious method whereby the pupils might learn not only flower painting, but flower arrangement. The Myrianthea, or Numberless Groups of Changeable Flowers, as it was called, contained seven plates for colouring, which included designs for a hand-screen and a card-rack. A number of flowers already coloured and cut out, or possibly to be coloured and cut out, together with bone spillikins with which to fasten the flowers into their urn or basket with 'taste', is extraordinary effective, and its dedication gave it a sufficient cachet.

To
Her Royal Highness
the
Duchess of Clarence,
Whose Liberally Conceded Patronage
Is Not Only Enhanced by Exalted
Station,
But by Highly Celebrated Taste
And Great Practical Skill in Drawing;
THE MYRIANTHEA,
By Her Royal Highness's Gracious
Permission
Is Humbly Dedicated
With the Most Profound Respect,
And the Most Sincere Gratitude,
By Her Royal Highness's
Most obliged and Devoted Servant,
JOHN BURGIS.

Contained in a cupid-decorated box, with traces of gilt still to be seen, the Myrianthea is undated, but the paper is watermarked 1823.
The care taken with these various artforms was admirable, indeed, incredible. A little book entitled *Wild Flowers and Their Teachings* was published in 1845 and at intervals thereafter, in which moral thoughts and verses alternated with no less than thirty-six pages of separate sprays of pressed flowers, each spray named and described. The books were sold at twenty-five

159

Far left: Eighteenth-century shell flower picture, presented to the Victoria and Albert Museum by Queen Mary. The making of shell nosegays was a popular Georgian pastime, and in the nineteenth century 'Sailor's Valentines' of shell work were brought from Barbados for keepsakes.

Left: Ornament in shell work. Note the passion flower on the left. Early 19th century, American. A fashionable pastime on both sides of the Atlantic. Shells could be bought for the purpose.

Below: English tile: cornflowers and wheat. One of six designed by Walter Crane. Victoria and Albert Museum, London. The flower was given the name of *Centaurea*, from the legend of the centaur Chiron, who was wounded by an arrow poisoned with the blood of the Hydra. He covered his wound with its blue flowers, which have retained their healing properties.

Right: Our Lady's Flowers. G. P. Fauconnet, *Flower-name Fancies*, 1918. Yesterday's flower-seller has a basket of Our Lady's flowers for sale: Lady's Slippers – Cypripedium; Lady's Shoes and Stockings – Birdsfoot trefoil; Lady's Nightcaps Canterbury bells; Lady's Mantle – Morning Glory; Lady's Garters – Brambles; and Lady's Laces – Dodder.

shillings, a high price for a small volume at the time, but one shudders to think of the sweated labour that these innocent-looking gifts must have entailed. Two footnotes are of interest. 'All the plants in this book are named, etc., from Hooker's *British Flora*, and are to be found in the neighbourhood of St Albans.' The second, under Whitlow Grass says, 'This plant grows abundantly on the graves in St Peter's churchyard, St Alban's, and only *on* the graves'. The anonymous compiler writes his preface from St Albans, too. Which leads one to the thought that perhaps these cherished little books were the work of some country vicar with a taste for botany, and that the sweated labour was perhaps, a labour of love.

As the century wore on, the young ladies' floral ingenuity was stretched to breaking point. Flowers were hand-painted on mirrors, on fire-screens, on slippers and fans. They were dried and pressed and framed in neat bouquets, a pleasing craft that has returned to fash-

ion once more. Flowers were counterfeited in shells, feathers and wax, in human hair and horse-hair, and, at their nadir, in Berlin wool. Fresh flowers were worn in the hair, on the bosom, tucked into the belt, and pinned on to furs and feather boas. My grandmother's ball-gowns were often described to me in my childhood, and always they seemed to be dotted with bunches of fresh geraniums, or violets, or philadelphus and maidenhair, or ivy leaves, with matching sprays for her hair, and in a little silver-gilt cornucopia which hooked into her belt, and which I still possess. The descriptions left me with an enchanting picture of grandmother's arrival at the ball, but a sense of misgiving as to her appearance some three or four hours later, when the cotillion was over – a wilting Cinderella. From Fabergé to grandma's, ballgowns is, perhaps, too far to have travelled in so short a space. It is about as far from the true craftsmen to the charming but attenuated efforts of the Interpreters of Flora.

XXIII
Floral
Calendars

LADY'S
SLIPPERS

LADY'S
NIGHT
CAP

LADY'S
THUMB &

LADY'S
LACES
& GARTERS

LADY'S
MANTLE

Time has as many divisions as there are seasons, months, weeks, days and hours, and reading of the past reminds us that a flower can be found to fit each one. The moon, the stars, and the signs of the Zodiac, as we have seen, can be consulted by those with faith. For many of us a flower calendar may hang on the wall to mark the passing days, or at the very least we can refer to the weekly gardening paper to see if it is time to plant the spinach. Time is in close liaison with growth, and repetition is the master of us all. Before the invention of calendars and clocks, the hours of light and darkness and the seasons of heat and cold were seen to be something to hold fast to. Emblems were understood before the written word, for an emblem, after all, is only an ingenious picture representing one thing to the eye and another to the understanding.

With the simple faith of the early Christians, flowers, with their annual miracle, were laid at the feet not only of the saints and martyrs, but of the Virgin herself. A Franciscan friar wrote:

> Mindful of the pious festivals which our Church herself prescribes, I have sought to make these charming objects of floral nature the timepieces of my religious calendar and the mementoes of the hastening period of my mortality. Thus I can light the taper to our Virgin Mother on the blowing of the white Snowdrop, which opens its floweret at the time of Candlemas; the Lady's-smock and the Daffodil remind me of the Annunciation; the Blue-Bell, of the festival of St. George; the Ranunculus of the invention of the Cross; the scarlet Lychnis, of St John the Baptist's Day; the white Lily, of the Visitation of Our Lady, and the Virgin's Bower, of her Assumption; and Michaelmas, Martinmas, Holy Rood, and Christmas have all their appropriate monitors.

In Germany it was the Virgin's Bower, the wild clematis, that sheltered Mary and the Child on their flight into Egypt. Lilies of the valley, *die Maiglockenchen*, little May bells, were dedicated to Whitsuntide.

There is an old verse which gives the flowers connected with the Christian year:

The Snowdrop, in purest white arraie,
First rears her head on Candlemas daie;
While the Crocus hastens to the shrine
Of Primrose love on St. Valentine.
Then comes the Daffodil, beside
Our Lady's Smock at Our Lady-tide.
Aboute S. George, when blue is worn,
The blue Harebells the fields adorn;
Against the day of Holie Cross,
The Crowfoot gilds the flowerie grasse,
When S. Barnabie bright smiles night
*   and daie,*
Poor Ragged Robin blooms in the hay.
The Scarlet Lychnis, the garden's pride,
Flames at S. John the Baptist's tide.
From Visitation to S. Swithin's showers,
The Lillie White reigns Queen of the
*   Floures:*
And Poppies, a sanguine mantle spred
For the blood of the Dragon S. Margaret
*   shed.*
Then under the wanton Rose, agen
That blushes for Penitent Magdalen,
Till Lammas daie, called August's
*   Wheel,*
When the long Corn stinks of Camamile.
When Mary left us here below,
The Virgin's Bower is in full blow;
And yet anon, the full Sunflowre blew,
And became a starre for Bartholomew.
The Passion-floure long has blowed,
To betoken us signs of the Holy Roode.
The Michaelmas Daisies, among dede
*   weeds,*
Blooms for S. Michael's valorous deeds;
And seems the last of floures that stode,
Till the feste of S. Simon and S. Jude –
Save Mushrooms and the Fungus race,
That grow till All-Hallow-tide takes
*   place.*
Soon the evergreen Laurel alone is greene,
When Catherine crownes all learned
*   menne.*
The Ivie and Holly Berries are seen,
And Yule Log and Wassaile come round
*   agen.*

In all Roman Catholic countries Corpus Christi Day was celebrated with flowers strewn along the streets; 'the common wayes with bowes are strewde, and every streete beside, and to the walles and windowes all, are boughes and braunches tide'. In the Churchwardens' Accounts of St Mary at Hill, in the City of London, the following entry occurs: 'For Rose-garlondis and Woodrove [Woodruff] garlondis on St. Barnebes' Daye, XJD'. St Barnaby's Day is 11 June. Evidently the booksellers made the most of their opportunities on saints' days, for in *New Essays and Characters*, by John Stephens the younger (1631), we read, 'Like a bookseller's shoppe on Bartholomew Day at London; the stalls of which are so adorned with Bibles and Prayer-bookes, that almost nothing is left within, but heathen knowledge'.

The monks compiled a flower saints' catalogue for every day of the year, and we find the primrose for St Agatha on 5 February, the heartsease for St Euphrasia on 13 March, and so on, throughout the year. At times it seems that the reverend fathers were a little hard put to it to complete the list. There was no shortage of saints, it is true, but when we find that the Four-Toothed Moss was offered to St Prisca on 18 January, the Alpine Hairy Blue Sowthistle laid before St Rheingarde on 6 June, and the Lurid Iris given to Bishop St Germain on 28 May, we feel that the flower catalogue is getting a little rarified. We long to know the connection between the Bishop and the Lurid Iris. But after searching the monastery garden, or thumbing through the herbals to produce such rarities as the Mixen Mushroom (St Marcellus), the Fennel-leafed Thickseed (St Quintin), and the Pellucid Heath (St Cyril), when the year drew to a close the ingenious fathers were finally defeated. On 31 December for poor St Sylvester, comes the unhappy admission, 'No flower appropriated'. Surely there must have been some small blossom left that could have been offered to a saint on the year's last day?

Many flowers were dedicated to the Virgin, and most of these were given some homely name indicating one of her possessions; her thimble, her cushion, or her slippers.

Lady's Smock – Cuckoo Flower,
    Meadow Cress

William Morris on the Seasons. A page from *A Book of Verse*, presented to Lady Burne-Jones, 1870. Victoria and Albert Museum. William Morris (1834–96), artist-craftsman, medievalist, poet and founder of the Kelmscott Press, was the fiery champion of Art for the People; his aim, 'not to have anything in the house but what one knows to be useful and thinks to be beautiful'.

THE LAPSE OF THE YEAR

SPRING am I, too soft of heart
Much to speak ere I depart:
Ask the summer-tide to prove
The abundance of my love.

SUMMER looked for long am I
Much shall change or ere I die
Prithee take it not amiss
Though I weary thee with bliss!

Laden AUTUMN here I stand
Weak of heart and worn of hand;
Speak the word that sets me free
Nought but rest seems good to me.

Ah, shall WINTER mend your case?
Set your teeth the wind to face
Beat the snow down, tread the frost
All is gained when all is lost.

Our Lady's Mantle – Morning Glory
Our Lady's Ribbons – Ribbon Grass
Our Lady's Laces – Dodder
Our Lady's Nightcap – Canterbury Bell
Our Lady's Thimble – Campanula
Our Lady's Tresses – Quaking Grass
Our Lady's Bedstraw – Galium verum
Our Lady's Cushion – Thrift
Our Lady's Candlestick – Oxlip
Our Lady's Taper – Mullein
Our Lady's Slippers – Cypripedium

Although some flowers were taken from the pagans and given to the saints, at the Reformation their old pagan names were restored, so that we still find names such as Venus' Looking-glass and Venus' Car; and a Protestant writer of the eighteenth century said, 'Botany, which in ancient times was full of the Blessed Virgin Mary, is now as full of the heathen Venus'. Many of St John the Baptist's flowers have discs with ray-like petals, for he inherits his day, 24 June, from Baldur the Beautiful, god of the summer sun. St Christopher takes over the Norse god Odin's flowers, Fleabane, Meadowsweet, Vetch and the Royal Fern, Osmunda. Edward the Confessor, King of the West Saxons, known as St Edward, was given the Crown Imperial as his flower.

In a manuscript dated 1536, in the Library of Balliol College, Oxford, comes a poem in which the Fleur-de-lis is made the image of Christ.

For His love that bought us all dear
Listen, lordings, that be here
And I will tell you in fere
Where-of came the flower delice.

On Christmas night, when it was cold,
Our Lady lay among beasts bold,
And there she bare Jesu, Joseph told.
And there-of came the flower-delice.

Sing we all, for time it is,
Mary hath borne the flower delice.

To the Chinese, every flower has a symbolic meaning, and theirs is the most ancient of all flower calendars. It is said that Ho Hsien-Ku, the Chinese Goddess of Flowers, decreed that reverence should be paid to a special flower for each month of the year. The following are the flowers of the Chinese Floral Calendar.

January – Plum Blossom
February – Peach Blossom
March – Tree Peony
April – Cherry Blossom
May – Magnolia
June – Pomegranate
July – Lotus
August – Pear Blossom
September – Mallow
October – Chrysanthemum
November – Gardenia
December – Poppy

The first chrysanthemum-viewing ceremony in China was held on the ninth day of the ninth month, 2000 BC. In Chinese folklore it is said that two most convenient trees grew at the court of Yao. On one side stood a tree which put forth a leaf every day for fifteen days as the moon waxed, and then, at the waning of the moon, it shed one leaf every day for another fifteen. In this way they measured the months. At the other side grew a tree which put forth a leaf once a month for six months, and then shed a leaf each month until the year was ended. Thus they measured the years. Almost as ancient is the Japanese Floral Calendar, their blooming seasons varying a little according to latitude and location in Japan's long stretch from north to south.

January – Pine
February – Plum
March – Peach and Pear
April – Cherry
May – Azalea, Peony and Wistaria
June – Iris
July – Morning Glory
August – Lotus
September – The Seven Grasses of Autumn
October – Chrysanthemum (as in China)
November – Maple
December – Camellia

Tree peony, *Paeonia suffruticosa*. By a Chinese artist working in Canton and Macao, 1812–1831. The tree peony has been cultivated in China from time immemorial. It was closely guarded in the garden of the Imperial Palace, and did not reach England until 1787. Its Chinese name means 'most beautiful', and it is the symbol of love and affection.

The Seven Grasses of Autumn are the Hagi Bush or Japanese Clover; Susuki Pampas Grass; Kuzu, Arrow-root; Nadeshiko, Wild Carnation; Ominaeschi Maiden Flower; Fujibakama, Chinese Agrimony; and Hirugao, Convolvulus or Wild Morning Glory.

There was also the Festival of the Seven Herbs, the Nanakusa, held on the morning of 7 January, when every orthodox Japanese ate rice-broth which contained Shepherd's Purse, Chickweed, Parsley, Cotton-weed, Radish, *Lamium amilexicula* and Turnip. So solemn was the festival, that in early days the plants were beaten in preparation at different times on the Nanakusa eve, namely:

Parsley – At the hour of the bird (6 p.m.)
Shepherd's Purse – At the hour of the dog (8 p.m.)

delicious picture of the fruits being grown in the English garden of the sixteenth century.

For December and January, and the latter part of November, you must take such things as are green all winter; holly; ivy; bays; juniper; cypress trees; yew; pine-apple-trees; fir trees; rosemary; lavender; periwinkle, the white, the purple, and the blue; germander; flags; orange trees; lemon trees; and myrtles, if they be stoved; and sweet marjoram warm set. There followeth, for the latter part of January and February, the mezereon tree, which then blossoms; crocus vernus, both the yellow and the grey; primroses; anemones; the early tulip; hyacinthus orientalis; chamairis; fritillaria. For March, there come violets, especially the single blue, which are the earliest; the yellow daffodil; the daisy; the almond-tree in blossom, the peach-tree in blossom; the cornelian-tree in blossom; sweetbriar. In April follow the double white violet; the wallflower, the stock gilliflower, the cowslip, flower-deluces, and lilies of all natures; rosemary flowers; the tulip; the double piony, the pale daffodil, the French honeysuckle, the cherry-tree in blossom, the damascene and plumb trees in blossom, the whitethorn in leaf, the lilac-tree. In May and June come pinks of all sorts; especially the blush pink; roses of all kinds, except the musk, which comes later; honeysuckles, strawberries, bugloss, columbine, the French marigold, flos Africanus, cherry-tree in fruit, rasps, vine flowers, lavender in flowers, the sweet satyrian, with the white flower; herba muscaria, lilium convallium, the apple-tree in blossom. In July come gilliflowers of all varieties, musk roses, the lime-tree in blossom, early pears and plums in fruit; gennitings codlins. In August come plums of all sorts in fruit; pears, apricots, berberries, filberts, muskmelons, monkshoods of all colours. In September come grapes, apples, poppey of all colours, peaches, melocotones, nectarines, cornelians, war-

Cotton-weed – At the hour of the rat (midnight)
Lamium amylexicula – At the hour of the bull (2 a.m.)
Turnip – At the hour of the tiger (4 a.m.)
Radish – At the hour of the hare (6 a.m.)

The time for the beating of the Chickweed is not given, but as the ceremony was accompanied by its own songs, it was obviously an exhausting procedure, and it is to be hoped that the resulting broth was found to be sufficiently restoring. At times these ingredients may have been in short supply, for different authorities list different herbs.
The earliest calendars in the west tend to be agricultural rather than floral, although Thomas Tusser, who farmed in East Anglia about 1557, had this advice

for the huswif in his *Five Hundred Points of Good Husbandrie*:

> *In March and in April, from morning to night,*
> *in sowing and setting, good huswives delight;*
> *To have in a garden or other like plot*
> *to trim up their house, and to furnish their pot.*

Many of Tusser's aphorisms, such as 'an ill wind', 'a pig in a poke', and 'a fool and his money', have become part of our language, yet today few of us remember his rough and ready verses, or even his name.
Soon after, in 1597, Francis Bacon's instructions to gardens tell us more of the growing of flowers for their beauty, ignoring the stern necessity of the pot, although he does give us a clear and

dens, quinces. In October and the beginning of November come services, medlars, bullaces, roses cut or removed to come late, holly-oaks, and such like.

John Evelyn's *Kalendarium Hortense, or the Gard'ners Almanac* (1664) tells us what to do 'Monethly, throughout the year, in the Orchard and the Olitory Garden', as well as the 'Parterre and Flower Garden', but his instructions, such as that for February, 'Gather worms in the evening after Raine', and 'Continue Vermine Trapps', are of a practical rather than a romantic nature. Evelyn's Calendar was the fore-runner of a spate of garden calendars, all more or less instructive, and many, like Phillip Miller's *Gardener's Calendar*, published in 1724, are classics in their own right.

It is Linnaeus' *Flower Calendar*, however, that gives the most vivid picture of the year's pattern of growing things. Linnaeus, as always, is a law unto himself, and his time is governed by the rhythm of nature, and not by the regulations of man. It was made in the climate of Uppsala in the year 1755, and differs from other calendars of its kind in as much as the months are divided according to the budding, and the duration of the blossoming, of the flowers. He divides the twelve months thus:

1. Reviving winter month from December 22 to March 19.
2. Thawing month from March 19 to April 12.

SPRING

3. Budding month from April 12 to May 9.
4. Leafing month from May 9 to May 25.
5. Flowering month from May 25 to June 20.

SUMMER

6. Fruiting month from June 20 to July 12.
7. Ripening month from July 12 to August 4.
8. Reaping month from August 4 to August 28.

AUTUMN

9. Sowing month from August 28 to September 22.
10. Shedding month from September 22 to October 28.
11. Freezing month from October 28 to November 5.

WINTER

12. Dead winter month from November 5 to December 22.

The year begins on a cautiously hopeful note.

REVIVING WINTER MONTH

From the Winter Solstice to the Vernal Equinox

12. 22. Butter shrinks and separates from the sides of the tub.
    23. Ash flower buds begin to open.
1. 1. Ice on lakes begins to crack.
    2. Wooden walls snap in the night. Cold frequently extreme at this time, the greatest observed was 55. 7.
    4. Horse dung spirts.

This is followed by a note which says that 'horse dung, in very severe frosts, throws out particles near a foot high, and that no other dung does the like', and we are full of joy that spring is round the corner and the horse dung is spirting. The days move from flower to flower in an endless saraband. The fish spawn. The frog comes forth and the swallow returns. Never has a calendar so teemed with life.

Linnaeus has so calculated this budding and blooming of the flowers that when the first snowdrop buds, the crocus will bud the second day after it, and so on. The hyacinth obediently blooms on the twelfth day. Even the cold weather has a metallic ring that should make us more philosophical when our favourite plants get nipped in the frost.

The lead cold – the brass cold – the iron cold – the very sounds freeze the blood. We hurry to the THAWING MONTH, 'From the first melting of the snow, to the

The month of November as seen through the rose-coloured spectacles of Robert Furber, a Kensington nurseryman, in his *Twelve Months of Flowers*. Hand-coloured engravings after the paintings of Pieter Casteels, 1730. The figures of Leda and the Swan support an urn whose numbered flowers include the Tree Candytuft and the White Egyptian Hollyhock.

1 Ficoides or fig Marigold.
2 White Periwinkle.
3 Earliest flowering Laurustinus.
4 Blew Periwinkle.
5 Tree Candy tufts.
6 Embroider'd Cranes bill.
7 Yellow spik'd Eternal.
8 Strip'd single Anemone.
9 Borage.
10 Thyme leav'd Myrtle.

11 French Marigold.
12 Colchicum Agrippina major.
13 Ilex leav'd Yasmines.
14 Great purple Cranes bill.
15 Arbutus or Strawberry tree.
16 Double Nasturtium.
17 Broad leav'd red Valerian.
18 Myrtle Cistus.
19 Virginian Aster.
20 Campanula Canariensis.

NOVEMBER

21 Pheasants Eye.
22 Perennial dwarf sun flower.
23 Double Feather few.
24 Carolina Star flower.
25 Scarlet Althæa.
26 Spanish white Jasmine.
27 Lavender with divided Leaves.
28 Golden Rod.
29 American Viburnum.

30 Yellow Dwarf Aloe.
31 Single blew Anemone.
32 Purple Ficoides.
33 Ground sell tree.
34 Pellitory with Daisy flower.
35 Scarlet single Anemone.
36 White Egyptian hollyhock.
37 Caper Bush.
38 Dwarf Colutea.

Printed for John Bowles at Mercers Hall in Cheapside.

Parr Sculp

floating of ice down the rivers'. We can afford to linger over the BUDDING MONTH, which takes us 'From the return of the White-Wagtail . . . to the coming of the swallow; or from the first flower to the leafing of the first tree, during the whole time of the flowering of the bulbous violet' (the early name of the snowdrop).

The year is now in full merry-go-round career until, at the REAPING MONTH, 'From the devil's bit to the blow of the meadow saffron', and the SOWING MONTH, 'From the first blow of the meadow saffron to the departure of the swallow', we gradually slow down in the SHEDDING MONTH, when 'From the first fall of the leaves of the trees to the last', we find ourselves back in the FREEZING MONTH, and 'The last green plant', and we reluctantly arrive at the winter solstice.

Even today, country books and flower books continue to be written in calendar form, but no floral calendar can ever rival in beauty Robert Furber's *Twelve Months of Flowers*, illustrated by Pieter Casteels and engraved by Henry Fletcher in 1730. The flower-bordered list of aristocratic subscribers is headed by Frederick, Prince of Wales, who had acquired Kew House and its gardens in the same year. Robert Furber, a Kensington nurseryman 'over against Hyde Park', issued these hand-coloured engravings in book form as an indication of the plants he could supply. The calendar for June shows the first sweet pea, the Purple Sweet Pea, to be offered for sale in this country, and a small and undistinguished flower it is too. Looking at the flower-filled urns which represent December, January and February one feels that sales-talk is nothing new, and that many of his customers might have been subject to more than a few disappointments.

Calendars of flower emblems are rare, but in 1825 *Floral Emblems* by Henry Phillips was published, and it remains quite the most original work of its sort. Henry Phillips, a flower historian, was a friend of John Constable. They first met in the fields outside Brighton, where Constable was painting and Phillips was botanizing. When Constable was at

170

The British Ewer, designed by Henry Phillips to commemorate the birthday of George IV. The date is symbolized by the arrangement of leaves and berries. Phillips does not say whether the ewer was presented to His Majesty. From *Floral Emblems*, 1825.

work on *The Cornfield*, Phillips sent him a list of flowers that might be expected to be in bloom in the hedgerows in the harvest season. Phillips was living in Brighton, having given up school-teaching in favour of botany, horticulture and landscape gardening. He had already designed a layout for the Kemp Town area of Brighton, with villas and gardens and a central park; a plan that was never executed. This was followed by an ambitious design for an Oriental

Garden, centred on a great Conservatory, with a library, museum, and school of science. Again the plan was abandoned, owing to that only too familiar reason, lack of funds. In 1832, Henry Phillips finally achieved at least part of his design, a domed conservatory, pre-dating Paxton's Great Conservatory at Chatsworth by three years.

Then, on 30 August 1833, on the eve of its official opening, Phillips's conservatory crashed to the ground, a heap of twisted iron and splintered glass. He has for memorial only his eight charming and scholarly books, and of these, only *Floral Emblems* concerns us at present.

The author starts with a series of numerical emblems, rather complicated sprays of leaflets and berries, by which any number from 1 to 1,000 may be symbolized. These, with the days of the week and the months of the year, were devised, he says, to enable the reader to record dates by floral symbols. As an example, he gives a striking illustration of the Emblematical British Ewer, on which, by means of his highly decorative floral signs, the date of the birthday of George IV is commemorated. He offers us an ingenious code of leaves for each day of the week, followed by floral emblems for the months, starting with a robin encircled in a garland of tussilage, *Tussilago fragrans*, a refreshing symbol for dreary January. The emblem for December is a holly wreath around a bunch of what Phillips describes as 'mirth-provoking mistletoe'. That Henry Phillips held strong views on the evils of drink is made clear by an illustration entitled 'Delicate and Lasting Pleasures arising from the Cup of Innocence', which shows Everlasting Sweet Peas, *Lathyrus*, arising from a goblet composed entirely of daisies, *Bellis perennis*, and containing, we must believe, nothing stronger than water.

Whether this book of seriously-intended emblems was put to useful purposes it is no longer possible to discover, but it is a charming and unusual gift book for any period, and one of the more innocent diversions of Regency Brighton, after Prinny had become King George IV.

XXIV
Flowers and Plants as Trade Signs

Among the ruins of Herculaneum and Pompeii, a number of shop-signs have been discovered. A few were painted, but as a rule, they were made of stone or terra-cotta, let into the pilasters at the side of the open shop fronts. Later it became the custom for a craftsman's tools to be sculptured on his house-front during his lifetime, and on his grave at death. It may thus be concluded that the shop-signs that became such a feature of the life of the Middle Ages were a development of the Roman custom. It was an effective form of advertisement in a day when few potential customers could read.

One of the most ancient and popular signs, the Bush, to indicate the sale of wine, was certainly known to the Romans. It was a bush, or bunch of evergreens, usually box or ivy, tied to the end of a pole, which gave rise to the proverb, 'Good wine needs no bush'. This bush, mounted on a pole, was depicted in the Bayeux tapestry. It also became the sign of an ale-house, and was known as an Alepole. In the western states of North America at the building of a new small town, a bunch of hay, or evergreens, was hung above a grocery or bar-room door, until such time as a sign-board could be provided. A green bush over a French peasant's door indicated that his vineyard was for sale.

The Myrtle Tree became a rare inn sign, and also the Rosemary Bush, and the Rosemary Branch marked the premises of a vendor of ass's milk in 1769, although the connection between the flower and this bygone trade is not known. The sign of the Green Man is thought to refer to the collector of herbs and simples, who used to distil the volatile oils from mint, thyme and other herbs. An inn would have been a convenient place to set up a still, which would account for the name of the Green Man and Still.

Some say the Green Man is the figure of Jack-in-the-Green, impersonated by young chimney-sweeps who, dressed in green leaves and boughs, led the May-day processions with dancing in the streets. Jack-in-the-Green also made his wild and leafy appearance on Lord Mayor's Day, and on St George's Day,

172

and on one occasion in an entertainment provided for Queen Elizabeth at Kenilworth Castle in 1575. An interpretation of the origin of the sign of the Green Man is given by one Bagford. 'They are called woudmen, or wildmen, thou' at thes day we in ye signe call them Green Men, covered with grene boues: and are used for singes (signs) by stillers of strong watters and if I mistake not are ye sopourters of ye king of Deanmarks armes at thes day; and I am abpt to beleve that ye Daynes learned us hear in England the use of those tosticatein lickers as well as ye brewing of Aele and a fit emblem for those that use that intosticating licker which berefts them of their sennes.' Man's spelling may have changed over the years, but he can still enjoy his 'tosticating lickers' at the Green Man. Yet another suggestion is that the Green Man is the figure of Robin Hood in his coat of Lincoln green.

Flowers as signs are disappointingly few, even for nurserymen, although about 1810 there was a Thomas Bailey at the Hand and Flower, and a Thomas Butler at the Thistle and Crown, both in Covent Garden. The Sign of the Acorne and Ye Signe of the Orange Tree were also used for nursery gardens, but the Hand and Flower more often denoted the ale-houses in the vicinity. The Two Blue Flower Pots was situated in Dean St. Soho, and the Two Flower Pots and Sun Dial near Drury Lane, and it is possible that these also were built on the sites of, or near to, old nursery gardens. There were several Flower Pot signs in London, from one of which, Dorothy Osborne wrote, she wanted to procure a quart of orange-flower water. The sign of the Flower Pot may have been taken from early pictures of the Annunciation, in which lilies were depicted in the hand of the Angel Gabriel, or in a vase at the feet of the Virgin. With the decline of popery, the angel was removed and the lily-pot became a vase of flowers; subsequently the Virgin too was omitted, and there remained only a pot of flowers.

The Flower-Pot that stood at the corner of Bishopsgate and Leadenhall Street remained until 1863, having been given

its death-blow by the introduction of the railway. For a time it languished as the starting-point for omnibuses, but it was finally demolished. The flower-pots depicted were usually flower-vases, and the Sign of a Blue Flower-Pot, or vase, was used by Cornelius a Tilborgh, 'sworn chirurgeon in ordinary to King Charles II, to our late sovereign King William, and also to Her Present Majesty Queen Anne'. As well as the blue vase at his front door in Lincoln's Inn Fields, his customers might recognize the house by a light at night over the door, and a blue ball at the back door. A writing-master of the name of James Seamer flourished in 1676 at the Flower de Luce in Fleet Street, and a similar

sign was used by an oilman of Leadenhall Street some sixty years later. A Blue Flower-de-Luce was the sign of a cabinet-maker near Drury Lane.

The Marigold, or Marygold, arose as a sign from its resemblance to the sun and its rays, and it was chosen to be the sign of the oldest bankers in London, Child's. Francis Child, the founder, was, in the reign of Charles I, apprenticed to William Wheeler, a goldsmith, whose shop stood on the site since occupied by the bank. He married his master's daughter, and thus laid the foundations of his immense fortune.

The Foxglove, source of the drug digitalis, was the sign painted on the shopfront of several apothecaries in France,

although the Coltsfoot seems to have been their official sign. In some Spanish chemists, flowers with medicinal virtues were painted on the walls, and the jars on the shelves contained such nature cures as Syrup of Honeysuckle, Cowslip and Squills.

The rose, as one might expect, turns out to be the most popular flower trade sign. Between 1766 and 1774, Stephen Garraway, Seedsman and Net-maker, kept a shop at the Rose, near the Globe Tavern, in Fleet Street. There was also Theophilus Stacy, at the Rose and Crown, without Bishopsgate. The Rose and Fan, a combination pregnant, one would have thought, with the Language of Love, turns out to have been merely the sign of a

Page 171: An apothecary's elegant bill-head. The names of Linnaeus, Haller, a distinguished Swiss anatomist and botanist (1708–1777) and Cullen, a Scottish physician and chemist (1710–1790), on the books and MS. at the head of the cartouche lend authority.

Left: At the Three Flower Pots. House sign in Dutch tiles, early 17th century. Note the arms of the families of Gorcham and Arkel on either side.

173

Upper right: A Linen Draper's billhead of 1761. The artichoke sign is a reference to the shopkeeper's name, Bigger.

Lower right: One of the many Rose and Crown trade signs. A bill-head of a file-cutter and small-tool maker's firm in the Minories, London.

Opposite above: There are various interpretations of the public house sign of The Green Man. The one here illustrated was possibly one of the Green-men who let off fireworks in the reign of James I. From Joseph Strutt, *Sports and Pastimes of the People of England*, 1903.

Opposite below: Inn sign: the Rose. A modern version of a still popular inn sign.

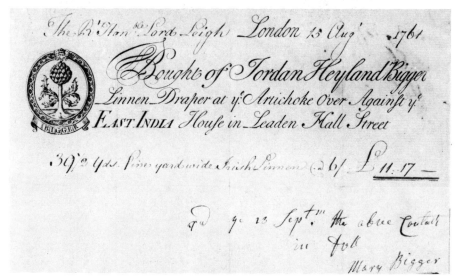

firm of glassmakers and cutters, who, in the eighteenth century, plied their trade at 'ye corner of Fleet Bridge'. Then we find a Rose in Bloom, a Rose and Fowler, and a Rose and Woolpack. Not all of these Roses had a good reputation. The Rose Tavern, in Covent Garden, was a noted place for debauchery in the seventeenth century. In this house, on 14 November 1712, a duel between the Duke of Hamilton and Lord Mohun was arranged, in which the latter was killed. During the reign of Queen Anne the place was still a well-known resort for loose women. It was mentioned in *The Rake Reformed* (1718):

Not far from thence appears a pendant sign,
Whose bush declares the product of the vine,
Where to the traveller's sight the full-blown
  Rose
Its dazzling beauties doth in gold disclose,
And painted faces flock in tallied cloaths.

The Rose in Wood Street was a spunging-house, where persons arrested for debt were kept for twenty-four hours, before they were lodged in prison. These houses were usually kept by a bailiff, and the unfortunate lodger spunged of all his money before he left. 'I have been too lately under their [the bailiffs'] clutches, to desire any more dealings with them, and I cannot come within a furlong of the *Rose spunging-house* without five or six yellow boys [gold sovereigns] in my pocket to cast out those devils there, who would otherwise infallibly take possession of me.' During the Wars of the Roses, the painted roses on the inn signs must have changed complexion on many occasions, according to which way the winds of battle blew. The Rose and Ball combined the Rose as the sign of a mercer, and the Ball, the device that silk dealers formerly hung outside their doors.

Thistle inn signs flourished north of the border, Shamrocks could be seen, and there was a Crown and Leek in Dean Street, Mile End. The possibly unique sign of a Shirley Poppy hangs on the outside of a public house built near the vicarage where the Reverend Wilkes bred the first flowers of that name. Just why the Artichoke, or Hartichook, as Susannah Fordham, owner of a haberdasher's business on 'ye Royall Exchange', called it,

was so popular a sign, cannot be discovered. It may have been the novelty of the plant; but it was used by a hosier, a lace-man, and a linen-draper, as well as by a seedsman. On the board of yet another draper the Artichoke was displayed in the incongruous society of Three Anchors.

Trees found considerable favour among appropriate trades, and we find the Buckthorn standing for apothecaries, the Cork Tree for cork cutters, the Fig Tree for grocers, the Olive and Lemon trees for the Italian warehousemen, the Mulberry for the silk-men, and, almost invariably, the Walnut for cabinet-makers. Painters of signboards themselves needed their own advertisements, and 'Thomas Proctor … announces that he selleth all sorts of signs, Bushes, Bacchus's, Bunches of Grapes', and Wili Steward also painted 'Bushes for Taverns . . . Laurells for Clubs', etc.

Pineapples frequently appeared on the signboards of confectioners, and dyers, scourers and silk dyers were to be found under the sign of the Cherry Tree. There were also punning devices, such as the charming emblem of William Norton, printer, in 1587, a Sweet William emerging from a cask or tun, on which appeared the letters NOR.

Where Olympia now holds its vast trade exhibitions, rare plants from North America, South Africa, Australia, Mexico, Russia, China and the West Indies, and, indeed, from all over the world, were to be seen in the nursery of Lee and Kennedy, under the Sign of the Vineyard. On the site of an old vineyard Lee and Kennedy set up their small nursery, which grew until they eventually produced in their greenhouses the exotic plants for which they became famous, and it was there that the first fuchsia was sold in England. How pleasant it would have been if Olympia had maintained the tradition, and held its exhibitions under the Sign of the Vineyard, or even the Sign of the Fuchsia.

APPENDIX I

The Official State Flowers of the USA and Floral Emblems in Heraldry

Each of the United States has its own emblematic flower, chosen in some cases by schools, and in some by common consent; but the largest number, the 'official' flowers, by state legislature. For instance, in Utah, the crops were destroyed annually between 1840 and 1851 by an infestation of crickets. Food was scarce, and many people were forced to eat the sego lily, which saved their lives. In gratitude, and because of the beauty of its flowers, in 1911 the legislature declared it the state flower of Utah. In Kansas, the status of the sunflower as official flower is older. It was adopted in 1903, because of its vital uses to the early pioneers. A textile fibre was produced from its stems, its leaves were used for fodder, a yellow dye was expressed from its flowers, and from its seeds valuable food and oil. Kansas has become known as the Sunflower State.

The first plant to be made a state symbol in America was the mistletoe. This was in Oklahoma in 1893. The violet grows in such profusion in the American countryside, that it has been adopted by three states: Rhode Island, chosen by the children in 1897, Illinois in 1908, and New Jersey in 1913. Ohio's scarlet carnation was adopted in memory of Governor William McKinley, whose favourite flower it was. The people of Vermont chose the red clover in 1894, because of its value to the farming community. The long-spurred blue columbine speaks to the people of Colorado of the blue skies, snowy mountains and the gold that brought the settlers in 1858. It was not adopted until 1899. Peach blossom was made the emblem of Delaware, the peach-growing state, as early as 1895.

From time to time the choice of flowers may be changed, but the following list has been accepted at the present time:

US State Flowers

Alabama	. .	Goldenrod
Arizona	.	Giant Cactus
Arkansas	.	Apple Blossom
California	.	Californian Poppy
Colorado	.	Blue Columbine
Connecticut	.	Mountain Laurel
Delaware	.	Peach Blossom
Florida	. .	Orange Blossom
Georgia	. .	Cherokee Ross
Idaho	. .	Lewis Mock-Orange
Illinois	. .	Native Wood Violet
Indiana	.	Zinnia
Iowa	. .	Wild Rose
Kansas	.	Sunflower
Kentucky	.	Goldenrod
Louisiana	.	Southern Magnolia
Maine	. .	Pine Cone
Maryland	.	Black-Eyed Susan
Massachusetts	.	Trailing Arbutus
Michigan	.	Apple Blossom
Minnesota	.	Showy Ladyslipper
Mississippi	.	Southern Magnolia
Missouri	.	Downy Hawthorn
Montana	.	Bitter Root
Nebraska	.	Goldenrod
Nevada	.	Sagebrush
New Hampshire	.	Purple Lilac
New Jersey	.	Violet
New Mexico	.	Yucca
New York	.	Rose
North Carolina	.	Dogwood
North Dakota	.	Prairie Rose
Ohio	. .	Scarlet Carnation
Oklahoma	.	Mistletoe
Oregon	.	Oregon Hollygrape
Pennsylvania	.	Mountain Laurel
Rhode Island	.	Violet
South Carolina	.	Yellow Jessamine
South Dakota	.	American Pasque-flower
Tennessee	.	Iris
Texas	. .	Texas Bluebonnet
Utah	. .	Sego Lily
Vermont	.	Red Clover
Virginia	.	Flowering Dogwood
Washington	.	Coast Rhododendron
West Virginia	.	Great Rhododendron
Wisconsin	.	Native Violet
Wyoming	.	Indian Paintbrush
Hawaii	. .	Hibiscus
Alaska	. .	Forget-me-not
District of Columbia		American Beauty Rose

Heraldic Emblems

Although in many English towns and counties trees and flowers are employed in the armorial bearings, Great Britain has not yet adopted the pleasant custom of endowing each county with its own flower. Geoffrey Grigson, in *A Herbal of All Sorts*, suggests that it would be of historic interest if Great Britain, too, had its county flowers, while yet wild flowers find root-room, and before the

Upper right: Worcester. The three pears in the arms of the city are said to commemorate a visit by Queen Elizabeth I.

Centre right: Saffron Walden in Essex proudly bears its castle, now in ruins, and three saffron crocuses, *Crocus sativus*, that once brought prosperity to the town.

Bottom right: Cheltenham. The circle enclosing wavy lines, and supporting a pigeon, represents the mineral waters which made Cheltenham an important spa. Two more pigeons on the shield indicate the belief that the flocking of pigeons around a saline spring led to its discovery.

Upper far right: Dundee. Our Lady's three lilies symbolize the patron saint of Dundee, the third city of Scotland.

Lower far right: Maine. From H. Ströhe, *Heraldischer Atlas*, 1899. In the charter granted by Charles I in 1639 Maine was named 'The Province or Countie of Mayne' because it was regarded as a part of 'the Mayne Lande of New England'. Leading occupations were agriculture, fishing, lumbering, ship-building and commerce.

concrete jungle engulfs us and them forever. He gives an unfinished list of nineteen counties, to encourage us. I quote three: the primrose for Cornwall (runners-up might be the squill and the triangulated leek), the wild daffodil or Lent lily for Gloucestershire, and the fritillary for Oxfordshire. Surely we should add the willowherb for London? Not indigenous, perhaps, but the flower that flew in on the healing country breezes to hide the battle scars of the blitz. Let us show our gratitude in a becoming way.

Meantime, it is encouraging to note that the fruit-growing county of Herefordshire had a wreath of hops with a collar of cider-apples for its sign; and Worcestershire, a pear tree. The three crocuses of Saffron Walden symbolize the saffron trade that one flourished in that district, and three parrot tulips are emblems of the tulip-growing districts of Lincolnshire. In another part of the county, a laurel wreath denotes its association with Lord Tennyson, once the Poet Laureate. Devonshire has the charming emblem of a Dartmoor pony holding a sprig of heather in its mouth; and the borough of Slough has honoured the simple Mrs Sinkins pink, born and bred in a workhouse garden, by incorporating it in its coat of arms.

Buckinghamshire's crest bears a crown from which rises a beech tree, in reference to the beeches of the Chiltern Hills, and Cheltenham has oak trees relating to those that line its wide and pleasant streets. Mansfield, as the chief town in Sherwood Forest, also has an oak, and Crawley New Town has adopted acorns, in reference not only to the forests that once surrounded it, but to the town's spectacular growth. The insignia of the Dorking and Horley Rural District also has twelve golden acorns, representing the twelve parishes of the district, and the motto, *E glande quercus*, 'From the acorn, the oak'. Rutland, also referring to the mighty potentialities within a small compass, used the same symbol. Dundee has for arms a bough-pot of lilies, because the Virgin is their patron saint. A similar device was used by the Crusaders, for the same reason. An old custom prevailed in Scotland

DEI DONUM

whereby each clan wore in its bonnets a distinguishing sprig of some local plant, usually an evergreen, which remained more or less unchanged throughout the changing seasons, so that men linked together for mutual assistance or ties of kinship might the more easily distinguish friend from foe. After the bloody battle of Culloden, the clans were dispersed, but in 1822 the custom was revived for the visit of George IV. Henry Phillips, in his *Floral Emblems* (1825), gives a list of the clans represented at the royal court of Edinburgh on that occasion, and of the emblems worn.

Buchanan	.	Birch
Cameron	.	Oak
Campbell	.	Myrtle
Chisholm	.	Alder
Colquhoun	.	Hazel
Cumming	.	Sallow
Drummond	.	Holly
Farquharson	.	Purple Foxglove
Ferguson	.	Poplar
Forbes	.	Broom
Frazer	.	Yew
Gordon	.	Ivy
Graham	.	Spurge Laurel
Grant	.	Cranberry Heath
Gunn	.	Rosewort
Lamont	.	Crab-Apple Tree
M'Allister	.	Five Leaved Heath
M'Donald	.	Heath Bell
M'Donnell	.	Mountain Heath
M'Dougal	.	Cypress
M'Farlane	.	Cloud Berry Heath
M'Gregor	.	Scotch Fir
M'Intosh	.	Boxwood
M'Kay	.	Bulrush
M'Kenzie	.	Deer Grass
M'Kinnon	.	St John's Wort
M'Lachlan	.	Mountain Ash
M'Lean	.	Blackberry Heath
M'Leod	.	Red Wortleberries
M'Nab	.	Rose Bush Berries
M'Neil	.	Sea Ware Bladder Fucus
M'Pherson	.	Variegated Box
M'Quarrie	.	Blackthorn
M'Rae	.	Club Moss
Menzies	.	Ash
Murray	.	Juniper
Ogilvie	.	Hawthorn
Oliphant	.	Great Maple

DIRIGO

MAINE

H. Ströhe

Robertson	.	.	Fern
Rose	.	.	Briar Rose
Ross	.	.	Bearberries
Sinclair	.	.	Clover
Stewart	.	.	Thistle
Sutherland	.	.	Cats-Tail Grass

In a household notebook, undated and quoted by an author unknown, was found this reference, which shows the profusion of plant sprigs gathered for an important occasion. 'To Donald Bain, for gaddering one greet creel of the Bir-ros [briar rose] flowers against the sword-playing in the Loch of Uvay a mutchkin of whiskey, he being sair wetted and defiled'.

Other plant emblems are found in other parts of the world. The birch tree is the emblem of Russia, the maple of Canada, and the ground-laurel of Nova Scotia. The tulip was the emblem of the Turkish rulers of the House of Osman. The chrysanthemum *Hironishi* is carried on the state crest of Japan. The edelweiss is Switzerland's symbol, and poets as well as historians would have us believe that all self-respecting Swiss maidens should demand of their lovers the flower of the edelweiss gathered from some mountainous crevice, the more inaccessible the better, as a proof of their devotion; although, in these days of equality of the sexes, the maiden would run considerable risk of being told to get it herself. And she probably would, too. It was also, according to a popular German song of the thirties, Adolf Hitler's favourite flower.

The flower that appears most frequently in heraldry is the rose, particularly the Tudor rose. The rose is the flower of English royalty, as the fleur-de-lys and the lily stand for the Bourbon kings of France. Henry III had a golden rose for his badge, and Edward IV a white. Elizabeth I chose for her motto, *Rosa sine spina*, 'The Rose without a Thorn'. The personal flag of our present queen bears an E with a crown above, within a chaplet of golden roses. The red rose still appears in the arms of Lancashire and a number of places in the county, just as the white rose does in the Yorkshire Ridings. So violent was the enmity between the white rose and the red during the

Wars of the Roses, that it has left its mark in today's superstition that it is unlucky to bring bunches of red and white roses into hospitals when visiting the sick.

Edward III added the fleur-de-lys to the shield of England by right of his mother, Isabella of France, during the Hundred Years' War. In 1630 he concluded with the French the peace of Bretigny by which he renounced the French crown. Five years later Charles V of France reduced the number of fleur-de-lys to three, and Henry IV followed suit. James I altered the arrangement of the shield by bringing in the arms of Scotland and Ireland, but it was not until 1801 that the French lily was removed from the British arms. Queen Victoria replaced the fleur-de-lys in her diadem with the shamrock, but the coronets of the younger members of the royal family still combine fleur-de-lys with strawberry leaves. The parents of Joan of Arc were ennobled with the surname of du Lys, and their arms were a crown of lilies above a sword and two lilies on a blue ground.

Washington Irving mentions in his *Sketchbook*, written in 1819, that 'Here [in Stratford on Avon] are emblazoned in stained glass the armorial bearings of the Lucy family for many generations, some being dated 1558. I was delighted to observe in the quarterings the three white luces, a pun on the family name.' When British schools and colleges were under the jurisdiction of the church, Our Lady's lily seemed a suitable symbol, and lilies appeared in the coats of arms of the University of Aberdeen, the schools of Winchester and Eton, and King's College, Cambridge.

Rue is one of the ancient plants employed in heraldry. In 1181, the first Duke of Saxony was given the right to bear a chaplet of rue on his arms. Just over six centuries later, in 1807, the first King of Saxony created the Order of the Crown of Rue. This order was conferred on King George V. When Ophelia said to the wicked Queen Gertrude, 'You may wear your rue with a difference', she was alluding to the Queen's hasty remarriage after the murder of the King, because 'difference' is an heraldic term

for an addition to, or change in, a coat of arms.

The Count of Dunois had the device of a bay-tree, with the motto, 'I defend the earth that bears me', for the bay-tree was believed to shield men from thunder and lightning, witches and devils.

The Prince de Condé, Louis II of Bourbon, known as the Great Condé, who was imprisoned at the time of the Fronde, occupied his time in the Bastille in cultivating carnations, and so his soldiers used the flower as a badge of bravery. The Ronsecco family have a red and white carnation emblazoned on their coat of arms.

Le Nôtre, who planted the gardens of Versailles, Saint-Cloud, the Tuileries and the Champs Elysees, was rewarded by a patent of nobility by Louis XIV. He chose for his arms a cabbage, with a spade and fork for supporters, so that his descendants might not forget to what the family owed its greatness.

Louis XV awarded to his physician, Quesnay, whom he called his 'Thinker', an armorial bearing of three pansies, the emblem of thoughts.

Pliny called the mulberry the most prudent of all trees, because it waits until winter is well over before it puts forth its leaves. Ludovico Sforza, who prided himself on his prudence, chose a mulberry tree for his device, and was called Il Moro.

There are three primroses in the arms of the Earls of Rosebery, whose family name is Primrose. The Merchant Company of Edinburgh has a sprig of broom as its device. A family by the name of Daisy has a coat of arms bearing three daisies, and in an old picture of Chaucer there is a daisy painted in the corner which is usually given to the coat of arms in a medieval painting.

Artists in the past have used a flower symbol as a signature to their paintings, as Whistler used the butterfly. A red carnation distinguishes more than one of the Italian painters. Benvenuto Tissio was called Il Girofalo for his device of a clove pink.

In 1851 a little book by Robert Tyas suggested a do-it-yourself combination of flowers and heraldry 'to be embroidered on chairs, worked on screens, painted on velvet, wrought on scarves and adapted in innumerable ways to add to the refinements of the home'. The full title of this charming book is *Flowers in Heraldry; or, Floral Emblems and Heraldic Figures, combined to express Pure Sentiments, Kind Feelings, and Excellent Principles, in a manner at once Simple, Elegant, and Beautiful.* There follows a delightful mixture of botany, the Language of Flowers and the most esoteric heraldic terms, made more acceptable to young embroidresses by the introduction of suitable verses and twenty-four emblazoned plates, the work of James Andrews, one of the best of the many excellent botanical artists of the period. The author claims that the use of flowers as emblems is even older than heraldry itself, and he chooses his flowers to express a sentiment, in the same way that flower language bouquets were assembled. There are also verses, such as the following, from which indefatigable needlewomen might conjure up their own designs.

On Azure field a Pale engrailed of gold
  Whereon a Fuchsia pendent lies,
Between six Daisies which unfold
  Their pearly face to sunny skies.
Where'er we seek in Nature, there we find
Sweet Innocence and Elegance combined.

Whatever the effects of the industrious young ladies' flashing needles on the refinements of the home, the book is a period piece of great charm, and the plates are irresistible.

Queen Elizabeth I, by Nicholas Hilliard (1547–1619). Walker Art Gallery, Liverpool. The Virgin Queen wears a splendid gown embroidered with the symbolic Tudor Rose – 'wrought ful wel, y-portreyd and y-wrought with floures'.

Telling the Time by Flowers

Here's Daisies for the morn, Primrose
  for gloom,
Pansies and Roses for the noontide hours:–
A wight once made a dial of their bloom,–
So may thy life be measured out by flowers.

— Thomas Hood

The wight in question was undoubtedly the learned botanist Linnaeus, who is known to have planted a Floral Dial which was supposed to mark the hours by the opening and closing of certain flowers. That there was some scientific basis for this we must presume, although in bad weather the Swedish sage must have been late at times for his appointments.

The dial which follows was copied with small variations in many of the Language of Flowers books.

	Opens A.M.		Closes Noon and Evening.	
	hours	minutes	hours	minutes
Goat's Beard	3	5	9	10
Late-flowering Dandelion	4	0	12	1
Hawkweed Picris	4	5	12	0
Alpine-Hawk's Beard	4	5	12	0
Wild Succory	4	5	12	0
Naked-stalked Poppy	5	0	7	0
Copper-coloured Day Lily	5	0	7	8
Smooth Sowthistle	5	0	11	12
Blue-flower Sowthistle	5	0	12	0
Field Bindweed	5	6	4	5
Spotted Cat's Ear	6	7	4	5
White Water Lily	7	0	5	0
Garden Lettuce	7	0	10	0
African Marigold	7	0	3	4
Mouse-ear Hawkweed	8	0	2	0
Proliferous Pink	8	0	1	0
Field Marigold	9	0	3	0
Purple Sandwort	9	10	2	3
Creeping Mallow	9	10	12	1
Chickweed	9	10	10	10

This timetable was arranged for Uppsala in Sweden. De Candolle gives another for Paris, and later one was arranged for the eastern states of America.

Linnaeus was not the originator of this fancy. The Horologe of Flora is mentioned by Pliny. Andrew Marvell knew of it, as we may read in 'The Garden':

How well the skilful gardener drew
Of flowers and herbs this dial new!

Left: The Floral Clock, Princes Street Gardens, Edinburgh. Edinburgh won the proud distinction of displaying the first weight-driven floral clock over a century ago.

Below: Eugene Rimmel's completely unscientific version of a floral clock. It is small wonder that the goddess is looking distraught. From Eugene Rimmel, *Book of Perfumes*.

There, from above, the milder sun
Does through a fragrant zodiac run,
And, as it works, the industrious bee
Computes its time as well as we.
How could such sweet and wholesome
* hours*
Be reckoned but with herbs and flowers.

There is mention of the Horologe of Flora in a description of Overton Lodge, which first appeared in *The Philosophy of Sport made science in earnest (1827).*

After winding for some distance through a path so closely interwoven with shrubs and trees that scarcely a sunbeam could struggle through the foliage, a gleam of light burst through the gloom, and displayed a beautiful marble figure, which had been executed by a Roman artist, representing Flora in the act of being attired by Spring. It was placed in the centre of the expanse formed by the retiring trees and at its base were flowering, at measured intervals, a variety of those plants to which Linnaeus had given the name of Equinoctial flowers, since they open and close at certain and exact hours of the day and thus by proper arrangement constitute the Horologe of Flora of Nature's timepiece. It has been constructed by Louisa Seymour, under the direction of her mother. The hour of the day at which each plant opened was represented by an appropriate figure of nicely trimmed box and these being arranged in a circle not only fulfilled the duty but exhibited the appearance of a dial.

The fashion continued, for Mrs Loudon, the wife and tireless assistant of John Claudius Loudon, gives a list of the opening and closing times of flowers in her *Encyclopaedia of Gardening,* and there is a description of a quite complicated design in *The Four Gardens* by Handasyde.

Lady Mary made a dial of flowers in her garden, whereby those who knew might have learnt the time of day. She laid it out in a little piece of waste ground, where flower-pots stood on a stone slab and an old rusty scythe, like an appropriate emblem, hung against the wall ... Lady Mary had set each plant of her horologe in a little square to itself, divided from the others by a tiny coping of brick; and behind the horologe she had put clumps of thyme and clusters of bright-coloured everlasting flowers, to show that the hours of the flying day are nothing beside time, which is eternal.

Sundials were sometimes cut in box, and these told the time by means of a moving shadow as other sundials do. They were laid out in the gardens of Broughton Castle, and Ascott, a country seat of the Rothschilds, as well as in some college gardens in Oxford and Cambridge. Lady Warwick described the box sundial in her own garden with affection. 'Never was such a perfect time-keeper as my sun-dial, and the figures which record the hours are all cut out and trimmed in Box, and there again on its outer ring is a legend which read in whatever way you please: Les heures heureuses ne se comptent pas. They were outlined for me, those words, in baby sprigs of Box by a friend who is no more, who loved my garden and was good to it.'

It is very possible that these flower dials were grown in monastery gardens, for in the Middle Ages every hour of the day had its flower symbol.

First hour	.	Budding roses
Second hour	.	Heliotrope
Third hour	.	White roses
Fourth hour	.	Hyacinths
Fifth hour	.	Lemons
Sixth hour	.	Lotus blossom
Seventh hour	.	Lupins
Eighth hour	.	Oranges
Ninth hour	.	Olive leaves
Tenth hour	.	Poplar leaves
Eleventh hour	.	Marigolds
Twelfth hour	.	Pansies and violets

A Franciscan friar wrote, 'I learn the time of day from the shutting of the blossoms of the Star of Bethlehem and the Dandelion, and the hour of night from the stars.'

Even the weather could be prophesied by the behaviour of some flowers. The pimpernel, which opens punctually at 7.08 a.m. and closes at 2.03 p.m., paying no attention to British Summer Time nor to continental time-tables, is also an hygrometer.

And if I would the weather know,
ere on some pleasure trip I go,
My scarlet weather-glass will show
whether it will be fair or no.

It may happen, in a cold late spring, that the weather clock runs slow, but Miss Mitford, the Pollyanna of the English countryside, finds something good in this that the rest of us fail to see. 'Nevertheless, there is something of a charm in this wintry spring, this putting back of the seasons. If the flower clock must stand still for a month or two, could it choose a better time than that of the primroses and violets?'

Since 1903 floral clocks have been moving with the times, as clocks should do, and flowers obediently tell us the hour, not by the opening and shutting of their petals, nor by the moving shadows cast by the sun, but, leaving nothing to chance and the vagaries of nature, they work with the help of ingenious mechanisms that are either weight-driven or electrically driven. The first weight-driven floral clock, which required daily winding, was seen in West Princes Street Gardens, Edinburgh; and four years later, another in Weston-super-Mare claimed the largest number of plants used so far, 40,000 for the dial and the surrounding bed. Not to be outdone, Hove has an electrically powered floral clock with two faces.

A matter of civic pride and a valuable tourist attraction, these splendid flowery time-tellers, the joy of their horologist and horticulturalist begetters, are most often to be seen in English seaside resorts, where they silently commend us when we make them the object of our pre-breakfast stroll, or, when the sun is sinking behind the pier, warn us that it is time to return to 'Bellevue' to change for dinner.

VOCABULARY

Flowers with the Sentiments which they Represent

A Broken Straw	Dissension; Rupture
A Rose Leaf	I never importune
A tuft of Moss	Maternal Love
Acacia	Platonic love
Acacia, Rose	Elegance
Aconite: Wolf's Bane	Misanthropy
Aconite-Leaved Crowfoot, or Fair Maid of France	Lustre
African Marygold	Vulgar minds
Agnus Castus	Coldness; to live without love
Agrimony	Thankfulness
Allspice (Calycanthus)	Benevolence
Almond Laurel	Perfidy
Almond-Tree	Indiscretion; Promise
Aloe	Acute sorrow; Bitterness
Althaea Frutex	Persuasion
Amaranth	Immortality
Amaryllis	Haughtiness: Pride
Ambrosia	Love returned
American Cowslip	You are my Divinity
Amethyst	Admiration
Angelica	Inspiration
Apple	Temptation
Apple Blossom	Preference
Arbor Vitae	Unchanging friendship; Old age
Ash-Tree	Grandeur
Aspen-Tree	Lamentation
Asphodel	My regrets follow you to the grave
Auricula	Painting
Austrian Rose	Very lovely
Azalea	Temperance
Bachelor's Buttons	Hope in love
Balm	Social intercourse
Balm-gentle	Pleasantry
Balm of Gilead	Healing
Balsam (Noli-tangere)	Impatience
Barberry	Sourness; Sharpness
Basil	Hatred
Bee Ophrys	Error
Bee Orchis	Industry
Beech	Prosperity
Bear's Breech (Acanthus)	The Arts
Belladonna	Imagination
Bilberry	Treachery
Bindweed	Extinguish
Broom	Humility
Bittersweet Nightshade	Truth
Black Mulberry Tree	I will not survive you
Black Poplar	Courage
Black Thorn	Difficulty
Bladder Nut Tree	Frivolous amusement
Blue Bottle Centaury	Delicacy

Blue Canterbury Bell . . .	Constancy
Blue Periwinkle . . .	Early friendship
Blue Violet . . .	Modesty
Borage	Bluntness; Courage
Box	Stoicism
Bramble	Envy
Branch of Currants . .	You please all
Branch of Thorns . .	Severity; Rigour
Bridal Rose . . .	Happy love
Broom	Neatness
Buckbean . . .	Calm; Repose
Bugloss	Falsehood
Burdock . . .	Importunity
Buttercups . . .	Ingratitude
Butterfly Orchis . . .	Gaiety
Cabbage	Profit
Cacalia	Adulation
Cactus	I burn
Calla	Magnificent beauty
Camellia Japonica . .	Unpretending excellence
Campanula, or	
Pyramidal Bell Flower .	Gratitude
Candy Tuft . . .	Architecture
Cardinal Flower . .	Distinction
Canary Grass . .	Perseverance
Carnation . . .	Pride and Beauty
Carolina Rose . .	Love is dangerous
Cashew Nut . . .	Perfume
Cedar of Lebanon . .	Incorruptible
Cedar Tree: Fennel . .	Strength
Camomile . . .	Energy in adversity
Chequered Fritillary .	Persecution
Cherry-Tree . . .	Good education
Chestnut-Tree . .	Do me justice
China Aster . . .	Variety
China, or Indian Pink .	Aversion
China, or Monthly Rose .	Beauty ever new
Chrysanthemum . .	Cheerfulness under adversity
Cinquefoil . . .	Beloved daughter
Citron	Beauty with ill humour
Clove scented Pink . .	Dignity
Coboea	Gossip
Cock's Comb (Crested Amaranth)	Singularity
Columbine . . .	Folly
Convolvulus, Blue . .	Repose
Convolvulus, Major .	Dangerous insinuator
Convolvulus, Pink . .	Worth sustained by judicious and tender affection
Coreopsis . . .	Always cheerful
Coriander . . .	Hidden merit
Corn Cockle (Rose Campion) .	Gentility
Cornell-Tree . . .	Duration (Apollo)
Coronella . . .	Success crown your wishes
Cowslip . . .	Pensiveness
Crown Imperial . .	Majesty; Power

Cuckoo Flower . . .	Paternal error
Cuckoo Pint . . .	Ardor
Cyclamen	Diffidence
Cypress and Marygold together .	Despair
Cypress-Tree . . .	Mourning
Daffodil . . .	Deceitful hope
Dahlia	Instability
Daisy, Michaelmas . .	Cheerfulness
Daisy	Innocence
Dandelion . . .	Oracle
Darnel, or Ray Grass . .	Vice
Dead Leaves . . .	Sadness
Dew Plant . . .	Serenade
Dittany of Crete . .	Birth
Dittany, White . .	Passion
Dodder of Thyme . .	Baseness
Dog's Bane (Apocynum) .	Deceit; Falsehood
Dragon Plant, Catchfly .	Snare
Ebony	Blackness
Eglantine, Sweet Briar .	Poetry
Elder	Compassion
Enchanter's Nightshade .	Fascination
Endive	Frugality
Evening Primrose . .	Inconstancy
Everlasting, or Cotton Weed	Never ceasing remembrance
Everlasting Pea . .	Lasting pleasure
False Narcissus . .	Delusive hope
Fern	Sincerity
Ficoides, or Ice Plant .	Your looks freeze me
Field Anemone . .	Sickness
Fig	Argument
Fig Marygold . .	Idleness
Fig-Tree . . .	Prolific
Fir-Tree . . .	Elevation
Flax	Domestic industry
Flax-leaved Goldylocks .	Tardiness
Flowering Fern . .	Reverie
Flower of an Hour . .	Delicate beauty
Fool's Parsley . .	Silliness
Foxglove . . .	Insincerity
Foxtail Grass . .	Sporting
Fraxinella . . .	Fire
French Honeysuckle .	Rustic beauty
French Marygold . .	Jealousy
Fumitory . . .	Spleen
Garden Anemone . .	Forsaken
Garden Daisy . .	I partake your sentiments
Garden Marygold . .	Uneasiness and jealousy
Garden Ranunculus .	You are rich in attraction
Garden Sage . .	Esteem
Garland of Roses . .	Reward of virtue
Geranium, Ivy . .	Bridal favour

186

Geranium, Nutmeg . . .	Expected meeting
Gillyflower . . .	Lasting beauty
Globe Amaranth . . .	Unchangeable
Goat's Rue . . .	Reason
Golden Rod . . .	Precaution
Goosefoot (Bonus Henricus) .	Goodness
Gorse	Enduring affection
Grass	Utility
Guelder Rose . . .	Winter of Age
Harebell . . .	Grief
Hawkweed . . .	Quick-sightedness
Hawthorn . . .	Hope. To the Romans, marriage
Hazel	Reconciliation
Heath	Solitude
Helenium . . .	Tears
Hellebore . . .	Female inconstancy
Heliotrope . . .	Devotion
Hemlock . . .	You will cause my death
Henbane . . .	Imperfection
Hepatica, or Noble Liverwort .	Confidence
Holly	Foresight
Hollyhock . . .	Fruitfulness
Honesty (Lunaria) . .	Honesty
Honey Flower . . .	Love, sweet and secret
Honeysuckle . . .	Bonds of love
Hop	Injustice
Hornbeam-Tree . .	Ornament
Horse-Chestnut . .	Luxury
House Leek . . .	Vivacity
Houstonia Cerulea . .	Content; Quiet happiness
Hoya	Sculpture
Hundred Leaved Rose . .	Graces
Hyacinth . . .	Game; Play
Hydrangea (Hortensia) . .	Boaster; You are cold
Indian, or Sweet Scabius . .	I have lost all
Indian Pink . . .	Always lovely
Iris	Message
Iris, German . . .	Flame
Ivy	Friendship in adversity
Japan Rose . . .	Beauty is your only attraction
Japanese Lilies . .	You cannot deceive me
Jasmine . . .	Amiability
Jasmine, Cape . .	Transport of joy
Jasmine, Carolina . .	Separation
Jasmine, Indian . .	I attach myself to you
Jasmine, Spanish . .	Sensuality
Jasmine, Yellow . .	Grace and elegance
Jonquil . . .	I desire a return of affection
Juniper . . .	Asylum; Protection
Kingcups . . .	Desire for riches
Lady's Mantle . . .	Fashion

Lady's Slipper . . .	Fickleness
Larch	Boldness
Larkspur . . .	Lightness; Levity
Larkspur, pink . .	Fickleness
Laurel	Glory
Laurestina . . .	I die if neglected
Lavender . . .	Distrust
Lemon	Zest
Lemon Blossoms . .	Fidelity in love
Lettuce . . .	Cold-heartedness
Lilac, Purple . . .	First emotions of love
Lilac, White . . .	Youthful innocence
Lily of the Valley . .	Return of happiness
Lily, White . . .	Purity; Sweetness
Lily, Yellow . . .	Falsehood; Gaiety
Linden or Lime Tree . .	Conjugal love
Liverwort . . .	Confidence
Liquorice, Wild . .	I declare against you
Lobelia . . .	Malevolence
Locust Plant . . .	Affection beyond the grave
London Pride . . .	Frivolity
Lotus Flower . . .	Estranged love
Love Lies Bleeding . .	Desertion. Hopeless, not heartless
Love in a Mist . .	Perplexity; Embarrassment
Lucern . . .	Life
Lupin	Veraciousness; Dejection
Lychnis . . .	Religious enthusiasm
Madder . . .	Calumny
Magnolia . . .	Love of nature; Magnificence
Mallow . . .	Mildness
Mandrake . . .	Horror
Maple	Reserve
Marjoram . . .	Blushes
Marygold . . .	Mental anguish
Marygold, African . .	Vulgar minds
Marygold, French . .	Jealousy
Meadow Saffron . .	My best days are past
Meadow Sweet . .	Uselessness
Mezereon . . .	Desire to please
Mignonette . . .	Your qualities surpass your charms
Milk Vetch . . .	Your presence softens my pains
Mimosa . . .	Sensitiveness; Courtesy
Mint	Virtue Dis
Mistletoe . . .	I surmount all difficulties
Mock Orange or Syringa (Philadelphus) .	Fraternal love
Monkshood . . .	Knight errantry
Moonwort . . .	Forgetfulness
Morning Glory . .	Affectation
Moschatel . . .	Weakness; Insignificance
Moss Rose . . .	Pleasure without alloy
Moss Rose Bud . .	Confession
Mountain Laurel . .	Ambition
Mouse-eared Chickweed .	Ingenuous simplicity
Mouse-eared Scorpion Grass .	Forget me not

Mullein . . .	Good nature
Mushroom . .	Suspicion
Musk Rose .	Capricious Beauty
Myrtle . . .	Love; Fertility
Narcissus . .	Egotism
Nasturtium . .	Patriotism
Nettle . . .	You are spiteful
Night-blooming Cereus .	Transient beauty
Nightshade . .	Falsehood; Dark thoughts
Nosegay . . .	Gallantry
Oak and Holly .	Hospitality
Oak leaf . .	Bravery
Olive branch . .	Peace
Orange Blossom .	Your purity equals your loveliness
Orange Tree . .	Generosity
Orchis . .	A belle
Osier . .	Frankness
Ox Eye . . .	Patience
Palm . . .	Victory
Pansy, or Heartsease .	Thoughts, Pensez à moi
Parsley . .	Entertainment; Feasting
Pasque Flower .	You are without pretension
Passion Flower .	Religious superstition when the flower is reversed, faith if erect
Pea, Everlasting .	An appointed meeting; Lasting pleasure
Pea, Sweet .	Departure; and Delicate pleasures
Peach blossom . .	I am your captive
Periwinkle . .	Sweet remembrances
Pheasant's Eye (Adonis) .	Sorrowful remembrances
Phlox . . .	Unanimity
Pimpernel . .	Assignation
Pine . . .	Pity
Pine-apple . .	You are perfect
Pink . . .	Lively and pure affection
Pink, Carnation .	Woman's love
Pink, Mountain .	Aspiring
Pink, Red Double .	Pure and ardent love
Pink, Variegated .	Refusal
Pink, White . .	Ingeniousness; Talent
Polyanthus . .	Pride of riches
Polyanthus, Crimson .	The heart's mystery
Polyanthus, Lilac .	Confidence
Pomegranate . .	Foolishness
Pomegranate, flower .	Mature elegance
Pompon Rose .	Genteel; Pretty
Poppy . . .	Consolation of sleep
Poppy, Scarlet .	Fantastic extravagance
Poppy, White . .	Sleep; My bane
Potato . . .	Benevolence
Potentilla . .	I claim, at least, your esteem
Primrose . .	Early youth and sadness
Primrose, Evening .	Inconstancy

Privet . . .	Prohibition
Purple Clover . .	Provident
Quaking Grass .	Agitation
Quince . .	Temptation
Ragged Robin .	Wit
Ranunculus . .	You are radiant with charms
Ranunculus, Wild .	Ingratitude
Raspberry . .	Remorse
Red Catchfly . .	Youthful love
Reeds . . .	Music
Restharrow . .	Obstacle
Rhododendron .	Danger; Beware
Rhubarb . .	Advice
Rocket . . .	Rivalry
Rock Rose (Cistus) .	Popular favour
Rose . .	Love
Rose, Austrian .	Thou art all that is lovely
Rose, Bridal .	Happy love
Rose, Burgundy .	Unconscious beauty
Rose, Cabbage .	Ambassador of love
Rose, Campion .	Only deserve my love
Rose, Christmas .	Tranquillize my anxiety
Rose, Daily .	Thy smile I aspire to
Rose, Damask .	Brilliant complexion
Rose, Deep red .	Bashful shame
Rose, Dog .	Pleasure and pain
Rose, Guelder . .	Winter. Age
Rose, Maiden Blush .	If you love me you will find it out
Rosa Mundi . .	Variety
Rose, Thornless .	Early attachment
Rose, White . .	I am worthy of you
Rose, Yellow . .	Decrease of love; Jealousy
Rose, York and Lancaster .	War
Rose, Full blown, placed over two buds . .	Secrecy
Rose leaf . .	You may hope
Rosemary . .	Remembrance. Your presence revives me
Rudbeckia . .	Justice
Rue . . .	Purification
Rush . . .	Docility
Saffron . . .	Mirth. Excess is dangerous
Saffron, Meadow .	My happiest days are past
Sage . . .	Domestic virtue
Sainfoin . .	Agitation
Saint John's Wort .	Animosity
Scabious . .	Unfortunate attachment; Mourning bride
Scarlet Fuchsia .	Taste
Scarlet Geranium .	Comforting
Scarlet Lily . .	High soul
Scarlet Lychnis .	Sunbeaming Eyes
Sea Lavender . .	Dauntlessness

Shamrock	Light-heartedness
Shepherd's Purse	I offer you my all
Snapdragon	Presumption, also No
Snowball Tree	Age
Snowdrop	Hope; Consolation
Southernwood	Jest; Bantering
Speedwell	Resemblance
Spider Ophris	Skill
Spiderwort	Transient happiness
Spindle Tree	Your charms are engraven on my heart
Spring Crocus	Youthful gladness.
Star of Bethlehem	Purity
Starwort, American	Cheerfulness in old age
Stephanotis	Will you accompany me to the Far East?
Stock	Lasting beauty
Stock, Ten Week	Promptness
Stonecrop	Tranquillity
Sunflower	False riches
Swallow-wort	Cure for heartache
Sweetbriar, American	Simplicity
Sweet Sultan	Felicity
Sweet William	Gallantry; Dexterity; Finesse
Syringa, Carolina	Disappointment
Tamarisk	Crime
Tansy	I declare war against you
Teasel	Misanthropy
Thistle, Common	Austerity; Independence
Thistle, Scotch	Retaliation
Thornapple	Deceitful charms
Thrift	Sympathy
Thyme	Activity; Courage
Tiger Flower	For once may pride befriend me
Toothwort	Secret love
Traveller's Joy	Safety
Trefoil	Unity
Truffle	Surprise
Trumpet Flower (Bignonia)	Fame; Separation
Tuberose	Dangerous pleasures; Voluptuousness
Tulip, Red	Declaration of love
Tulip, Variegated	Beautiful eyes
Tulip, Yellow	Hopeless love
Tulip-Tree	Fame

Turnip	Charity
Tussilage	Justice shall be done you
Valerian	An accommodating disposition
Venus's Car	Fly with me
Venus's Looking Glass	Flattery
Verbena, Pink	Family union
Verbena, Scarlet	Unite against evil; Church unity
Verbena, White	Pray for me
Vernal Grass	Poor but happy
Veronica	Fidelity
Vervain	Enchantment
Vine	Intoxication
Violet, Blue	Faithfulness
Violet, Dame's	Watchfulness
Violet, Yellow	Rural happiness
Virginia Creeper	I will cling to you both in sunshine and shade
Virgin's Bower	Filial love
Viscaria Oculate	Will you dance with me?
Wake Robin	Ardour
Wallflower	Fidelity in adversity
Water Lily	Eloquence; Purity of heart
Water-Melon	Bulkiness
Wheat	Riches
White Daisy	I will think of it
White Mulberry-Tree	Wisdom
White Mullein	Good nature
White Rose (dried)	Death preferable to loss of innocence
White Violet	Candour
Willow Herb	Pretension
Willow, Weeping	Mourning
Winter Cherry	Deception
Wisteria	Welcome, fair stranger
Witch Hazel	Spell-bound
Wood Sorrel	Maternal tenderness
Wormwood	Absence
Yarrow, Milfoil	War
Yellow Day Lily	Coquetry
Yew	Sorrow
Zephyr Flower	Expectation
Zinnia	Thoughts of absent friends

Sentiments and the Flowers by which they are Represented

A belle	Orchis
Absence	Wormwood
Accommodating disposition	Valerian
Activity; Courage	Thyme
Acute sorrow; Bitterness	Aloe
Admiration	Amethyst
Adulation	Cacalia
Affection beyond the grave	Locust Plant

Age	Snowball Tree
Agitation	Quaking Grass
Always cheerful	Coreopsis
Always lovely	Indian Pink
Amiability	Jasmine
Architecture	Candy Tuft
Ardour	Wake Robin
Argument	Fig
Arts (The)	Bear's Breech (Acanthus)
Aspiring	Mountain Pink
Assignation	Pimpernel
Asylum; Protection	Juniper
Austerity; Independence	Common Thistle
Aversion	China, or Indian Pink
Bantering; Jest	Southernwood
Bashful shame	Deep Red Rose
Beautiful eyes	Variegated Tulip
Beauty is your only attraction	Japan Rose
Beauty ever new	China, or Monthly Rose
Beauty, Delicate	Flower of an Hour
Beauty, Lasting	Stock
Beauty, Magnificent	Calla
Beauty, Rustic	French Honeysuckle
Beauty, Unconscious	Burgundy Rose
Beauty with ill humour	Citron
Belief; Religious superstition when reversed, faith if erect	Passion Flower
Beloved daughter	Cinquefoil
Belle	Orchis
Benevolence	Potato
Birth	Dittany of Crete
Blackness	Ebony
Bluntness; Courage	Borage
Blushes	Marjoram
Boaster; You are cold	Hydrangea (Hortensia)
Boldness	Larch
Bonds of love	Honeysuckle
Bravery	Oak leaf
Brilliant complexion	Damask Rose
Bulkiness	Water-Melon
Calm Repose	Buckbean
Calumny	Madder
Candour	White Violet
Capricious beauty	Musk Rose
Charity	Turnip
Charms, deceitful	Thornapple
Cheerfulness in old age	Starwort, American
Cheerfulness under adversity	Chrysanthemum
Cheerfulness	Daisy, Michaelmas
Cold-heartedness	Lettuce
Coldness; to live without love	Agnus Castus
Comforting	Scarlet Geranium
Compassion	Elder
Confession	Moss Rose Bud

Confidence	Hepatica or Noble Liverwort
Conjugal love	Linden or Lime Tree
Consolation; Hope	Snowdrop
Consolation of sleep	Poppy
Constancy	Blue Canterbury Bell
Coquetry	Yellow Day Lily
Courtesy; Sensitiveness	Mimosa
Crime	Tamarisk
Cure for heartache	Swallow-wort
Danger; Beware	Rhododendron
Dangerous insinuator	Convolvulus, Major
Dark thoughts; Falsehood	Nightshade
Dauntlessness	Sea Lavender
Deceit; Falsehood	Dog's Bane (Apocynum)
Deceitful charms	Thornapple
Deceitful hope	Daffodil
Deception	Winter Cherry
Declaration of love	Red Tulip
Decrease of love; Jealousy	Yellow Rose
Delicacy	Blue Bottle Centaury
Delicate pleasures	Sweet Pea
Delusive hope	False Narcissus
Desire for riches	Kingcups
Desire to please	Mezereon
Despair	Cypress and Marygold together
Devotion	Heliotrope
Dexterity; Gallantry; Finesse	Sweet William
Difficulty	Black Thorn
Diffidence	Cyclamen
Dignity	Clove Scented Pink
Disappointment	Syringa, Carolina
Dissension; Rupture	A Broken Straw
Distinction	Cardinal Flower
Distrust	Lavender
Do me justice	Chestnut-Tree
Docility	Rush
Domestic industry	Flax
Domestic virtue	Sage
Duration	Cornell-Tree
Early youth and sadness	Primrose
Elegance	Acacia Rose
Elevation	Fir-Tree
Eloquence; Purity of heart	Water Lily
Enchantment	Vervain
Entertainment; Feasting	Parsley
Error	Bee Ophrys
Estranged love	Lotus Flower
Expectation	Zephyr Flower
Extinguish	Bindweed
Falsehood	Bugloss
False riches	Sunflower
Fame	Tulip-Tree
Family union	Pink Verbena

Fantastic extravagance	. . .	Scarlet Poppy
Fascination	. .	Enchanter's Nightshade
Fashion	. . .	Lady's Mantle
Felicity	. . .	Sweet Sultan
Female inconstancy	. .	Hellebore
Fickleness	. .	Lady's Slipper, and Pink Larkspur
Fidelity	. . .	Veronica
Fidelity in adversity	. .	Wallflower
Fidelity in love	. .	Lemon Blossoms
Filial love	. .	Virgin's Bower
Fire	. . .	Fraxinella
First emotions of love	.	Purple Lilac
Flame	. . .	German Iris
Flattery	. . .	Venus's Looking Glass
Fly with me	. .	Venus's Car
Folly	. . .	Columbine
Foolishness	. .	Pomegranate
Foresight	. .	Holly
Forgetfulness	. .	Moonwort
For once may pride befriend me	.	Tiger Flower
Forsaken	. . .	Garden Anemone
Frankness	. .	Osier
Fraternal love	. .	Philadelphus, Mock Orange or Syringa
Friendship in adversity	. .	Ivy
Frivolity	. . .	London Pride
Frivolous amusement	.	Bladder Nut Tree
Frugality	. .	Endive
Fruitfulness	. .	Hollyhock
Gaiety; Falsehood	. .	Yellow Lily
Game; Play	. .	Hyacinth
Generosity	. .	Orange Tree
Genteel; Pretty	. .	Pompon Rose
Glory	. . .	Laurel
Good education	. .	Cherry Tree
Good nature	. .	Mullein
Goodness	. .	Goosefoot (Bonus Henricus)
Gossip	. . .	Coboea
Grace and elegance	. .	Yellow Jasmine
Grandeur	. .	Ash-Tree
Gratitude	. . .	Campanula, or Pyramidal Bell Flower
Grief	. . .	Harebell
Happy love	. .	Bridal Rose
Hatred	. . .	Basil
Haughtiness; Pride	. .	Amaryllis
Healing	. . .	Balm of Gilead
Hidden merit	. .	Coriander
High soul	. .	Scarlet Lily
Honesty	. . .	Honesty (Lunaria)
Hope. To the Romans, marriage	.	Hawthorn
Hope in love	. .	Bachelor's Buttons
Hopeless love	. .	Yellow tulip
Hopeless, not heartless; Desertion		Love Lies Bleeding

Horror	. . .	Mandrake
Hospitality	. . .	Oak and Holly
I am your captive	. .	Peach Blossom
I am worthy of you	. .	White Rose
I attach myself to you	.	Indian Jasmine
I claim, at least, your esteem	.	Potentilla
I declare against you	.	Wild Liquorice
I declare war against you	.	Tansy
I die if neglected	. .	Laurestina
I desire a return of affection	.	Jonquil
If you love me you will find it out	Maiden Blush Rose
I have lost all	. . .	Indian, or Sweet Scabius
I never importune	. .	A Rose Leaf
I offer you my all	. .	Shepherd's Purse
I partake your sentiments	.	Garden Daisy
I surmount all difficulties	.	Mistletoe
I will not survive you	.	Black Mulberry-Tree
I will think of it	. .	White Daisy
Idleness	. . .	Fig Marygold
Imagination	. .	Belladonna
Immortality	. .	Amaranth
Impatience	. .	Balsam (Noli-tangere)
Imperfection	. .	Henbane
Importunity	. .	Burdock
Inconstancy	. .	Evening Primrose
Incorruptible	. .	Cedar of Lebanon
Independence; Austerity	.	Common Thistle
Indiscretion; Promise	.	Almond-Tree
Industry	. . .	Bee Orchis
Ingeniousness; Talent	.	White Pink
Ingenuous simplicity	.	Mouse-eared chickweed
Ingratitude	. .	Buttercups
Injustice	. . .	Hop
Innocence	. . .	Daisy
Insincerity	. .	Foxglove
Inspiration	. .	Angelica
Instability	. .	Dahlia
Intoxication	. . .	Vine
Jealousy	. . .	French Marygold
Justice	. . .	Rudbekia
Justice shall be done you	.	Tussilage
Knight errantry	. .	Monkshood
Lamentation	. .	Aspen-Tree
Lasting beauty	. .	Stock
Lasting pleasure	. .	Everlasting Pea
Lightness; Levity	. .	Larkspur
Life	. . . .	Lucern
Lively and pure affection	.	Pink
Love; Fertility	. .	Myrtle
Love is dangerous	. .	Carolina Rose
Love of Nature; Magnificence	.	Magnolia
Love returned	. .	Ambrosia

Lustre	Aconite-leaved Crowfoot, or Fair Maid of France
Magnificent beauty . . .	Calla
Majesty; Power . .	Crown Imperial
Malevolence . . .	Lobelia
Maternal Love . . .	A tuft of Moss
Maternal tenderness . .	Wood Sorrel
Mature elegance . .	Pomegranate Flower
Message	Iris
Mildness . . .	Mallow
Mirth; Excess is dangerous .	Saffron
Misanthropy . . .	Aconite, Wolf's Bane
Mourning . . .	Weeping Willow
My happiest days are past .	Meadow Saffron
My regrets follow you to the grave	Asphodel
Never ceasing remembrance .	Everlasting, or Cotton Weed
No, also Presumption .	Snapdragon
Obstacle . . .	Restharrow
Oracle . . .	Dandelion
Ornament . . .	Hornbeam-Tree
Painting . . .	Auricula
Passion . . .	White Dittany
Patience . . .	Dock
Patriotism . . .	Nasturtium
Peace . . .	Olive branch
Pensiveness . . .	Cowslip
Perfidy . . .	Almond Laurel
Perplexity; Embarrassment .	Love in a Mist
Persecution . . .	Chequered Fritillary
Persuasion . . .	Althea Frutex
Pity	Pine
Platonic love . .	Acacia
Pleasure and pain . .	Dog Rose
Pleasantry . . .	Balm-gentle
Pleasure without alloy .	Moss Rose
Poetry	Eglantine, Sweet Briar
Poor but happy . .	Vernal Grass
Pray for me . . .	White Verbena
Precaution . . .	Golden Rod
Preference . . .	Apple Blossom
Pretension . . .	Willow Herb
Pride and beauty . .	Carnation
Pride of riches . . .	Polyanthus
Profit . . .	Cabbage
Prohibition . . .	Privet
Prolific . . .	Fig-Tree
Promptness . . .	Ten-Week Stock
Prosperity . . .	Beech
Pure and ardent love .	Red Double Pink
Purification . . .	Rue
Purity	Star of Bethlehem
Purity; Sweetness .	White Lily

Quick-sightedness . .	Hawkweed
Reconciliation . .	Hazel
Refusal . . .	Variegated Pink
Religious enthusiasm .	Lychnis
Remorse . . .	Raspberry
Repose . . .	Blue Convolvulus
Resemblance . . .	Speedwell
Reserve	Maple
Retaliation . . .	Scotch Thistle
Return of happiness . .	Lily of the Valley
Reverie . . .	Flowering Fern
Reward of Virtue . .	Garland of Roses
Rivalry	Rocket
Rural happiness . .	Yellow Violet
Riches	Wheat
Sadness	Dead Leaves
Safety	Traveller's Joy
Sculpture . . .	Hoya
Secret love . . .	Toothwort
Sensitiveness; Courtesy .	Mimosa
Sensuality . . .	Spanish Jasmine
Separation . . .	Carolina Jasmine
Separation; Fame . .	Trumpet Flower, Bignonia
Serenade . . .	Dew Plant
Sickness . . .	Field Anemone
Silliness . . .	Fool's Parsley
Sincerity . . .	Fern
Singularity . . .	Cock's Comb, Crested Amarant
Skill	Spider Ophris
Sleep; My bane . .	White Poppy
Social intercourse . .	Balm
Solitude	Heath
Sorrow	Yew
Sorrowful remembrances .	Pheasant's Eye (Adonis)
Sourness; Sharpness . .	Barberry
Spell-bound . . .	Witch Hazel
Spleen	Fumitory
Sporting . . .	Foxtail Grass
Stoicism	Box
Strength . . .	Cedar-Tree; Fennel
Success crown your wishes .	Coronella
Sunbeaming eyes . .	Scarlet Lychnis
Surprise	Truffle
Sympathy . . .	Thrift
Sweet remembrances .	Periwinkle
Taste	Scarlet Fuchsia
Tears	Helenium
Temperance . . .	Azalea
Temptation . . .	Apple
Thankfulness . . .	Agrimony
The heart's mystery . .	Crimson Polyanthus
Thoughts, Pensez à moi .	Pansy, or Heartsease
Thoughts of absent friends .	Zinnia

192

Thy smile I aspire to . .	.	Daily Rose
Tranquillity . . .	.	Stonecrop
Transient beauty . .	.	Night-blooming Cereus
Transient happiness . .	.	Spiderwort
Transport of joy . .	.	Cape Jasmine
Treachery . . .	.	Bilberry
Truth . . .	.	Bittersweet Nightshade
Unanimity . . .	.	Phlox
Unchangeable . .	.	Globe Amaranth
Unchanging friendship; Old age .		Arbor Vitae
Unconscious beauty . .	.	Burgundy Rose
Unfortunate attachment;		
Mourning Bride . .	.	Scabius
Unite against evil; Church unity .		Scarlet Verbena
Unity . . .	.	Trefoil
Unpretending excellence .	.	Camellia Japonica
Uselessness . .	.	Meadow Sweet
Utility . . .	.	Grass
Variety . . .	.	China Aster
Variety . . .	.	Rosa Mundi
Vice . . .	.	Darnel, or Ray Grass
Victory . . .	.	Palm
Virtue . . .	.	Mint
Vivacity . . .	.	House Leek
Veraciousness; Dejection .		Lupin
Voluptuousness; Dangerous		
pleasures		Tuberose
Vulgar minds . . .		African Marygold
War . . .	.	Yarrow, Milfoil

War . . .	.	York and Lancaster Rose
Watchfulness . . .		Dame's Violet
Weakness; Insignificance .	.	Moschatel
Welcome, fair stranger .	.	Wisteria
Will you accompany me to the		
Far East? . . .	.	Stephanotis
Will you dance with me? .	.	Viscaria Oculata
Winter of age . . .		Guelder Rose
Wisdom . . .	.	White Mulberry-Tree
Worth sustained by judicious		
and tender affection .	.	Pink convolvulus
You are my divinity . .	.	American Cowslip
You are perfect . .	.	Pine Apple
You are radiant with charms .		Ranunculus
You are without pretention		Pasque Flower
You please all . . .		Branch of Currants
You will cause my death .	.	Hemlock
Your charms are engraven		
on my heart . . .		Spindle Tree
Your looks freeze me .	.	Ficoides, or Ice Plant
Your presence revives me;		
Remembrance . .	.	Rosemary
Your presence softens my pains .		Milk Vetch
Your purity equals your loveliness		Orange Blossom
Your qualities surpass your charms		Mignonette
Youthful gladness . .		Spring Crocus
Youthful love . . .		Red catchfly
Zest . . .	.	Lemon

BIBLIOGRAPHY

All mentions of Parkinson, Gerard or Culpeper in the text refer to:
Parkinson, John, *Paradisi in Sole Paradisus Terrestris*, London, 1629.
Parkinson, John, *Theatrum Botanicum*, London, 1640.
Gerard, John, *Herball*, 3rd edn, London, 1633.
Culpeper, Nicholas, *Complete Herbal*, Manchester, 1826.
Quotations from the Language of Flowers come from various small Victorian books, too numerous to mention individually, and the Vocabulary is chiefly compiled from Adams, H. G., *The Language and Poetry of Flowers*, New York, 1858; Ingram, John, *Flora Symbolica*, London, c. 1875; and 'L.V.', *The Language and Sentiment of Flowers*, 1866.

CHAPTER I
Bowra, C. M., *The Oxford Book of Greek Verse in Translation*, Oxford, 1938
Brewer, E. Cobham, *Dictionary of Phrase and Fable*, London, 1901
Ingram, John, *Flora Symbolica*, London, c. 1875
Kennedy-Bell, M. G., *The Glory of the Garden*, London, 1923

CHAPTER II
Barrett, W. A., *Flowers and Festivals*, London, 1868
Deas, Lizzie, *Flower Favourites, Their Legends, Symbolism and Significance*, London, 1898
Kennedy-Bell, M. G., *The Glory of the Garden*, London, 1923
Langhorne, Dr John, *The Fables of Flora*, London, 1804

CHAPTER III
Calthrop, Dion Clayton, *The Charm of Gardens*, London, 1917
Hone, William, *Table Book*, London, 1878

CHAPTER IV
Eastwood, Dorothy, *Mirror of Flowers*, London, 1953
Pratt, Anne, *Flowering Plants of Great Britain*, London, c. 1870
Rohde, Eleanour Sinclair, *The Old English Herbals*, London, 1972

CHAPTER V
French, E. N. (ed.), *A Countryman's Day Book*, London, 1929
Hazlitt, W. Carew, *Gleanings in Old Garden Literature*, London, 1887
Parkins, Dr, *The English Physician*, London, 1826

CHAPTER VI
Mackay, Charles, *Memoirs of Extraordinary Popular Delusions*, 2nd edn,
    Vol II, London, 1852
Thistleton Dyer, T. F., *The Folk-Lore of Plants*, London, 1889

CHAPTER VII
Friend, Rev. Hilderic, *Flowers and Flower Lore*, London, 1884
Grigson, Geoffrey, *The Englishman's Flora*, London, 1960
Thistleton Dyer, T. F., *The Folk-Lore of Plants*, London, 1889

CHAPTER VIII
Green, John R., *A Short History of the English People*, London, 1874,
    reprinted 1915
Hazlitt, W. Carew, *Gleanings in Old Garden Literature*, London, 1887
Hulme, F. Edward, *Natural History Lore and Legend*, London, 1895
Lee, Henry, *The Vegetable Lamb of Tartary*, London, 1887
Lee, Mrs R., *Trees, Plants and Flowers*, London, 1859
Parley, Peter, *Tales about Plants*, London, 1839
Porteous, Alexander, *Forest Folklore, Mythology and Romance*, London,
    1928
Porteous, Crighton, *The Beauty and Mystery of Well Dressing*, Derby,
    1949
Rhind, William, *A History of the Vegetable Kingdom*, London, undated
Savage, F. G., *The Flora and Folk Lore of Shakespeare*, London, c. 1923

CHAPTER IX
Grigson, Geoffrey, *The Englishman's Flora*, London, 1960
Moldenka, Harold N., *American Wild Flowers*, New York, 1949
Pratt, Anne, *Flowering Plants of Great Britain*, London, c. 1870
Synge, Patrick M., *Plants With Personality*, London, undated
Taylor, J. E., *Flowers, Their Origins, Shapes, Perfumes and Colours*,
    London, undated
Taylor, J. E., *The Sagacity and Morality of Plants*, London, 1884

CHAPTER X
Amherst, The Hon. Alicia, *A History of Gardening in England*, London,
    1896
Hillier, Bevis, *A Bouquet for Flowers*, London, 1976
Phillips, Henry, *Flora Historica*, London, 1824
Rohde, Eleanour Sinclair, *The Old English Herbals*, London, 1972
Rohde, Eleanour Sinclair, *The Story of the Garden*, London, 1932
Weeks, N., and Bullen, V., *The Bach Flower Remedies*, London, 1964

CHAPTER XI
Grieve, Mrs M., *A Modern Herbal*, London, 1976
Hemphill, Rosemary, *Herbs and Spices*, London, 1966
Leyel, Mrs C. F., *Herbal Delights*, London, 1937

Philbrick, H., and Gregg, Richard B., *Companion Plants*, London,
    1976
Saneki, Kay N., *Discovering Herbs*, London, 1973

CHAPTER XII
Bean, W. J., *The Royal Botanic Gardens, Kew*, London, 1908
Drewitt, F. Dawtrey, *The Romance of the Apothecaries Garden at Chelsea*,
    London, 1924
Günther, R. T., *Oxford Gardens*, Oxford, 1912
Heine, Heinrich, *Confessions*, London, 1961
Sieveking, Albert F., *The Praise of Gardens*, London, 1885
Taylor, Gladys, *Old London Gardens*, London, 1953

CHAPTER XIII
Grigson, Geoffrey, *Gardenage*, London, 1952
Rothery, Agnes, *The Joyful Gardener*, new edn, 1951
Walker, Winifred, *All the Plants of the Bible*, London, 1959

CHAPTER XIV
Ellacombe, Henry N., *The Plant-Lore and Garden-Craft of Shakespeare*,
    London, c. 1896
Flower, Newman, *Through My Garden Gate*, London, 1945
Green, J. R., *A Short History of the English People*, London, 1915
Hulme, Edward, *Familiar Wild Flowers*, London, c. 1900
Macaulay, Thomas B., *History of England*, new edn, Vol. 1, London,
    1915
Wilkinson, Lady, *Weeds and Wild Flowers*, London, 1858

CHAPTER XV
Crane, Walter, *Flora's Feast*, London, 1889
Crane, Walter, *Flowers From Shakespeare's Garden*, London, 1901
Grandville, Albert, *Les Fleurs Animées*, Paris, 1851
Hale, Mrs Sarah Josepha, *Flora's Interpreter*, Boston, 1852
Lear, Edward, *Nonsense Botany*, numerous editions
Marryat, Captain, *The Floral Telegraph*, London, c. 1859
Miller, Thomas, *The Poetical Language of Flowers*, London, c. 1847
Zaccone, Pierre, *Nouveau Langage des Fleurs*, Paris, 1860

CHAPTER XVI
Calthrop, Dion Clayton, *The Charm of Gardens*, London, 1917
Earle, Alice Morse, *Old Time Gardens*, New York, 1902
Rohde, Eleanour Sinclair, *The Scented Garden*, London, 1948

CHAPTER XVII
Ault, Norman (ed.), *Elizabethan Lyrics*, London, 1925
Ellacombe, Henry N., *The Plant-Lore and Garden Craft of Shakespeare*,
    London, c. 1896
Savage, F. G., *The Flora and Folk Lore of Shakespeare*, Cheltenham,
    c. 1923

CHAPTER XVIII
Gosse, Edmund, *Father and Son*, London, 1907
Patmore, Coventry, *The Toys*, London, 1916
Randall, Vernon, *Wild Flowers in Literature*, London, 1934
Stevenson, Robert Louis, *A Child's Garden of Verses*, London, undated

CHAPTER XIX
Brand, John, *Observations on Popular Antiquities*, London, 1813
Carruthers, Miss, *Flower Lore*, Belfast, undated
Irving, Washington, *The Sketch Book of Geoffrey Craym, Gent*, numerous
    editions 1820–1929
Jefferies, Richard, *Field and Hedgerow*, London, 1900

CHAPTER XX

Brand, John, *Observations on Popular Antiquities*, London, 1813
Brewer, E. Cobham, *Dictionary of Phrase and Fable*, London, 1901
Carruthers, Miss, *Flower Lore*, Belfast, undated
Dobson, Austin, *Eighteenth Century Vignettes*, London, 1906

CHAPTER XXI

Carruthers, Miss, *Flower Lore*, Belfast, undated
Deas, Lizzie, *Flower Favourites, Their Legends, Symbolism and Significance*, London, 1898
Hazlitt, W. Carew, *Gleanings in Old Garden Literature*, London, 1887

CHAPTER XXII

Bainbridge, H. C., *Peter Carl Fabergé*, London, 1966
Kredel, Fritz, *Glass Flowers from the Ware Collection*, New York, 1940
Paston, George, *Mrs Delany, a Memoir*, London, 1900

CHAPTER XXIII

Earle, Alice Morse, *Old Time Gardens*, New York, 1902

Handasyde, *The Four Gardens*, London, 1924
Kennedy-Bell, M. G., *The Glory of the Garden*, London, 1923

CHAPTER XXIV

Lamb, Cadbury, and Wright, Gordon, *Discovering Inn Signs*, Tring, 1970
Larwood, Jacob, and Hotten, J. C., *The History of Signboards*, London, 1875

APPENDIX I

Evans, F. E., *Discovering Civic Heraldry*, Tring, 1968
Grigson, Geoffrey, *A Herbal of All Sorts*, London, 1959
Phillips, Henry, *Floral Emblems*, London, 1825
Tyas, Robert, *Flowers in Heraldry*, London, 1851

APPENDIX II

Bacon, Francis, *Of Gardens*, Guildford, 1903
Coats, Alice, *Henry Phillips*, Reading, *c.* 1973
Ingram, John, *Flora Symbolica*, London, *c.* 1875
Kennedy-Bell, M. G., *The Glory of the Garden*, London, 1923

ACKNOWLEDGEMENTS

Photographs and illustrations were supplied or are reproduced by kind permission of the following:

Black and White
Author's collection: 9, 17, 20, 21, 25, 26, 27, 30, 31, 52, 58, 63, 70–1, 86, 104, 106, 111, 112, 122, 127, 130, 138, 158, 163, 169, 170; Society of Antiquaries: 165; Bibliotheque Nationale: 153t; British Tourist Authority: 142 ml, 175; British Library: 19; Brighton Public Libraries: 143; Bildarchiv der Osterreichisches National Bibliotek: 76l; British Museum: 23, 39, 69; BM (Natural History): 28, 37, 53, 66, 92, 93, 94, 96, 167; Bodleian Library: 50, 54 (filmstrip 196c), 67 (filmstrip 196c), 80 (filmstrip 196c), 102 (filmstrip 173d) Biblioteca Medicea-Laurenziana: 73, Chelsea Physic Garden: 84, Courtesy the Earl of Derby: 89; Liches des Musees Nationaux: 120, 149; College of Arms, London: 151; Kunsthistorischen Museum: 14, 34-5, 39, 146; Laing Art Gallery: 78, Mansell Collection: 10, 24, 32, 33, 38, 60, 90; Manchester City Art Gallery: 125; Museum National d'Histoire Naturelle: 88; National Monuments Record: 155; John Nott – Picton House Gallery: 142l; National Gallery, London: 12, 13, 18, 22, 147; Rimmel International: 114–15, 119; The Scotsman: 183e; Tate Gallery, London: 95; Sotheby's Belgravia: 135; Victoria and Albert Museum, Crown Copyright: 109, 113, 116, 126, 128–129, 133, 141, 142r, 145, 150, 159, 160, 161, 162, 171, 172, 174; Walker Art Gallery, Liverpool: 181; Courtesy Wartski; 156. Duke of Westminster 153b;

Colour
Author's collection: 42, 43, 44, 45; Bodleian Library: 41; Bodleian Library (filmstrip 227.2): 48; Botanical Museum Harvard University: 45t; British Library: 47; City of Manchester Art Gallery: 46b; Victoria and Albert Museum (Crown Copyright): 46t.

INDEX

Botanical names, and nicknames not in general use, have been indexed only occasionally, usually as a means of identification when a plant is referred to by different names on different pages. The plants in the following lists have not been indexed: US state flowers, p. 177; Scottish clans, pp. 179–80; floral clock, p. 182; and Language of Flowers, pp. 185–94. A number in brackets immediately after a page number indicates separate references to the subject on that page. Figures in *italics* refer to illustrations.